Exploring the Ideas of Tadeusz Kowalik

Grzegorz Konat • Gavin Rae
Editors

Exploring the Ideas of Tadeusz Kowalik

Crises, Transformations and Alternatives

palgrave
macmillan

Editors
Grzegorz Konat
SGH Warsaw School of Economics
Warsaw, Poland

Gavin Rae
Department of Social Sciences
Kozminski University
Warsaw, Poland

ISBN 978-3-032-09282-3 ISBN 978-3-032-09283-0 (eBook)
https://doi.org/10.1007/978-3-032-09283-0

This Palgrave Macmillan imprint is published by the registered company Springer Nature Switzerland AG.
The registered company address is: Gewerbestrasse 11, 6330 Cham, Switzerland

Tadeusz Kowalik in the Chochołowska Valley (Western Tatras), 2010.
(Photo by Małgorzata Kula, from the collection of and courtesy of Małgorzata and Jan Kula)

Preface

Tadeusz Kowalik (1926–2012) was a professor of economics and humanities whose academic career spanned nearly six decades. His work focused primarily on the history of ideas, particularly economic thought, and included comparative studies of economic systems, with special emphasis on Poland's systemic transformation during the final two decades of the twentieth century. He authored, co-authored, and edited several dozen monographs and hundreds of scholarly articles and book chapters. The high academic standing of his work is reflected in its translation into multiple languages. He also spent extended periods at major research centres around the world, and his stature is affirmed by the recognition he received from economists both in Poland and internationally (Konat, 2024, p. 1).

Jan Toporowski described Kowalik as "one of the great political economists of the twentieth century", placing him "alongside ... Oskar Lange, Michał Kalecki and, of course, Rosa Luxemburg". Toporowski further added that "Tadeusz Kowalik not only laid out the foundations of twentieth century political economy. He has also provided us with a political economy for the twenty-first century" (Toporowski, 2012, p. 14).

Kowalik witnessed ten decades and lived through three distinct economic and political systems in Poland. He consistently integrated his academic pursuit of economic ideas with his socialist vision of a more equitable and just society. After his passing, numerous obituaries appeared both in Poland and abroad. Those who knew him personally recalled him as a man of strong principles, who lived in accordance with the ideals he espoused (Rae, 2025, p. 1). As Toporowski observed, Kowalik "remained a person of a rare personal modesty, for whom the condition of humble people and the ideas of scholars who recognised the value of those ordinary people, were far more important than his own individual achievements" (Toporowski, 2013, p. 56).

The importance of Kowalik is evidenced by the fact that since his death, a number of academic works devoted to his achievements have been published (including at least four books: two volumes of a *festschrift* dedicated to him (Bellofiore et al., 2014a, 2014b) and one by each of the undersigned authors). It is largely due to Tadeusz Kowalik's enormous intellectual authority—and in commemoration of the 10th anniversary of his death—that an international academic conference entitled "Exploring the Ideas of Tadeusz Kowalik: Crises, Transformations and Alternatives" was organised in Warsaw in 2022. Here, scholars from several countries on three continents remembered Kowalik, analysed his thought, and developed it further in order to gain a better understanding of the contemporary world.

The work we are presenting to the Reader not only shares title with that conference, but is also largely its material outcome: Seven of the ten texts it contains are revised and expanded versions of papers delivered on 9 July 2022.

The book opens with an introduction by Marcin Kula, entitled "A Twisted Reality ... and Choosing a Consistent Course in Life. Tadeusz Kowalik (1926–2012)" (Chap. 1). The text is a comprehensive biographical and intellectual portrait of Tadeusz Kowalik, tracing his life from a modest childhood through his involvement in socialist thought, critical Marxism, and opposition to both Stalinist and neoliberal models. It highlights his moral integrity, political activism, and unwavering commitment to social justice, including his criticism of Poland's post-1989 transformation. The author emphasises Kowalik's enduring belief in market socialism as a humane alternative to both capitalism and authoritarian socialism.

It is worth mentioning here that we had previously intended to write an introduction to this book ourselves, briefly discussing the figure of Tadeusz Kowalik and his life. However, after reading Professor Kula's text, we decided that we could not have done it any better and that this stands as an ideal introduction to Kowalik and the book.

The rest of the book is divided into three parts. The first part, entitled "Tadeusz Kowalik and His Ideas", contains five chapters.

The second chapter, written by Riccardo Bellofiore, is entitled "The 'Political Aspects of Full Employment' and the '*Crucial Reform* of Capitalism': A Discussion with Jan Toporowski on Kalecki and Kowalik" (Chap. 2). Bellofiore critically analyses Jan Toporowski's interpretation of

Kalecki's work, arguing that Kalecki's 1943 and 1970 writings reflect a shift from a radical critique of capitalism to a more reformist stance. He reinterprets Kalecki's evolving views through his lesser-known studies of the US economy and positions his theory within a Marxian framework centred on exploitation and labour discipline. The chapter also traces Tadeusz Kowalik's later return to a Marxist critique, ultimately calling for a theory that goes beyond reformism to confront capitalism's systemic limits.

In the third chapter ("Tadeusz Kowalik Between Oskar Lange and Michał Kalecki", Chap. 3), Jan Toporowski explores Tadeusz Kowalik's intellectual ties to Oskar Lange and Michał Kalecki, highlighting his key role in editing their collected works. While Kowalik is often seen as reconciling their differing interpretations of Marxism and socialism, his writings suggest a growing affinity with Kalecki's perspective. His major research on Rosa Luxemburg marks a notable turn towards Kalecki's approach.

The fourth chapter is entitled "The Wandering Intellectual: The Influence of Sociology on Tadeusz Kowalik" (Chap. 4) and was written by Gavin Rae. The author examines the influence of sociology on the intellectual development of Tadeusz Kowalik. Kowalik drew heavily on sociological insights to critique both socialist and capitalist economic systems. He was influenced early on by Ludwik Krzywicki and Oskar Lange, which drew him towards examining issues such as alienation, institutional diversity, and the interdependence of economy and society. Kowalik's opposition to the positivisation of economics and his commitment to embedding economic analysis within a broader social setting led him to engaging with the work and ideas of sociologists. By tracing Kowalik's evolving relationship with sociology across Poland's shifting political landscape—from state socialism through the post-socialist transformation—the author underscores Kowalik's position as a public intellectual who advocated for economic systems grounded in social justice, democratic planning, and pluralism.

In the following chapter ("Tadeusz Kowalik vs. 'Western Marxism': Two Attempts to Conceptualise the Post-1989 Changes in East Central Europe as 'Bourgeois Revolutions'", Chap. 5), Grzegorz Konat introduces a comparative analysis of two interpretations of the post-1989 transformation in East Central Europe as a "bourgeois revolution" published in the mid-1990: one by Tadeusz Kowalik and the other by Colin Barker and Colin Mooers. Barker and Mooers provide a robust and systematically Marxist framework, making their analysis appear convincing. In contrast, while Kowalik's thesis is noted for its originality, the author argues it lacks theoretical depth and rigour. Konat attempts to show how this could have resulted from Kowalik's break with Marxism beginning in the 1980s.

The subsequent chapter is entitled "Tadeusz Kowalik: Personality and Living Ideas" (Chap. 6). Its author, Paweł Kozłowski, presents a reflective tribute to Kowalik, portraying him as a principled economist, humanist, and moral voice rooted in the ideals of social justice and democratic pluralism. Kozłowski highlights Kowalik's critique of neoliberalism and his advocacy for a mixed economy and real utopias grounded in solidarity. The author argues that Kowalik's legacy remains vital in confronting today's global inequalities and market-driven policies.

The second part of the book, entitled "Contemporary Socio-Economic Problems Viewed Through the Lens of Tadeusz Kowalik's Thought", contains three texts.

The first of these (Chap. 7 of the book) is by Hanna Szymborska and Janusz Szymborski and is entitled: "How Neoliberalism Undermines the Health of the Polish Population". The text critically examines the evolution of neoliberal policies in Poland's healthcare system over three decades, linking them to worsening public health outcomes, including during the COVID-19 pandemic. It highlights the implementation of market mechanisms in public health institutions and the ideological justification of these reforms despite their failure to deliver promised improvements. Drawing on the work of Tadeusz Kowalik, the authors advocate for a reorientation of the system to address these negative trends.

In Chap. 8 ("From Reform to Reality: The Polish Pension System and Socioeconomic Justice"), Janina Petelczyc examines the post-1999 transformation of the Polish pension system in light of Tadeusz Kowalik's thesis that Poland developed one of the most unjust socio-economic systems in Europe. She analyses key reforms—including the shift from a Defined Benefit to a Defined Contribution model, partial privatisation via Open Pension Funds, and the treatment of privileged groups—through the lens of solidarity and justice. The chapter also considers whether any of these reforms have helped reduce inequalities or instead reinforced them, using data from the Social Insurance Institution (ZUS).

Meanwhile, Janusz J. Tomidajewicz, in his text entitled "The Welfare State and the New World Order" (Chap. 9), explores contemporary models of socio-economic governance within the context of shifting global political and economic dynamics. He criticises the limitations of neoliberalism and, drawing on the ideas of Tadeusz Kowalik, advocates for the construction of a democratic welfare state, particularly through deeper European integration. The author also examines the key obstacles to such transformation in Poland and the European Union.

The entire content of the third part of the book, entitled "Kowalik on Kowalik", is a very extensive interview given by Tadeusz Kowalik to Edward Chudziński, Paweł Kozłowski, and Filip Ratkowski in 2004 (Chap. 10). The text, which appeared in the magazine *Zdanie*, was entitled *Trzech na jednego. Musztarda przed obiadem* [*Three against One. Mustard Before Dinner*], where the first part was the permanent title of a series of conversations published in this periodical, while the second was a direct reference to an excerpt from Kowalik's interview. We decided not to change this title.

Until the publication of an intellectual biography by one of us (Rae, 2025), this interview stood as the most important source of knowledge about the life and intellectual evolution of Tadeusz Kowalik, and to this day it remains the most important source of information about Kowalik's life from the person himself. Thanks to its translation and inclusion in this volume, English-speaking readers will be able to read this text for the first time.

* * *

We would first of all like to thank all the authors of the chapters in this book, which cover a range of topics related to the work and life of Tadeusz Kowalik. We owe deep gratitude to Jan Toporowski, for his support and encouragement throughout the preparation of the conference and book and during our ongoing engagement with the work of Tadeusz Kowalik. Also, Paweł Kozłowski has been extremely supportive during our endeavours and was particularly helpful in us gaining acceptance to republish the interview with Tadeusz Kowalik that appears in this book. Of course, we would like to express our gratitude in this regard to the other two co-authors of the interview, Edward Chudziński and Filip Ratkowski, as well as to the editors of *Zdanie*.

As already mentioned, this book is largely an outcome of a conference held in Warsaw in 2022, marking the tenth anniversary of Kowalik's death. We are grateful to everyone who participated in this conference, either through giving presentations or contributing during the discussion. This includes Tadeusz Kowalik's wife, Irena Kowalik, and son, Mateusz Kowalik, who have also given us great encouragement when researching and publishing on Tadeusz Kowalik. We are extremely thankful for the generous support provided by the Rosa Luxemburg Foundation in Poland, and especially from the invaluable Piotr Janiszewski, which made the conference in Warsaw possible. We would also like to extend our gratitude to the co-organisers of the conference: The Polish Economic Society, and in particular Elżbieta Mączyńska; and the Książka i Prasa publishing house, especially its director—Stefan Zgliczyński.

Finally, we thank the editorial and production team at Palgrave Macmillan, including Wyndham Hacket Pain, Asma Azeezullah and Aashika Philomi, who have been extremely helpful during the preparation of this book.

Warsaw, Poland

Grzegorz Konat
Gavin Rae

References

Bellofiore, R., Karwowski, E., & Toporowski, J. (2014a). *The legacy of Rosa Luxemburg, Oskar Lange and Michał Kalecki,* Vol. 1 of *Essays in honour of Tadeusz Kowalik.* Palgrave Macmillan.

Bellofiore, R., Karwowski, E., & Toporowski, J. (2014b). *Economic crisis and political economy,* Vol. 2 of *Essays in honour of Tadeusz Kowalik.* Palgrave Macmillan.

Konat, G. (2024). *The Polish transformation: Tadeusz Kowalik on the Epigonic Bourgeois revolution of 1989.* Brill.

Rae, G. (2025). *Tadeusz Kowalik and Poland's return to capitalism through socialism: Full circle.* Manchester University Press.

Toporowski, J. (2012). Tadeusz Kowalik a współczesna ekonomia polityczna. In T. Kowalik (Ed.), *Róża Luksemburg. Teoria akumulacji i imperializmu,* (pp. 7–14). Instytut Wydawniczy Książka i Prasa.

Toporowski, J. (2013). Tadeusz Kowalik: Radical political economist, solidarity advisor and critic of globalised capitalism. *PSL Quarterly Review, 66* (264), 50–57.

Contents

1 Introduction: A Twisted Reality … and Choosing a Consistent Course in Life. Tadeusz Kowalik (1926–2012) 1
Marcin Kula

Part I Tadeusz Kowalik and His Ideas

2 The "Political Aspects of Full Employment" and the "'Crucial Reform' of Capitalism": A Discussion with Jan Toporowski on Kalecki and Kowalik 19
Riccardo Bellofiore

3 Tadeusz Kowalik Between Oskar Lange and Michał Kalecki 43
Jan Toporowski

4 The Wandering Intellectual: The Influence of Sociology on Tadeusz Kowalik 55
Gavin Rae

5 **Tadeusz Kowalik vs. "Western Marxism": Two Attempts to Conceptualise the Post-1989 Changes in East Central Europe as "Bourgeois Revolutions"** 67
Grzegorz Konat

6 **Tadeusz Kowalik: Personality and Living Ideas** 103
Paweł Kozłowski

Part II Contemporary Socio-Economic Problems Viewed Through the Lens of Tadeusz Kowalik's Thought

7 **How Neoliberalism Undermines the Health of the Polish Population** 121
Hanna Szymborska and Janusz Szymborski

8 **From Reform to Reality: The Polish Pension System and Socio-economic Justice** 147
Janina Petelczyc

9 **The Welfare State and the New World Order** 171
Janusz J. Tomidajewicz

Part III Kowalik on Kowalik

10 **Three Against One. Mustard Before Dinner** 191
Tadeusz Kowalik, Edward Chudziński, Filip Ratkowski, and Paweł Kozłowski

Index 249

Notes on Contributors

Riccardo Bellofiore was formerly a professor of political economy at the University of Bergamo, Italy. His research combines Marxian, Keynesian, and monetary circuit approaches to macroeconomics and capitalist dynamics. He has written extensively on the economics of Michał Kalecki and Tadeusz Kowalik, and on the broader tradition of critical political economy. Bellofiore has edited volumes on Marx, Luxemburg, Minsky, and Sraffa, and has contributed to the rethinking of the relationship between full employment, capitalist reform, and structural crisis. His work foregrounds the role of labour, money, and institutions in shaping the contradictions of modern capitalism.

Grzegorz Konat is an assistant professor in history of economic ideas at the SGH Warsaw School of Economics. He has published on the history of economic thought, including co-edited volumes *Paradoksy ekonomii. Rozmowy z polskimi ekonomistami* [*Economic Paradoxes: Conversations with Polish Economists*] (Warsaw 2016) and *Realny kapitalizm. Wokół teorii kapitału monopolistycznego* [*Real Capitalism: Exploring Monopoly Capital Theory*] (Warsaw 2018). His most recent book is *The Polish Transformation: Tadeusz Kowalik of the Epigonic Bourgeois Revolution of 1989* (Leiden-Boston 2024).

Paweł Kozłowski is a sociologist and economist, professor at the University of Warsaw. He is interested in the relationship between ideas, the economy, and society. His publications include *Z Polski i o Polsce. Korespondencja z lat 2004–2006* [*From Poland and About Poland: Correspondence from 2004–2006*, with Andrzej Walicki, 2007], *Dziennik* *profesora nadzwyczajnego* [*Diary of an Associate Extraordinarius*, 2015], *Niekiedy. Dziennik profesora nadzwyczajnego—kontynuacja* [*Sometimes: Diary of an Associate Professor—Continuation*, 2019], *Przeciw systemowi* [*Against the System*, 2020], *Spotkania z Andrzejem Walickim* [*Meetings with Andrzej Walicki*, 2021], *O socjologii w Polsce Ludowej rozmów jedenaście* [*Eleven Conversations on Sociology in People's Poland*; an extended interview with Jerzy J. Wiatr, 2022], *Przeciw systemowi 2. Rozmowy nie tylko z książkami* [*Against the System 2. Conversations Not Only with Books*, 2023].

Marcin Kula is a retired professor at the University of Warsaw. He studied history and sociology at the University of Warsaw. He completed his doctoral studies at the then Main School of Planning and Statistics (now the SGH Warsaw School of Economics), but obtained his doctorate at the Institute of History of the Polish Academy of Sciences. He initially worked there. He then took up a position at the University of Warsaw and, at various times, at the Koźminski University and the Theatre Academy in Warsaw. He specialised in the history of Latin America, the history of Poland after World War II, social movements and historical sociology. His most recent publication is: *Rola społeczna. Pojęcie, wokół którego możemy się spotkać jako historycy i socjologowie?* [*The Social Role: A Concept We Encounter as Historians and Sociologists?*] (Warsaw 2024).

Janina Petelczyc is a researcher specialising in social security systems, with a focus on pension policies, welfare state reforms, and labour market institutions. She works at the Department of Social Insurance at the SGH Warsaw School of Economics and collaborates with the European Insurance and Occupational Pensions Authority (EIOPA). Her research interests include the sustainability and equity of pension systems, the social impacts of economic reforms, and sustainable investments in private pension funds.

Gavin Rae is an associate professor in sociology at Koźminski University in Warsaw. He has researched and written on issues relating to Poland and Central and Eastern Europe, "post-socialist" capitalism, and the welfare state. His intellectual biography of Tadeusz Kowalik has recently been published by Manchester University Press and its Polish edition—by Wydawnictwo Heterodox.

Hanna Szymborska is an independent researcher currently working in the UK public sector, with over 7 years of experience in academia. She holds a PhD from the University of Leeds, specialising in inequality, financialisation, and economic policy through the lens of heterodox schools of thought. She is committed to promoting pluralism and inclusivity in economics. She sits on the Executive Board of Diversifying and Decolonising Economics and has contributed numerous peer-reviewed and policy publications in *Journal of Post Keynesian Economics*, *Feminist Economics*, *Review of Black Political Economy*, *International Journal of Political Economy*, *Review of Evolutionary Political Economy*, *Structural Change and Economic Dynamics*, *PSL Quarterly Review*, *and UNU-Wider working paper series* and edited volumes published by Oxford University Press, Routledge, Palgrave Macmillan, and Edward Elgar.

Janusz Szymborski is a professor of paediatrics. After 25 years of clinical work, he has been involved in the field of public health for almost three decades. He has held the following positions: Deputy Chairman of the Commission of Health in Parliament of Poland (1989–1991), Director of National Research Institute of Mother and Child in Warsaw (1996–2001), Member of the Government Population Council (2002–2024), professor at the Wszechnica Polska University in Warsaw (2003–). He has authored or co-authored approximately 350 scientific publications and 25 monographs, including *Assumptions of Population Policy in Poland* (2016), *Health Crisis in Poland During the Pandemic – Conclusions*, Supreme Audit Office (2023), *The Health of Children and Youth in Poland; Native Traditions of Care; Contemporary Goals* (forthcoming).

Janusz J. Tomidajewicz is a retired professor at the Poznań University of Economics and Business and the University of Zielona Góra. He is author and editor of studies on economic and social policy issues in Poland and the European Union, as well as on the sources and methods of combating the financial and economic crisis, published in, among others: *A New All-European Development Model in an Enlarged EU. Social and Economic Aspects* (Poznań 2004), *Privatisation in Poland and the Formation of the European Social Model* (Poznań 2009), *Does the Current Financial Crisis Mean the Crisis of Liberal Capitalism?* (Timisoara 2010), *Les réponses à la crise. Une épreuve pour l'integration européenne* [*Responses to the Crisis. A Test for European Integration*] (Paris 2012) and *Pensions in 30 years, Social Policy Issues 2022.* Team leader and editor of periodic reports on the economic and social situation in Poland, published as the Economic Observatory of the Polish Economic Society.

Jan Toporowski is a professor of economics at King's College London and the London School of Economics. His research is concentrated on monetary theory and policy, finance, and the work of Michał Kalecki. He is on the Editorial Boards of the *Journal of Post-Keynesian Economics*, the *Review of Political Economy*, and the *Review of Keynesian Economics*. Jan Toporowski has published two volumes of biography of Michał Kalecki and over 350 books, articles, and papers on economics and finance. Before becoming an academic, he worked in fund management, international banking, and central banking. He has been a consultant for the United Nations Development Programme, the United Nations Conference on Trade and Development, the UN Economic Commission for Africa, and the Economist Intelligence Unit. His most recent book is *Interest and Capital: The Monetary Economics of Michał Kalecki* (Oxford 2022).

List of Figures

Fig. 7.1	Average life expectancy at birth between 1990 and 2022 in Poland	124
Fig. 7.2	Total number of deaths in 2020 as a share of the 2015–19 average, adjusted for population	126
Fig. 7.3	Excess mortality by month as a share of additional deaths compared with average monthly deaths in 2016–19	127
Fig. 7.4	Composition of health spending, 2019	135
Fig. 7.5	Mortality rates from preventable causes, 2019	135
Fig. 8.1	Financial flows from contributions before and after the 1999 pension reform	154
Fig. 8.2	Percentage of individuals receiving pensions of a specified amount from the new and old systems in December 2022	159
Fig. 8.3	Average accumulated capital (in PLN) by year of birth and gender in the first quarter of 2024	160
Fig. 8.4	Number of retirees receiving pensions below the minimum level (in thousands)	162
Fig. 9.1	Types of socio-economic governance	178

List of Tables

Table 7.1 Number of excess deaths in Poland compared to the average over the last 50 years 122
Table 8.1 Polish pension system in 1999 154
Table 8.2 Projections of demographics, pension expenditures, and replacement rates for Poland 2022–2070 158

CHAPTER 1

Introduction: A Twisted Reality … and Choosing a Consistent Course in Life. Tadeusz Kowalik (1926–2012)

Marcin Kula

There is a saying, sometimes directed at someone who is wished badly: 'May you live in interesting times!' This so-called folk wisdom has perfectly recognised that interesting times are difficult and sometimes even life-threatening. There is another saying: 'What does a Jew do when a story comes out? He enters the nearest gate so that it does not trample him'. This saying comes from Eastern European Jewish folklore and reflects situations that are bad for the community, not necessarily the Jewish community. Well, Tadeusz Kowalik lived in interesting times and did not 'run to the gate', but faced and sought solutions to them.

Kowalik was born in 1926 in the village of Kajetanówka in the Lublin region.[1] It was a poor region and a poor village. His family, always close to him, did not have much money. This deprivation gave him, I suspect, a certain fortitude and even allowed him to acquire skills. He was able to do

M. Kula (✉)
University of Warsaw (emeritus), Warsaw, Poland
e-mail: j.m.kula@uw.edu.pl

G. Konat, G. Rae (eds.), *Exploring the Ideas of Tadeusz Kowalik*,
https://doi.org/10.1007/978-3-032-09283-0_1

a lot of everyday things on his own, which a person coming from an urban intelligentsia family, would certainly not be able to do, such as mend his own shoes or clothes. When, during a holiday with the Kowaliks, my wife tore a piece of her clothing, he just said: 'give it to me for the evening, I'll fix it for you'. Until his late years, despite his nagging illness (he joked: 'I manage three types of cancer'), he remained active. He swam and skated and he was simply brave in life. I guess his own starting point also sensitised him to the issue of the plight of the poor in society. Perhaps from these times he retained an ease of contact—despite all his later social advancement—with less educated people. His funeral was attended by a highland family of friends from the Zakopane area, together with their children, all dressed in highland costumes.

Tadeusz was 13 when the war broke out, an age when you already understand a lot. Yet, in 1939 it was very difficult to understand anything. Probably under the influence of the victory over the Bolsheviks in 1920, and also as a result of the large role of the army and the military in the life of the country, there was an opinion in Poland that the country was strong. However, Hitler quickly defeated Poland. Although it later turned out that France also fell quickly, and in the USSR the Nazis initially advanced like a knife through butter, the sensation of the defeat in Poland was enormous, and the occupation heavy. On the other hand, the Red Army entered Poland from the East, supposedly bringing freedom to its Ukrainian and Belorussian brothers. It is debatable whether it really went there to bring them freedom, but it certainly brought misery to the Poles. In some localities, the Poles already preferred the Germans to the Red Army, although they soon saw that the occupier was just as much an occupier. I do not know, because I did not happen to discuss these matters with Tadeusz Kowalik, to what extent the deportation of people to exile by the Russians, German persecution, the Holocaust, and other misfortunes affected him. It is certain that these events touched him, even if he was only a teenager at the time.

The post-war times were also not easy, although they were very different to what came before. Poland had new borders, outlined by Stalin and approved by the Western Allies. The Lublin region thus became the first Polish region where the Red Army (since 1946 called 'Soviet') and the Polish troops going with it entered in 1944. They were only part of the Polish army, fighting on the fronts of the Second World War. Other Poles fought on the Western Front. The liberators, whom were regarded as new occupiers by some people, proceeded to organise the Polish authorities.

Anti-Communist resistance in the forests was still very much alive, and some continued to distance themselves from the new system in a number of forms. For example, in July 1949, the faithful supposedly saw tears in the eyes of the Virgin Mary depicted in the painting at the Lublin Cathedral. Crowds of people flocked to Lublin to watch the 'miracle', the miraculous nature of which was not recognised by the Catholic Church.

It was obvious to those in the know that overt or subliminal opposition did not stand a chance. It was difficult to believe in the prospect of a third world war fought by the Western Allies over Poland. Even the people of the underground, who had been hiding a Polish national 'relic' from the Nazis in Lublin throughout the occupation—Matejko's painting 'The Battle of Grunwald'—decided to hand it over to the new authorities (which would have been ruined if it had lain in hiding for a while longer). The new rulers placed the greatest possible emphasis on the Polish character of the newly created government. Their first created body with government functions was called the 'Polish Committee of National Liberation'. This was highly distinctive, even if the word 'Polish' was added to it by Vyacheslav Molotov, who had earlier signed the Ribbentrop Pact and referred to Poland as a 'bastard offspring' of the Treaty of Versailles (Zaremba, 2001, p. 138). The demonstrations organised by the new authorities were surprising. The first parade of the Polish Army, which came to Poland with the Red Army, took place on 15 August, the regular Polish Army holiday in pre-war Poland. Moreover, this was the anniversary of the defeat of the Bolsheviks in the Battle of Warsaw in 1920. Meanwhile, on the tribune, as a representative of the USSR government, stood General (soon to be Marshal) Nikolai Bulganin, who had participated in that battle in 1920. On the Bolshevik side, of course (Zaremba, 2001, p. 140).

One can, of course, ask whether the new authorities were sincere in such and further demonstrations of Poland's rebirth. There is, for example, the well-known sentence of Jakub Berman, a very important figure in the then and later authorities, when proposing the celebration of the national holiday of 3 May: 'We are undoubtedly aiming to abolish the 3rd of May, we are aiming for the national holiday to be linked to a new state act that will replace the [constitution of the] 3rd of May, but this is for the future. At present, 3 May is a moment of bringing together and mobilising the broad masses of the nation' (Zaremba, 2001, p. 141). He was, however, saying this to his propagandists (in April 1945), and the Polish symbolism was visible to all. It was similarly visible later in Warsaw. Few people—and even fewer of the city's many new residents—immediately after the war thought about how Stalin halted Soviet troops in 1944 on the eastern side of the Vistula in order not to help the Warsaw Uprising. In fact, immediately after the war, the Uprising was not held in such veneration as it was later. Instead, the new government set about rebuilding Warsaw. Incidentally, a little known fact is that Stalin opposed the idea of moving Poland's capital to the unruined city of Łódź, stating that Warsaw was to remain the capital after reconstruction. Last but not least, and certainly important from Tadeusz Kowalik's point of view, the new Polish authorities announced a rebuilding of the system towards social democratisation. As previously mentioned, Kowalik had seen poverty in the Polish countryside, supposedly even helping farmers to write applications for the rectification of various injustices affecting them. Perhaps this inspired him to study law ('He wanted to be a lawyer, to defend the poor and the wronged' (Osiatyński, 2012, p. 9)). The new regime was supposed to modernise the country, make up for its backwardness, and improve the material existence and social advancement of people who at first had very limited opportunities. How all this would be accomplished was another matter.

In 1946, Tadeusz Kowalik joined a communist youth organisation, the Union of Youth Struggle, and in 1948 he joined the Polish Workers' Party (the future Polish United Workers' Party). Incidentally, it was peculiar that the party, effectively communist, adopted the name 'Workers'. Most probably, his affiliation with it, led Kowalik to occupy low-level positions, connected with the authorities, s. In the years 1945–1946, he was an accountant in the Provincial Office for the Control of the Press, Publications, and Public Performances (actually: censorship) in Warsaw, and later, until 1947 in Lębork, he was a district plenipotentiary of the Gdańsk Provincial Office of the same institution. In the following years, he studied law at the University of Warsaw. He graduated in 1951 and even took up a lowly post [*asesor*] in the Warsaw County Court (1950–1951).

Already with a degree from Warsaw University, Kowalik became associated with an institution to which a few words need to be devoted. In the years 1951–1954, he was an *aspirant* (in today's terminology: a doctoral student) at the Institute for Training Scientific Cadres, attached to the Central Committee of the Polish United Workers' Party (IKKN), and between 1954 and 1957 he was a lecturer in economics there. As the name suggests, this institution was to train new cadres for science and higher education. In Poland, relatively few old professors were removed from the universities. At times, they were 'only' sidelined and not allowed to teach. Nevertheless, the communists wanted to create a cadre that the party could rely on. The IKKN was modelled on the once-existing Institute of the Red Professorship in Moscow. Today, the materials produced in this university are hard to read and sometimes downright frightening.[2] At the same time, at least two things are surprising about the functioning of this institution. It recruited many very intelligent students, which was usually not the case for the PZPR. The second surprising thing is that many of its students later came into conflict with the party. At the time of the 'thaw', a number of them became a milieu then and *ex post* were referred to as 'revisionists'. Why this name? It came from the fact that they did not renounce Marxism, nor did they want to turn back from the path of socialism, but they wanted both of these things to be different from the practiced reality. It is important to realise that, whatever one thinks of Marx's theory, it is difficult to recognise as Marxism something that was preached here. If the 'bible' of Marxism preached was to be 'A Short Course' (*History*, 1939), then anything that was desired by those in power in Moscow and Warsaw—and certainly in other capitals of the Soviet camp—could be regarded as Marxism. The revisionists wanted to 'revise' the system and bring its ideological basis closer to a more genuine Marxism. Although this was certainly naïve, this group included some outstanding individuals, such as Kołakowski, Baczko, and Brus. A tangible proof of their naivety—though at the time still only expressed in words—was the pronouncement in 1957 by Władysław Gomułka, First Secretary of the Central Committee of the Communist Party (1956–1970), that revisionism was a tuberculosis for the party, while hard dogmatic tendencies were at best a flu.

Why exactly did such people end up in the IKKN? First of all, as I have mentioned, because there were many intelligent, though certainly infatuated, people there. In spite of the absurdities signalled earlier, they had opportunities to read extensively. After all, as they were being prepared to fight their ideological opponents, they had to have some knowledge about them. Sometimes, unlike the average party apparatus, they had to be familiar with what was going on in the country, as they were the cadres at the forefront of building the new reality. And last but not least: in authoritarian or even totalitarian regimes, in certain situations it is easier for cadres close to the centre to express doubts than for people standing at a distance and rejecting everything. Those standing close, in turn, are more likely to express a desire to repair the system than to reject everything *en bloc*.

The aforementioned revisionists became more deeply involved in the wave of opposition to the system, which was sweeping the country, including the PZPR itself, after Stalin's death. A number of important events occurred, including Khrushchev's 'Secret Speech' at the 20th Congress of the CPSU in 1956, the death of the leader of Stalinist Poland, Bolesław Bierut; the escape to the West of one of the most important officers of the local secret police; and the broadcasting over the 'Radio Free Europe' of his story about how communist Poland actually functioned. In June 1956 came a dramatic moment: the workers' demonstrations and then the riots in Poznań, which were bloodily suppressed by the army. Nominally the workers' state fired on the workers. October 1956 saw the plenary meeting of the Central Committee of the Polish United Workers' Party (PZPR), which is regarded as the symbolic and real pinnacle of de-Stalinisation in Poland. Kowalik was active in the revisionist current. He participated in an important discussion club at that time called the Crooked Circle Club and, more importantly, between 1956 and 1957 he was editor-in-chief of the first-rate economics' weekly *Życie Gospodarcze* [Economic Life]. During this period and under his direction, the magazine promoted the relaxation of the rigours of central planning (the cornerstone of economics under real socialism!) as well as greater independence of enterprises and the increased participation of workers in their management. In Poland at the time, there was much talk of the Yugoslav model, and demands to imitate its economic system.

All these discussions, held in ever-widening circles before 1956 and immediately after the changes of the time, did not last long. Poland, however, never returned to Stalinist terror. Even if the concrete structure of the system survived to its end, people's fear diminished, the pressure on farmers to create collective farms on the model of Soviet kolkhozes ceased, censorship became more political than ideological, and more trips were made to Western countries, which were beneficial to economists, historians, and sociologists, among others. More or less formalised centres for the exchange of ideas among intellectuals emerged, especially in the aforementioned disciplines. Kowalik was very active in all this. He researched the leftist, or socialist, current in the history of Polish economic thought (Rosa Luxemburg, Edward Abramowski, Ludwik Krzywicki, Michał Kalecki, Oskar Lange). At various times he stayed, also as a lecturer, at the universities of Oxford, Cambridge, Toronto, or Washington.

Although Stalinist-type terror had not returned, the second half of the 1960s brought more and more alarming symptoms. An unreformed, or at best insufficiently reformed economy, was malfunctioning. Conflict with the Catholic Church was growing. Leaving aside the finer points of contention, two are worth mentioning. The first was a letter from the Polish bishops to the German bishops calling for reconciliation between the nations. Gomułka was upset that the Church was interfering in the matter of foreign relations, and he did not at all want to diminish the fear of Germans amongst Poles, which was so convenient for him in domestic politics. The second conflict revolved around the celebration of the millennium of the Polish statehood and the 'baptism of Poland'. The Church was organising a nationwide celebration of the baptismal anniversary, while the state, under the leadership of the PZPR, was organising a celebration of the millennium of statehood. However, there existed no other date before the baptism that could be invoked by the party-state side as the foundation date of Poland. There is a legend about a ruler named Popiel who was eaten by mice. However, it is difficult to make a millennium celebration of a ruler being eaten by mice. Despite this, Gomułka's position was that the baptism was the work of an already existing state. Whatever the truth of this matter, many competing celebrations and demonstrations were held throughout the country.

Gomułka also began a conflict with intellectuals and universities. This coincided with growing divisions amongst generational and political groups within the PZPR itself. The culmination of these frictions was the mass student demonstrations in various university towns in 1968 (just like in the West!), and later the anti-Semitic campaign launched by one of the party factions. As a consequence of the latter, some 13,000 Polish citizens of Jewish origin were pushed out of Poland (Stola, 2010, p. 222). Subsequently, numerous students were expelled from universities and various repressions were undertaken against them, and a group of prominent professors were also removed. Tadeusz Kowalik was then expelled from the PZPR. Luckily for him, he worked at the Polish Academy of Sciences, and it was from the universities that 'revisionists' and 'Zionists' (as they were absurdly called) were expelled.

In 1968, among the leaders of the countries of the Soviet camp, Gomułka was one of the most insistent on the Warsaw Pact providing 'brotherly aid' to Czechoslovakia. He feared that the revisionist tendency (which he was very familiar with) would strengthen there—and spill over into Poland which was still riven with conflicts.

He was also afraid of the growing influence in Czechoslovakia—as he imagined it—of West Germany.[3] It was only two years later that Gomułka himself brought about the signing of a border treaty between West Germany and Poland, that is, the recognition of the Polish character of the lands Germany had lost as a result of the Second World War. Ostensibly, this was illogical, since Poland recognised East Germany as a separate state and it was East Germany, not West Germany, that bordered Poland. But both the nations, and most likely Gomułka personally, knew well which of the two states truly represented Germany.

Strengthened, as he must have believed, by the signing of the treaty, Gomułka decided to drastically increase food prices. It should be remembered that in a centrally planned economy, it was the state, not the market, which set prices. Not only was the increase very large, but it was introduced shortly before Christmas, when people buy a lot of food. The result was riots, especially in the port cities on the Baltic coast, which were bloodily suppressed. The nominally workers' state again fired on the workers. Gomułka, who had assumed power in the wake of the shooting of workers in Poznań in 1956 and who was the only First Secretary of the Central Committee of the PZPR to be genuinely welcomed by the nation, ended his rule by shooting at the workers again.

Edward Gierek replaced Gomułka as First Secretary. During the first period of his rule, he seemed to realise better that the country needed to be modernised. However, he acted in a very unwise and short-sighted way, without any sensible reform of the economic system. As a result of importing investment funds to modernise the production processes in many factories—beyond the capacity to absorb these funds—he indebted the country. He decided to construct new large steelworks: probably primarily to build his own future legacy. He had crazy ideas, such as regulating the Vistula, perhaps necessary but very difficult and expensive to achieve. His craziest idea, luckily not taken up, was the idea of building a Polish island near Antarctica for krill fishing. He had probably been told that this marine crustacean could play an important role in feeding humanity, which some believed at the time.

The Poles were at first happy with Gierek. He was in better touch with the people than Gomułka, especially at the end of his rule. It was pleasant to live better on money borrowed from the West, to have small passenger cars manufactured under a FIAT license, and to enjoy the finally rebuilt Royal Castle in Warsaw. In the mid-1970s, however, the situation quickly began to deteriorate again. In 1975, a group of intellectuals, Tadeusz

Kowalik among them, wrote a letter to Gierek calling for fundamental systemic changes. The wheels of history, however, were already turning in another direction.

In 1976, an increase in the price of groceries was announced. This resulted in a wave of demonstrations, the largest of which was in the city of Radom. These evolved into riots, which were brutally suppressed, though without the use of weapons. Gierek remembered well what had happened in Poznań in 1956 and on the Coast in 1970. He had decided that, under his rule, weapons would not be used against workers, and he never wavered from this decision. Nevertheless, people were beaten, arrested, put on trial, sentenced to prison, and idiotic rallies in support of the First Secretary, against the demonstrators, took place all over the country. Then, in 1977, a group of intellectuals, mainly but not exclusively from Warsaw, organised an association called the Workers' Defence Committee, with the aim of helping those arrested and their families. Tadeusz Kowalik was among the signatories of the movement's founding declaration. What was new—in the entire Soviet camp—was not only the founding of such an organisation, the use of the words 'defence of the workers' in its name (in a country nominally ruled by workers!), but also the openness of its activities. To some extent, this was made possible by a progressive change in the atmosphere in Poland, the USSR, and internationally (a reduction in fear!). However, it was also the result of a desire to tell people not to be afraid, to act, even though they would face unpleasantness, trouble, police searches of homes, arrests, and so on. In the same year, Kowalik and his colleagues began to organise lectures for students, outside the universities, on topics that were either ignored or biased in university teaching. This movement was modelled on a nineteenth-century example, taken from Poland under the Russian partition, taking from it the name: *Towarzystwo Kursów Naukowych* (Society for Academic Courses). Kowalik was one of the signatories of the founding declaration. He taught classes on 'Economic history and the history of economic thought in contemporary Poland'. The Society's activities were obviously extra-legal, and militias of young people loyal to the system were sent to disrupt lectures or even to beat up attendees.

And then, in August 1980, came a key moment in the growing conflict. Mass workers' strikes were ignited in Poland. The Marxist vision was actually being realised: the working class was acting, not against the owners of the means of production in the literal sense, but against their collective owners, or at least their disposers. It meant nothing that these 'owners of

People's Poland' sometimes came from working-class families, may have been poor in their youth and had undergone rapid social advancement. Marx's thesis that the social and economic system creates forces that destroy it was also confirmed. People's Poland built—it is another matter how sensibly—large industrial plants and it was the workers of these plants who protested. Marx wrote that the bourgeoisie, by creating industry, unites the proletariat, and this thesis was also confirmed. Even if it was not the bourgeoisie that built the industry, it was the working class that united: first in the factories and then much more widely.

Of course, the movement developed under different slogans. Workers went on strike and many Poles joined the movement in the name of better living conditions, a better place for the Church and religion in public life, opposition to censorship and for greater cultural freedom, even in opposition to communism and the liberation of the country from Soviet domination. Some of these slogans were deliberately held back by the protestors, for fear of provoking Soviet intervention. Not all today are equally recalled as slogans of the movement. Today, this movement is spoken of as a fundamental step towards Poland regaining its independence from Soviet domination. Even General Jaruzelski, hardly stated, when announcing the imposition of martial law, that the aim was to save communism in Poland. He said that he was saving Poland, and the implication was that he was saving it from potential Soviet intervention. This is not the place to consider whether Poland actually faced the threat of such an intervention, although it is my belief that the General took into account the possibility of it. Rather, he sensed that he could only appeal to people using this argument. It is for this reason, therefore, that the mass movement of this time is still regarded as being one for national independence. However, this movement did not 'only' have such a character. The eminent late journalist Ryszard Kapuściński characterised the striking workers of the Gdańsk Shipyard, the epicentre of the strikes, to whom he travelled as follows:

> On the Coast, the workers shattered the stereotype of the labourer that had been lingering in official cabinets and elite salons. The labourer does not discuss—he executes the plan. If one wants the prole [*robol*] to speak out, it is only for the sake of promises and assurances. The prole only cares about one thing: how much he earns. When he leaves the factory, he carries screws, ropes and tools in his pockets. If it weren't for the management, the workers would rob the whole plant. Then they stand in front of the beer stalls. Then they sleep. In the morning, on the train to work, they play cards. When they

> arrive at the factory, they queue up to see the doctor and take sick leave. It's a hard life managing workers. There is nothing to talk to them about. There is a lot of sighing about it at all the important meetings.
>
> Meanwhile, on the Coast, and then all over the country, from beyond this vapour of contented self-restraint, a young face of a new generation of workers has emerged—thinking, intelligent, aware of their place in society. (Kapuściński, 1990, pp. 29–30)

Kapuściński continued:

> Whoever tries to reduce the coastal movement to wage and living standard matters has not understood anything. For the main motive of these occurrences was human dignity, there was a striving to create new relations between people, in every place and at all levels, there was the principle of mutual respect binding everyone without exception, the principle according to which the subordinate is also a partner. (Kapuściński, 1990, p. 31)

Importantly, Kapuściński drew a general conclusion: 'For the August strike was both a dramatic struggle and a celebration. A struggle for one's rights and a Celebration of Straightened Arms, Lifted Heads' (Kapuściński, 1990, p. 29).

For Tadeusz Kowalik, what was happening at that time was a reopening of the road he had already entered immediately after the war and which, in this first edition, was growing increasingly distasteful to him. He quickly signed an appeal by well-known intellectuals, calling on the communist authorities to respect the striking workers and enter into negotiations with them. He is believed to have initiated taking the text of this appeal to the shipyards. On the spot, he became one of the experts of the Inter-Union Strike Committee, organised in the shipyard first by the striking workers of the Coast and then more widely.

For the strikers, the support of outsiders alone was important. It also raised the visibility of the strike abroad. It had a practical significance in terms of their ability to formulate demands and negotiate with the authorities. As a consequence of the strike, the Solidarity trade union was born: the first (apart from the Catholic Church and smaller churches) nationwide structure independent of the communist regime. Between 1980 and 1981, Kowalik was an advisor to the Solidarity leadership and an advisor to the leadership of the union's intellectual agency, the Centre for Social and Professional Work. He clearly pushed to maintain the union's leftist direction, which was not an easy task. 'Solidarity' intrinsically contained many characteristics of a left-wing movement and so did many of its demands. However, left-wing discourse was then largely appropriated in Poland by the communist establishment and the right-wing discourse was therefore often dominant. Moreover, in the economy, after the discrediting of communist economics, liberal capitalism appeared to many people as the only sensible solution.

The collapse of communism in Poland in 1989 was a phenomenon dictated by many factors on the ground, in the USSR, and in the world. It took a lot of people by surprise. The journey from socialism to capitalism could not have been predicted by Marx, nor—many years later—was it likely to have been predicted by Tadeusz Kowalik. In Poland, the working class—to use Marxian terminology—won capitalism, or at least contributed to its reign. In addition, especially in the first moments of the transition, it was a wild capitalism. The path illuminated by, to name symbolically, Margaret Thatcher and Ronald Reagan, was radically pursued. Numerous social groups—people who were losing their jobs—found themselves in a very dramatic situation. The workers who went on strike against communism in 1980 would have been the first to be surprised to learn that registered unemployment alone between 1990 and mid-1994 would affect 16.6% of the labour force (Pańków & Ziółkowski, 2001, p. 100). The transition was carried out in a politically dangerous way, strengthening the nationalist-populist right wing, which to this day plays on the notion of social solidarity and helping the less well off. The right wing also raises issues of dependence on the West, sometimes describing Poland as having become a semi-colonial country.

Tadeusz Kowalik distanced himself from the accepted path of reform. He did not take part in the Round Table talks, although he supported the negotiations between Solidarity and the communist authorities—like the vast majority of people who wanted change and preferred to achieve it without the risk of bloodshed. After the fall of communism, he did not take up any state position, like many of his colleagues from the milieu of intellectuals that had initially opposed the PZPR. He was very critical of the free-market economic plan of reform, called the 'Balcerowicz Plan' (named after the leading reformer, Leszek Balcerowicz, Deputy Prime Minister and Minister of Finance in 1989–1991 and 1997–2000 and President of the National Bank of Poland in 2001–2007).

Thanks to the transition, Kowalik was given the long-overdue professorial title, this is a state appointment in Poland, which he had been denied during communism. In 1992, however, he co-founded the left-wing party

'Labour Union'. However, after the experience of communism, left-wing thinking had little chance of wide acceptance in Poland, although parties and politicians originating from the PZPR even came to power over time, and today the left has a certain voice in the political life of the country. Kowalik did, however, develop leftist thinking in the sphere of economic reflection. Let me quote his letter to me, written in 2006.[4] In it, he criticises an article I published at the time (Kula, 2006).[5] Although I was not sure whether to publish this letter, I have decided to do so as I am the subject of his criticism, although I am not convinced he was right. In this article I wrote a nuanced analysis of the transformation, which for Kowalik was not sufficiently critical. I am, however, somewhat comforted that the subject heading of the email was: 'praise+polemic'. His email read:

> Dear Marcin
> I briefly absorbed your article in 'Europa'. It is an important text, which I will probably
> return to again. But in the heat of the moment, perhaps more sharply than it deserves, I will note two things that aroused my opposition.
> 1) the consolation that 'despite all the weaknesses, the Polish transformation does not present itself too badly'. If it weren't for the fact that I hold both of you,[6] in high esteem—whenever I think of you, and I'm glad you exist—I would have written an ironic letter to 'Europa' as follows:
> 'Sure it's not bad, we only have an unemployment rate two or three times higher than the EU average and above that of our comparable neighbors like the Czech Republic and Hungary. Only 87.5% of the registered unemployed do NOT[7] receive benefits. Only half of the people of working age are economically inactive. In the last ten years the number of those living below the biological minimum level only rose by two and a half times. In 16 years the number of people living below the subsistence minimum increased and, as yesterday's *Rzepa*[8] reported, only one in ten children living in the country's capital city go hungry.'
> 2) 'We dreamed of Western efficiency... welfare-oriented'.[9] This is a cliché used by official sociologists, which is unworthy of you. Read more often social policy studies. Or perhaps—as pointed out in numerous works by Gardawski, Gilejko and many others—we dreamed of a West German system, Swedish capitalism? Would you believe that the West outside America has moved away from the welfare state? So what and to what extent is, as you write, 'scary'?[10] How does this scariness affect your assessment of what has happened in Poland?

> I insist that one of the most unjust social systems experienced in Europe in the second half of the last century was established in Poland. And I have been insisting on this for ten years now.
> I am hugging you tightly, to the point of encouraging you to self-reflect - Tadeusz

What do I say after re-reading this letter after 18 years? I think I will maintain my formerly nuanced opinion. Maybe, in the end, Poland came out better from the 'shock therapy' than the countries which chose more gradual paths of reform. Maybe, after all, some protective measures towards marginalised social groups were possible at the time. It is well known, for example, that in the democratisation of Germany after the Second World War, great care was taken not to create groups that threatened democracy because of their situation. It is clear that, for various reasons, these situations were not comparable, and unfortunately I no longer have a discussion partner such as Tadeusz Kowalik to reflect on such matters. I will therefore limit myself to taking up at the end the words of my one-time pupil and now colleague, Adam Leszczyński, about Tadeusz Kowalik: 'To the end of his life, he was an advocate of the search for an economic system that would be devoid of the defects of capitalism—the pursuit of profit, the exploitation of workers, cyclical crises—and at the same time of the defects of the planned socialist economy, with its inefficiency and wastefulness. His ideal has always been market socialism, an economic system with a human face: guaranteeing equality and universal social security, but also growth and market efficiency' (Leszczyński, 2012). I leave hanging (with regret!) the question of whether such a thing is possible.

Translated from Polish by Grzegorz Konat and Gavin Rae

Notes

1. I am familiar with many elements of Professor Kowalik's biography thanks to my long-standing friendship with him. While writing these pages I also used his biography contained in the publication (Halbersztadt, 2000) and in the biographical sketch by Beata Losson from the website 'Encyklopedia Solidarności' [Encyclopedia of Solidarity] (the latter is no longer available; editors' note).
2. Here are some topics of papers written by IKKN students: 'Marxism-Leninism on the role of the proletarian state in the period of the construction of socialism', 'The leadership role of the PZPR in the struggle for

socialism in Poland', 'The development of historical materialism in the works of Comrade Bierut', 'The Marxist-Leninist theory of proletarian revolution', 'PPS revisionism: the ideology of the agent of the bourgeoisie', 'The influence of Marxist-Leninist philosophy on the Polish intelligentsia of the interwar period (Rudniański, Spasowski, Czarnowski)', 'The significance of the work of Maria Curie-Skłodowska for the further development of dialectical materialism', 'The reactionary role of neo-positivism in Polish philosophy of the interwar period', 'Critique of the views of T. Twardowski', 'Critique of the views of T. Kotarbiński', 'Critique of the views of K. Ajdukiewicz', 'Reactionary face of phenomenology in Poland (Ingarden)', 'Critique of the sociology of F. Znaniecki', 'Critique of rural research in Polish bourgeois sociology of the interwar period (Bujak, Chałasiński, etc.)', 'Critique of Bystroń's sociology', 'The reactionary role of bourgeois sociology of the interwar period', 'The place of the views of St. Czarnowski in the sociology of the interwar period', 'Evaluation of the work of Ludwik Krzywicki' (Tematyka prac dysertacyjnych 1952, pp. 359–361). I thank Dr Krzysztof Persak for drawing my attention to this inventory.

3. At the time, the name 'German Federal Republic' was used in Poland, thus abbreviated to 'GFR'. The idea was to emphasise that there were supposedly two equal German states: the West German state and the German Democratic Republic, abbreviated as the GDR.
4. The letter was dated 11 January 2006. Clearly written quickly, it contained many typos, which I have corrected here.
5. I wrote this article in October 2005.
6. The author addresses me and my wife, Małgorzata Kula (an economist at the University of Warsaw).
7. Capital letters in the original.
8. Daily newspaper *Rzeczpospolita*.
9. The full passage in print read: 'We dreamt of Western productivity while retaining many socialist solutions at the same time. We wanted Western wealth and a state in its own way (like a socialist state) that was welfare-oriented'.
10. A reference to an excerpt from my article: 'If it had been said in 1980 that, as a result of the transition, unemployment would reach almost 20 per cent and Warsaw housing prices would reach prices close to Manhattan, few would have believed it. Nevertheless, although the former utopianism increases the psychological effects of a hard landing, they are still terrible even without it'.

References

Halbersztadt, J. (2000). Tadeusz Kowalik. In A. Dudek, J. Skórzyński, M. Strasz, & P. Sowiński (Eds.), *Opozycja w PRL. Słownik biograficzny. 1956–89* (Vol. 2, pp. 171–173). Ośrodek Karta.

History of the Communist Party of the Soviet Union (Bolsheviks): Short Course. (1939). New York: International Publishers.

Kapuściński, R. (1990). *Lapidarium*. Czytelnik.

Kula, M. (2006, January 11). Solidarność w 80 procentach. *Fakt*, supplement *Europa*, 2, 8–9.

Leszczyński, A. (2012, July 31). Nie żyje prof. Tadeusz Kowalik, wybitny ekonomista, krytyk Balcerowicza. *Wyborcza.pl*. Retrieved May 9, 2024, from https://wyborcza.pl/7,75398,12226083,nie-zyje-prof-tadeusz-kowalik-wybitny-ekonomista-krytyk-balcerowicza.html.

Osiatyński, J. (2012, August 7). Tadeusz Kowalik. 1926–2012. *Gazeta Wyborcza, 183*, 9.

Pańków, J., & Ziółkowski, M. (2001). Przemiany w sferze gospodarczej. Produkcja – praca – zatrudnienie – bezrobocie. In E. Wnuk-Lipiński & M. Ziółkowski (Eds.), *Pierwsza dekada niepodległości. Próba socjologicznej syntezy* (pp. 91–115). Instytut Studiów Politycznych PAN.

Stola, D. (2010). *Kraj bez wyjścia? Migracje z Polski 1949–1989*. Instytut Pamięci Narodowej and Instytut Studiów Politycznych PAN.

Tematyka prac dysertacyjnych z materializmu dialektycznego i historycznego w Instytucie Kształcenia Kadr Naukowych przy KC PZPR. (1952). *Myśl Filozoficzna, 1, 359–361*

Zaremba, M. (2001). *Komunizm, legitymizacja, nacjonalizm. Nacjonalistyczna legitymizacja władzy komunistycznej w Polsce*. TRIO and Instytut Studiów Politycznych PAN.

PART I

Tadeusz Kowalik and His Ideas

CHAPTER 2

The "Political Aspects of Full Employment" and the "'Crucial Reform' of Capitalism": A Discussion with Jan Toporowski on Kalecki and Kowalik

Riccardo Bellofiore

Introduction

'The Political Aspects of Full Employment', Kalecki's (1943) justifiably famous article published, is still worth reading today. Its significance is controversial: all the more so if we focus the discussion on the relationship of this article to the later one written by Kalecki together with Kowalik in 1970 and published in Italian in *Politica ed Economia* in 1971.

Jan Toporowski on *Contributions to Political Economy* (Toporowski, 2023) has returned to that article with many considerations with which I largely agree. There are, however, a few key points on which I would venture a dissenting opinion. In the following, in the spirit of dialogue, I present my objections and some alternative conclusions.[1]

R. Bellofiore (retired) (✉)
University of Bergamo, Bergamo, Italy

G. Konat, G. Rae (eds.), *Exploring the Ideas of Tadeusz Kowalik*,
https://doi.org/10.1007/978-3-032-09283-0_2

Full Employment Capitalism?

I agree with most of Toporowski's account of Kalecki's, 1943 article, but I disagree with how he summarises its message. We are told that Kalecki was optimistic that in a capitalist democracy the resistance of business leaders to full employment would be overcome. The Second World War confirmed the lesson of the First, that full employment was possible and that it had become an urgent social demand 'from below'. The traditionally accepted policy instruments for increasing employment through interest rate policy to boost private investment are not very effective. Private investment had to be boosted by public investment, if not by subsidising consumption, to reach that goal.

Kalecki affirms that full employment can be achieved through government spending but reminds us that there are objections to this popular view. These objections, although couched in economic terms, are essentially political. The first objection concerns the business community's aversion to government intervention, in general, and in the level and composition of employment, in particular. The second objection is that public spending competes with private initiatives. The third objection is that permanent full employment threatens labour discipline: if full employment persists, workers would no longer be controlled by the threat of lay-offs; hence, political stability could also unravel.

These objections explain the paradox of business resistance to the full-employment policies of Roosevelt and/or Keynes,[2] even though higher output and employment would benefit business profitability. Instead, when 'sound finance' prevails, the capitalist class powerfully directs investment and employment and controls government policy through the so-called 'state of confidence'. Toporowski refers to Kalecki's preference for economic policies that support mass consumption through welfare payments, pensions, family allowances, or subsidies to maintain low prices for basic necessities.

Kalecki asserts that *if* capitalism can accommodate full employment, this would amount to a 'crucial reform'. This fundamentally different capitalism requires new social and political institutions reflecting the increased power of the working class. This adaptation is the *conditio sine qua non* if capitalism is not to be discarded as an obsolete system. Toporowski sees in this line of thought Kalecki's convergence with Keynes and other progressives who maintained that mass unemployment was not necessarily a permanent feature of capitalism.

The conclusion is that the 1943 article contains the core of a kind of *full employment road to socialism*. A straight line leads to the 1970 article with Kowalik in *Politica ed economia*, according to which the tension between a policy of reform and revolutionary struggles is replaced by a fundamental reform that radically changes the system without abolishing capitalist relations of production.

I would like to propose a very different argument. 'Political Aspects of Full Employment' argues that *permanent* full employment, although necessary for a fully developed democracy, is *incompatible* with capitalism. The 1970 Kalecki-Kowalik 'crucial reform' article *contradicts* this earlier view. To properly understand the evolution of Kalecki's thinking, we need to look at a few articles he wrote in Polish about the United States in the 1950s and 1960s, where the economist argued that a kind of permanent full employment (and with it a fundamental reform) was *actually* already taking place, but according to peculiar modalities that worried Kalecki as a Marxian. His article with Kowalik can be understood as a development from these Polish articles.

In my view and in retrospect, unexpectedly the 1943 article amount to a prophetic outlook. Kalecki was able to predict some factors relevant to understanding the collapse of what has later been called as the Fordist configuration of capitalism in the *Trente Glorieuses*. On the contrary, the 1970 article with Kowalik on the crucial reform turned out to be short-sighted. This led Kowalik to change his views a few years later.

In the following pages I will try to put some flesh on the bones of this argument.

Mass Unemployment Is Inevitable Under Capitalism

The first comment I would like to make is that it is certainly true that in 1943 Kalecki believed that the pressure of the masses could overcome the opposition of the business world. He added, however, that even in this case full employment in a capitalist situation could only be *temporary*: this does not mean, of course, that it is not a reasonable goal for democratic movements and socialist policies. He may have had in mind the experience of the 1937–1938 recession during the second Roosevelt administration.

The reason for the temporary nature of full employment is that the *maintenance* of full employment would bring about social and political changes which would give new impetus to the opposition of the business leaders. Much more than Toporowski, I would emphasise the 'if' behind

Kalecki's argument. That is why, for me, Kalecki's answer in 1943 to the question 'if' an interventionist policy in favour of full employment would give way to a fundamentally different capitalism would be: *definitely not.* Capitalism cannot 'accommodate' full employment; it can only do so *briefly* and *locally.*

Toporowski is right that it is important to see Kalecki's contention on full employment against the background of Fascism and Nazism, but I fear that his interpretation short-circuits different lines of reasoning that were different at different stages. Kalecki's discussion of the Blum episode in France would be also important here, but I will not go into it too much and will only discuss aspects of his comments on the United States during the New Deal and in the 1950s and 1960s.

With regard to the Blum episode, I shall confine myself to the following considerations. For Kalecki, in periods of proportional increases in money wages and prices, corporate profits and productive workers' money incomes rise faster than the money incomes of those on fixed incomes who have little bargaining power in the market for productive resources. Kalecki sees this as the cause of a conflict of interests between wage increases in favour of the working class versus the purchasing power of the petty bourgeoisie. The doctrine of 'sound finance' demanded by the entrepreneurial bourgeoisie may be supported by the petty bourgeoisie, which sees it as a protection of its own interests against the workers... The big financiers and the 'passive' capitalists are hostile to a deficit policy. The fear of currency devaluation fuels the tendency to export capital abroad. The *de facto* devaluation of the currency, which is provoked in this way, confirms the fear itself.

Let me return for now to the 1943 article. A point that is usually not emphasised enough is that for Kalecki unemployment is not just a means of influencing wages, but more fundamentally of controlling workers' effort in capitalist labour processes. This is what 'labour discipline' actually means. It is well known that Kalecki never referred to the so-called 'labour theory of value': either endorsing or rejecting it. As I understand it, the 'labour theory of value' is not primarily a theory of price: here Kalecki had his own view of price determination in an oligopoly setting and rightly regarded 'free competition' as a dangerous myth. The labour theory of value is instead a genetical theory about the *constitution* of the value added in the period, and hence of the origin of surplus value.

The capitalist process strictly depends on the 'exploitation' of human beings as living bearers of labour power, and hence on the 'use' of that labour power hired on the labour market. The ‘sucking’ of living labour which is going on in capitalist labour processes is, however, conditional on the outcome of ‘class struggle in production’ (a term coined by Etienne Balibar). Production for ‘capital as a whole’, which has at its disposal money as capital and the means of production, is *nothing but* the ‘consumption’ of workers as ‘living labour power’. That is why the value added in the period exhibits *only* labour.

Kalecki, in 1943, fully understands that Keynesian policies, if successful and permanent, would endanger capital as a ‘social relation in production’. This argument is strictly consistent with the labour theory of value as I have described it, as it is the idea that this conflicts in the buying and selling of labour power and in the immediate valorisation process can create negative expectations about wages and productivity, so that investment is not forthcoming, and in this case no investment, no surplus value. This is what, according to some authors (e.g. Napoleoni, the early Aglietta, the late Glyn and others), partly, and perhaps even crucially, accounts for the downturn phase of Fordism, which began since the mid-late 1960s, well before the onset in 1973–1974 of the oil crisis.

The ‘political business cycle’ safely maintains capitalist social relations. That is why a Marxian, *not* a Keynesian, like Kalecki, should oppose this kind of policies. But even a non-Marxian progressive should oppose a regime of modest economic fluctuation just below the level of full employment: it does not ensure *permanent* full employment. The fact that permanent full employment is beyond the reach of Keynesian policies is not a *technical* difficulty. It is, of course, a *political* difficulty, but that means appropriate to capitalist *social* relations. No more and no less. We are not in an economics discourse, but in a political economy discourse, where economic, social, political cannot be divorced.

If the conclusion of the 1943 article is precisely to argue that mass unemployment is inevitable under capitalism, this is a significant contrast with Keynes and most of the heterodoxy that today urges a ‘rethink’ of capitalism. Toporowski seems rather to see a continuity between Kalecki, Keynes, and the progressives. He writes [Toporowski, 2023: p. 12, my italics] that

> [t]he purpose of his article was to show *how this could be done*. But he also recognised that a regime of full employment would change the fundamental conditions under which capitalism was used to operating. At the end of his life, in 1970, as an alternative to ‘the problem of reconciling the struggle for

> reform with the revolutionary struggle', Kalecki suggested a 'Crucial Reform' that '*will strengthen, not weaken, the revolutionary potential of mass movements*'. Such a reform would arise when '... the strong pressure of the masses leads to such a radical reform of the system that, without abolishing the existing relations of production, a new valve is opened for the development of the forces of production. There will then be a paradoxical situation: a 'crucial reform' imposed on the ruling class may *stabilise* the system, temporarily at least. (Kalecki & Kowalik, 1971, p. 467)

Consumption and Socialisation of Investment

Let us stay with the 1943 article for a while. In his argument, Kalecki responds to the objection that the government would have nothing to show for its money if it subsidised consumption. He insists that such subsidies would ensure a higher standard of living for the population, adding the rhetorical provocation: 'Isn't this [consumption] the purpose of all economic activity?' Kalecki is right in general, but the point is that we live *in capitalism*, where this is not the goal.

Under capitalism, as Kalecki well knew, the *composition* of production is indirectly but powerfully determined by capitalist enterprises: including that between those goods which are made available to workers as consumers and those which are not. What *monetary* subsidies can buy on the market depends on the *real* production that capitalist enterprises sell on the market. Moreover, there is no purpose of economic activity 'in general'. The purpose of capitalist economic activity is surplus value, not household consumption. Capitalism should not be confused with socialism.

The rhetorical nature of Kalecki's question is obvious. The idea of the mainstream(s) in economics is that the economic process is a one-way street from resources to consumption, according to Sraffa's brilliant characterisation. Unfortunately, Keynes himself writes in the *General Theory* that '[c]onsumption—to repeat the obvious—is the sole end and object of all economic activity' (Keynes, 1973, pp. 104–106). He should have known better, for in 1933 he wrote,

> Karl Marx ... pointed out that the nature of production in the actual world is not, as economists seem often to suppose, a case of C-M-C', i.e. of exchanging commodity for money in order to obtain another commodity. *That may be the standpoint of the private consumer. But it is not the attitude*

> *of business, which is a case* of M-C-M', i.e. *of parting with money for commodity in order to obtain more money.* (Keynes, 1979, p. 81, my italics)

Capitalism is a circular process of producing (more) commodities by means of commodities, (more) money by means of money, in fact (more) value by means of value. What should be fixed is not monetary subsidies but welfare payments *in kind*, which is indeed the argument of authors as diverse as Graziani and Minsky.

I agree with Toporowski's criticism of what he calls *Business Keynesianism*. It looks very much like the economic policy favoured by the Neoclassical Synthesis: although, to get the full picture, one should add to private investment a fiscal policy aimed at manipulating consumption. In his 1975 *John Maynard Keynes* Minsky called it the high-profit-high-investment economy.

Minsky is also an interesting read on another subject that Toporowski touches on in these pages: the socialisation of investment. Toporowski writes that 'Kalecki's sceptical remarks about the difficulties of coordinating private investment do not quite put an end to the "socialisation of investment" that Keynes called for at the end of his *General Theory*' (Toporowski, 2023, p. 11). Minsky was far more critical of Keynes's view of the socialisation of investment.

Keynes wrote that

> a somewhat extensive socialisation of investment will prove the only means of securing an approximation to full employment... But beyond this there is no obvious case for a system of state socialism which would embrace most of the economic life of the community. It is not the ownership of the means of production which it is important for the State to take over. Once the State is able to determine the full employment of resources, all that is necessary will have been achieved and no break with the general tradition of society will be necessary. If central control succeeds in establishing, as far as possible, an aggregate volume of production corresponding to full employment, the classical theory comes into play again. There is no objection to the classical theory as to what private self-interest determines what is produced, in what proportions the factors of production are combined to produce it, and also as to the distribution of value. (Keynes, 1973, p. 378)

It is a contradictory view. The towering heights of the economy must be socialised, and high consumption, in the sense of collective consumption, must be achieved. Minsky wants *more* socialisation of investment than Keynes, and he pushes for *communal* consumption rather than private consumption. I see collective consumption as part of autonomous demand, just as indebted consumption was in Neoliberalism (though socially they are opposite), and just as private investment and capitalist consumption. The gulf between this heretical view of society and the economy is that, to quote Minsky,

> [w]e are inevitably forced back to the normative question of for whom the game should be set and what kind of output should be produced. It is clear that if reasonably full employment is the dominant objective, then the system of perpetual waste and want has so far been successful. (Minsky, 1975, p. 164)

This means not only that the risk of 'it' (a Great Depression) should not be repeated, but also that the deterioration of the biological and social environment associated with 'Keynesian' policies must be stopped.

The pandemics have reminded us of the lesson we should have learned from the War and the New Deal, which is more radical than Keynesianism: that the core of controlling the economy should concern determining 'how', 'how much', 'where', 'what', and 'for whom' to produce. This implies a radicalisation of Minsky's notion of socialisation into that of a 'social production economy'.[3] And it is somehow a reformulation of Walter Benjamin's plea for revolution as pulling of the emergency brake on the runaway train of capitalist accumulation. I think that this Minskyan perspective needs to be articulated with Kalecki's view, and this requires original thinking out of the repetition of one's own views.

On the other hand, Toporowski emphasises an opposition between Kalecki and Keynes that may be based on a misunderstanding. Toporowski claims that Keynes was sanguine about the employment possibilities of 'filling old bottles with banknotes' or building pyramids. Instead, Kalecki believed that public works had to satisfy some need. But in the *General Theory*, we read

> It is curious how common sense, struggling to escape from absurd conclusions, has been apt to arrive at a preference for wholly 'wasteful' forms of credit expenditure rather than for partly wasteful forms which, because they are not wholly wasteful, tend to be judged on strict 'business' principles. For example, unemployment relief financed by loans is more readily accepted than the financing of improvements at a cost below the current rate of interest; while the form of digging holes in the ground known as gold-mining,

> which not only adds nothing to the real wealth of the world but involves the disutility of labour, is the most acceptable of all solutions. If the Treasury were to fill old bottles with banknotes, bury them at suitable depths in disused coal mines, which are then filled to the surface with urban rubbish, and leave it to private enterprise, on the time-honoured principles of laissez-faire, to dig up the notes (the right to do so being acquired, of course, by tendering for leases), there need be no more unemployment, and with the help of the repercussions the real income of the community, and also its capital wealth, would probably become a good deal greater than it actually is. *It would indeed be more sensible to build houses and the like; but if there are political and practical difficulties in the way, the above would be better than nothing.* (Keynes, 1936, p. 129, my italics)

Keynes was pushing for something socially useful that would meet public needs: 'digging holes' is better than nothing because of the effect on employment. But the real question is a different one. Why should a writer who in 1929 argued that a three-hour day was already feasible, and who despised the 'love of money' as a disgusting morbidity, change his mind in 1936 and argue for more work and employment rather than a reduction in working hours for all? The answer lies in a date between the writing of *Economic Possibilities of Our Grandchildren* and *The General Theory*: 1933. It is probably the same answer that must be given to the question of why Keynes was prepared to accept a wasteful 'better than nothing' solution to mass unemployment.

Fascism and the Articles on the United States in the 1950s and 1960s

Fascism was a political response to the conflict Kalecki highlighted between full employment and social stability: political pressure replaces the economic pressure of unemployment. I agree with Mariano D'Antonio (1978) when he writes that Kalecki was acutely aware that the state in a representative democratic regime is a battleground for the assertion of conflicting interests. Adhering to a 'classical' interpretation of politics within Marxism, he maintains that, as long as capitalism and its system of social values persist, there will be insurmountable limits to the political and material emancipation of the working class. These limits are enforced by the ruling class either through the direct use of the state, that is, by Fascism and the suppression of political freedoms, or indirectly through the objective force of the economic process, by the emergence of unemployment as a result of a deliberate budgetary policy.

However, it is extremely interesting to look at what Kalecki wrote in two articles in Polish, which I was able to read in Italian translation already in 1975 in a collection of essays *Sul capitalismo contemporaneo* [On Contemporary Capitalism] edited by Alberto Chilosi. They are now available in English translation in the *Collected Works* edited by Jerzy Osiatyński, Volume VII and Volume II.

In the first, collected in Volume VII, 'The Economic Situation in the USA as Compared with the Pre-War Period', Kalecki reiterates that the imbalance between the development of the productive forces and the markets is one of the main contradictions inherent in the capitalist system, and that this contradiction became more acute in the period 1937–1955. The relative share of big business's accumulation of the national product increased, mainly absorbed by armaments. However, there was a decrease in unemployment mainly due to an increase in the armed forces and in government employees, but this did not have the expected effect on the standard of living.

According to Kalecki, the militarisation of the US economy led to the full utilisation of its productive forces for two reasons. One was that the expenditure from the imperialist military system counteracted the expansionary effect on capacity of the higher share of big capital accumulation in national income. The other was that the higher number of military and civil servants allowed a significant reduction in unemployment. These two factors held back the potential growth of the standard of living by reducing the share of consumption in the national income, in favour of armaments and the associated trade balance surplus, and also by increasing the number of unproductive workers in relation to the total number of people employed in the production of consumer goods and services.

Although lower unemployment and a significant rise in living standards confirm the trend towards the disintegration of monopoly capitalism, Kalecki argues that these results have a political significance that should not be underestimated. To make a proper assessment, one fact must be taken into account: that in the United States the means of information and propaganda (the press, cinema, radio, and television) are de facto under the full control of the ruling class. Hence the conclusion. With a high level of employment and a standard of living that was considerably higher than before the war (as a result of the increase in labour productivity), an effective propaganda conquered the broad masses of the population.

> This explains the fact that in the USA there is no significant opposition to armaments and the cold war; that the anti-capitalist undercurrent which characterized the New Deal period has slackened; and that the trade unions are part and parcel of the military imperialist setup. Workers in the USA are not duller and trade union leaders are not more reactionary 'by nature' than in other capitalist countries. Rather, the political situation in the USA is simply, in accordance with the precepts of historical materialism, the unavoidable consequence of economic developments and of characteristics of the superstructure of monopoly capitalism in its advanced stage. (Kalecki, 1997, p. 286)

This is a Classical Marxist view, but at the same time stands in contrast to the 1943 article. In 1943 the Marxian proposition was that full employment is *incompatible* with capitalism. In 1956 the argument tries to reconcile the fact that, in spite of that, something like permanent full employment *actually* occurred, with Kalecki's understanding of US capitalism as imperialist and driven by militarism and arms spending. It is a *new* political-social-economic situation in which, in order to guarantee the subordination of the working class, there is now *no need of extensive labour unemployment*, nor of the use of political coercion as in Fascism and Nazism, nor of the political business cycle as defined in 1943.

Let us see how the discussion develops in his other article in Polish, *The Economic Situation in the USA, 1956–1961*, published in 1962 and now collected in Volume II. I am not referring here to the details of the conjunctural analysis, but to the general conclusions he drew about the nature of US capitalism. As Kalecki himself explained in the introduction to the Polish collection in which he included the article I am referring to, the latter is a paper closely related to the 1943 article.

Kalecki contrasts his approach with four views. The most extreme views are that capitalism is rejuvenated and dynamic (yet capitalism still has a tendency to recession if not for government budget interventions), and that nothing has really changed in capitalism. The other two views are that there is now 'planning in capitalism' through the joint action of big capital and government (which Kalecki judges to be pure fantasy), and that the role of the capitalist government is just of softening recessions and accelerating business upswings. For Kalecki, anti-crisis interventionism, let alone 'planned' capitalism, is not characterised by consistent actions by the ruling class.

As far as the overall representation is concerned, Kalecki now designs an alternative version of the picture he gave in 1956. The post–Second World War period reflected a favourable economic situation. There was a rapid rise in the standard of living and low unemployment compared to the pre-war period. The absence of serious crises changed the mentality of the US masses. In them there is not much left of the vehement anti-capitalism that was typical after the great crisis of the 1930s, Kalecki writes: a very different opinion from that behind his 1943 article. However,

> there is a new factor which will gradually but persistently work in the opposite direction. The standard of living is now increasing very slowly. Since 1950 it has increased by only 1.5% p.a. For the present, this probably does not have a great effect on the masses, since they still tend to compare their situation now with that before the war. However, if, as is likely, the growth rate of the standard of living continues to be low, its jump from the pre-war period to 1950 will be forgotten as time goes on and dissatisfaction will spread, especially among the less affluent groups of the population. Hence the attitude of the American masses towards capitalism will gradually change, intensified still further as the growth rate of the USA lags behind that of the socialist countries. (Kalecki, 1991, p. 401)

As the editors of the *Collected Works* observe in relation to this article, '[c]ertain aspects of the changes in socio-political relations and in the conditions and forms of the class struggle in the developed capitalist countries after the Second World War, connected with the working class and the masses becoming more conformist, were taken up by Kalecki later' in the article with Kowalik on the 'crucial reform' (Kalecki, 1991, p. 585).

As Mariano D'Antonio (1978) has pointed out: on the one hand, Kalecki's political analyses are very much conditioned by the concrete circumstances to which they refer, and they are accompanied by the temptation to generalise and derive 'laws' from the observed phenomena. On the other hand, however, the Polish economist is much more wary than other scholars of proclaiming as irreversible phenomena what are peculiar features that have emerged in the historical events of contemporary capitalism.

An Aside on the Monetary Aspect of Kalecki

I will not discuss section 3 of Toporowski (2023) on the 'monetary and financing aspects'. I find it excellent as an exposition of Kalecki's thinking. There is only one point, though not a minor one, where my understanding may differ from Toporowski.

Are we sure that what Kalecki's argument about the financing of government deficits does not depend on the fact that, in his view, the velocity of circulation can change in such a way as to achieve the desired result? This is in fact partially spelled out by the same Toporowski (p. 6):

> Financing the deficit through the issue of bonds allowed the government to use the monetary resources *that were already there* to finance a current fiscal deficit that would put the money back into the portfolios of capitalists. Servicing the resulting national debt through a capital levy, as a charge on those monetary resources, would take money out from those portfolios, and put the money back in as payments on the national debt. In this way, the fiscal deficit and the servicing of the national debt can be *accommodated by accelerating* the financial circulation of money between government accounts, and the accounts of big business.

Of course, in this way the 'technical' aspects, as Kalecki would say, are pushed into the background. One of the merits of Toporowski's writings on Kalecki is the insistence on entrepreneurial capital as a necessary precondition for investment decisions and hence for business expansion. It is certainly true that there is a continuity here with a Classical-Marxian emphasis on the ownership of means of production. But I would not be so sure that this is linked to the idea of the necessity of a prior availability of money capital. This last thesis can lead to a confusion between the historical fact of accumulated wealth and the logical monetary investigation of a capitalist process. Moreover, while it is true that any level of investment is self-financing, Toporowski follows Kalecki in downplaying the key role of finance to production. As Messori (1991) has clarified,

> [f]irms as a whole must increase the amount of money wages *before* receiving a corresponding increase in their monetary proceeds. The time-lag between the payment of money wages and consumption expenditures is determined by the production period of the composite consumption good. Throughout this production period, either the assets or the liabilities of the capitalist class with regard to the banking system must, respectively, decrease or increase.

> Kalecki can implicitly exclude these possibilities by means of [the] assumption [that] the productions of the two composite goods do not take time. Thus *he reduces the economic process to a point of time*: the firms' payment of the money wages and realisation of monetary proceeds are *simultaneous.* (p. 307, my italics)

and

> *it is incorrect to restrict the analysis of financing to an increase in investment* … if the production of the composite consumption good takes time, the capitalist class will need financing to pay the money wages in advance. Moreover, without government intervention and external exchanges [there is] the need to maintain that firms as a whole hold bank deposits at the opening phase of any period. The only possible source of these deposits is bank credit obtained in the opening phase of some previous period and not reimbursed at its closing phase. … this is equivalent to the affirmation that commercial banks *renewed* their credits. Thus we may hereafter assume that the aggregate of firms must finance the entire amount of money wages through bank credit. (pp. 307–308)

The danger of Toporowski's Kaleckian analysis is that it confuses *investment financing* and *production financing.*

The Crucial Reform

What does my interpretation say about the article published in *Politica ed economia* in 1971? Can we accept Toporowski's position that Kalecki and Kowalik see the 'Crucial Reform' as a new capitalist configuration which, contrary to the standard assessment in the socialist movement, will strengthen and not weaken the revolutionary potential of mass movements?

I don't think so. Rather, I believe that Kalecki and Kowalik do not present a suggestion, but they do envision a 'problem' to be dealt with by critical social theory. To understand their argument, we need to follow closely their rethinking of the old opposition between (radical) reform and (socialist) revolution:

> The *problem* of reform in capitalism is most often posed in socialist literature as the problem of *reconciling the struggle for reform with the revolutionary struggle*—that is, the struggle to change the social system altogether—and of conducting the fight for immediate and partial goals so that it will

> strengthen, not weaken, the revolutionary potential of mass movements. (Kalecki & Kowalik, 1971, p. 467, my italics)

The problem should be re-examined anew contemplating an 'extreme' situation, where

> the strong pressure of the masses leads to such a radical reform of the system, in spite of the opposition of the ruling class, that, without abolishing existing relations of production, a new valve is opened for the development of productive forces. There will then be a *paradoxical* situation: a 'crucial reform' imposed on the ruling class may *stabilize* the system, *temporarily* at least. As we argue below, *we have to do with just such a situation in contemporary capitalism.* (p. 467, translation altered my italics)

What we have here, then, is a 'fact' that leads to a 'paradox'. The Italian translation was revised by Paolo Sylos Labini and is slightly stronger than the English, as in Collected Works, Volume II: *tale situazione si verifica appunto nel capitalismo contemporaneo* [such a situation occurs precisely in contemporary capitalism]. The reference to Sylos Labini, 'who corrected the linguistic deficiencies', is taken from Antonio Pesenti's editorial note, appended as a preface to the article. The article was published in 1971, after the death of Kalecki, who had sent the article with Kowalik to Pesenti in a letter dated 3 April 1970, proposing it for *Critica Marxista*. Kalecki anticipated that the review would not want to 'take responsibility' for the argument, which he expected to be controversial, but also theoretically and politically relevant. He would have no objection to an editorial introduction. *Politica ed economia* presented the article after this editorial note by Pesenti as *lo scritto di Kalecki* [Kalecki's paper]. Kowalik, however, appeared in the title preceding the letter and in the editorial note.]

Pesenti faithfully summarised the main thesis of the article as follows. The paradox was that the winning social pressure 'from below' would determine a high degree of *economic* stability in the system and its acceptance by the masses: stability in the structural spheres would lead to a consequent greater *social* stability. The break from conformity, that is, from the accepted dominance of the bourgeois apparatus, could only come from the new, not yet integrated generations, as the current student movement (the so-called movement of 1968) shows. Pesenti then proceeded to a criticism of Kalecki and Kowalik that I would not consider here.

I prefer to return to Kalecki and Kowalik's own line of thought. After reviewing previous debates, they give a synthetic picture of capitalism since the 1920s. Apart from the conquest of the 8-hour day and the extension of social security, they argue that it was almost the same capitalism as before the First World War. The turning point was the crisis of 1929–1933, when the period of 'crucial reform' began, especially in Germany and the United States. Mass unemployment was countered by state intervention filling the gap of insufficient demand. During the Second World War, capitalism was centrally managed, but controls weakened considerably after the end of the conflict. What allowed the realisation of accumulated profits was the constitution of a capitalist system of large corporations with complementary markets guaranteed by state purchases, mainly of armaments.

It is clear, then, that (contrary to the 1943 article) the process of 'crucial reform', that was supposedly *already in motion* in the 1930s, was *accelerated* in the 1940s by the War and by some of the experiences of the 1950s and 1960s, especially in the United States. State intervention in the expansion of markets *became an institution*, making it possible to limit unemployment to a few per cent and thus *to conform in practice something like the 'right to work' slogan of 1848.* Consistent with his articles on the United States in 1956 and 1962, in 1971 Kalecki, now with Kowalik, observes that this state of affairs

> led to a certain *transformation of the working class*, which on the whole became *radically reformist* in its attitude toward capitalism. As a result of high employment rates workers got a satisfactory level of real income, anti-capitalist attitudes have weakened considerably. They ceased to fight for a reduction in armaments and have become very sensitive to adhering to the 'rules of the game'. (Kalecki and Kowalik, 472, my italics)

Moreover:

> The relative stability of reformed capitalism depends on a *high degree of social conformity*. One can express the cautious opinion that *recent student movements* seem to be an omen of the declining ability of the bourgeois power apparatus to manipulate new generations entering the historical scene. This phenomenon is all the more serious since, with the rapid progress in science and technology, *intellectuals* are beginning to play an ever greater role as a social group. For the time being, student movements in some cases have contributed to intensified protests of the working class against violating the

> 'rules of the game', and to widening the appeal of slogans calling for mass dissent. (Kalecki and Kowalik, 476, my italics)

With some oscillations, the argument is clear. Workers are *integrated* and their struggles are only *reactive* to capitalists breaking the rule of the game of an implicit social pact. The only hope for revolution—since, make no mistake here, Kalecki *disliked* this crucial reform—are the intelligentsia and the student movement.

Second Aside on Pauperisation

Although it is not strictly necessary for the discussion of the positions of Kalecki and Kowalik, it should be noted that there is one point at which Toporowski expresses what appears to be a Kalecki-inspired critique of Marx. Referring to the 1943 statements that

> 'Full employment capitalism' will need 'new social and political institutions which will reflect the increased power of the working class. If capitalism can adjust itself to full employment, a fundamental reform will have been incorporated in it. If not, it will show itself an outmoded system which must be scrapped.' (Toporowski, 2023, p. 13)

Toporowski continues claiming that

> This may be contrasted with the traditional Marxian view that capitalism progresses through the *immiseration* of the working class, whose coming together in factories allows them to resist '*pauperisation*' and 'cuts from under its feet the very foundation on which the bourgeoisie produces and appropriates products.' (Toporowski, 2023, p. 13, my italics)

An interpretation like this is definitely wrong, unless 'Marxian' is not limited to the Marx of the 1848 *Communist Manifesto*. Certainly, it does not reflect the mature Marx. Not to spend much time on this, I limit myself to a long quote from Lucio Colletti:[4]

> Here it only remains to turn to a consideration of the so-called theory of the '*absolute* immiseration' or long-term impoverishment of the masses, which, since Bernstein, has been often attributed to Marx by a variety of commentators: notably, until a few years ago, by the most primitive exponents of 'dialectical materialism' in the Soviet Union. *Not only is such a theory absent*

> *in Marx, but it would have been impossible for him to have produced it.* [Marx's] is a theory, in other words, of *relative* immiseration or an increase in the imbalance or inequality of the workers' conditions in relation to the conditions of the class that owns the means of production. … Hence *not only does Marx's theory not exclude increases in real wages*, but this increase, whatever Bernstein and Joan Robinson may think, proves absolutely nothing which contradicts Marx's thought. Indeed, *the theory of increasing exploitation holds good even in the case where wages have risen.* … This is, in fact, the decisive point in the entire Marxist theory of exploitation … [i]t is the dependence which ties the workers to the will of the capitalist class, and not their absolute poverty, that represents 'the *differentia specifica* of capitalist production'. (Colletti, 1972, pp. 101–102, my italics)

Kowalik in the 1970s: The Entries in *Enciclopedia Einaudi*

In two very long essays—two entries which together actually form a book and were published only in Italian in the *Enciclopedia Einaudi* ('Capitale' [Capital], 1977, and 'Crisi' [Crisis], 1978)—Kowalik proposed his own broader perspective on capitalism and its gradual development through structural crises.[5]

In the entry on *Capital*, he linked the notion of capital to that of socio-economic formation, showing how original accumulation and the formation of the (national and world) market allowed multiple ways of constituting capitalist social relations, thanks to the hegemony that the bourgeoisie conquered and also thanks to state intervention. The key authors with whom Kowalik engages in a dialogue here are Marx and Weber. Kowalik judges reductive the view of capitalism as an instrument for rationalising economic calculation within the management of companies: something that is discredited by the ubiquitous presence of waste in contemporary capitalism, but also by the systematic recurrence of crises. We may also (but not exclusively) see here the influence of the *Monthly Review* tradition.

In the entry on 'Crisis', the discourse is presented on a larger scale than in Kowalik's book on Rosa Luxemburg (rightly interpreted not as an underconsumptionist but as a theorist of an underinvestment crisis), although the key reference, along with Schumpeter, is once again Kalecki. After a historical overview of the (exogenous) crises of pre-capitalist economies and societies and the (endogenous) periodic alternation of prosperity and depression in capitalism, he confronts the contradictions and limitations of Keynes and the Keynesian tradition. The cornerstone of cycle and crisis lies in the dual and ambiguous role of investment. Investment, along with capitalist consumption, is the main autonomous and unstable component of effective demand; at the same time, it is also a new addition to productive capacity that needs ever-expanding markets. Because of this duality, the solution to the problem of effective demand cannot but lead to the cycle, and the cycle to periodic structural crises.

In Kowalik's view, Neo-mercantilist and Keynesian economic policies can only be deeply inadequate, and it is understandable that they have led to paradoxical results. The expansion of foreign trade shifted the crises to the underdeveloped countries, while deficit spending took the form of armaments and militarism. But the main reason for the difficulties lies in the very nature of capitalism, in the inherent instability of a system driven by the capitalists' need for investment. Crises cannot be overcome without overcoming capitalism.[6]

In these two entries, Kowalik explicitly argues that full employment can only be *temporary*. In this way, Kowalik rescued the Kaleckian tradition from the straitjacket of left Keynesianism and placed it firmly within an original development of the Marxian tradition. The reference to the 'crucial reform' disappears, and Kowalik's thinking is clearly far removed from the theses of the 1970 article with Kalecki. In fact, the same phenomena discussed there are recalled, but often with opposite conclusions.

> State interventionism, developed on a large scale since the 1930s and 1940s, undoubtedly helped to dampen economic fluctuations ... Despite this, *unemployment is still one of the most serious social problems*. ... However, the average level of employment has been higher than in several previous decades, and unemployment benefits have become one of the stabilisers ... Even during the first quarter of the century after the war (whose relative prosperity now seems more and more a thing of the past), the economies of the capitalist countries continued to develop along cyclical lines. This was decidedly contrary to the expectations and assurances of most Keynesian economists. ... *The right to work*, guaranteed by law in some countries and officially proclaimed by the United Nations, *has remained a stated intention but not translated into practice*. ... The 1970s witnessed events that seemed to go far beyond the pre-existing situation of dampened cyclical fluctuations. Fluctuations between a state of near-full employment and a state of unemployment at the level of several percentage points gave way to *an almost constant high level of unemployment of a structural nature*. What is

> more, unemployment, hitherto regarded as the most effective barrier against inflation, has begun to go hand in hand with a rapid and general rise in prices.

It is easy to see how this picture agrees with, and contrasts with, the one sketched in 'Observations on Crucial Reform'. But Kowalik does not stop there and asks, *from the perspective gained in the 1970s*, why full employment proved *unattainable* in the long run and why cyclical growth did *not* give way to stable growth. In the entry on 'Crisis' it is said that the limitations of state interventionism are not due to deep-rooted prejudices and intellectual conservatism, or to the contrast between sound theory and flawed economic policy. The real causes are the *class antagonism between capital and labour*, the *conflicts between capitalist fractions* and *the delusion that the state is neutral.* Kowalik quotes Sweezy sympathetically when he says that the Keynesians take the economic system out of its social context and treat it as if it were a machine to be sent to the repair shop to be overhauled by an engineering state.

The tendency towards the *globalisation* of capital undermines countercyclical intervention, while planning proposals within capitalism do not undermine the institutional foundations of decision-making processes that are at the origin of cyclical fluctuations, nor do they have any impact on the power of large corporations.

Similar views are expressed in the entry on 'Capital'. The most realistic theory of the limits of the capitalist system, though not entirely free of error, is said to be that developed by Baran and Sweezy. The 'normal state' of capitalism in the monopoly capital phase is one of expansion and stagnation. Even if it should be toned down, the stagnationist hypothesis is still a serious argument for changing the system. After the great crisis of the 1930s and the programmes of full employment, it became clear that capitalism could *not* guarantee one of the most basic human rights: *the right to work.* The inability of the system to solve traditional problems such as *cyclical crises* and *mass unemployment*, which does not disappear even in periods of expansion, as well as the inability to combat inflation effectively, both underline capitalism's inability to plan on a global scale and therefore to cope with the new problems, which can only be solved only by planning.

The conclusion is radical and pessimist. For Kowalik, it is becoming increasingly clear that, even in the highly industrialised countries, capitalism is no longer fulfilling its historical mission of creating the conditions for the full development of each individual.

> It is not very likely that the working class more educated and conscious of its own value, will accept for too long the servile role assigned to it by capitalist relations. All of this suggests that the further survival of capitalist relations of production is destined to explode, with general dissatisfaction, growing social conflicts and crises. The socialist challenge coincides with that of the Third World, which is no less dangerous for capitalism. ... Clear in their Eurocentrism sound the following phrases of Kautsky today: 'Where are today the barbarians not yet invaded by the 'spirit of capitalism' and in possession of sufficient military and political strength and intelligence to abolish the existing state order and establish a new order in its place?' .... Certainly, a 'rejuvenation of society from within' is a much more rational method of development; but the experience of the great crisis shows that these internal renewing forces manifest themselves when capitalism is on the brink of catastrophe.

Conclusion: The Final Rejoinder by Kowalik

These words may be closer to us than we think: they do not correspond to our time, and therefore they are useful to fight against this time and for a better time to come. What happened between the article and the entries can be partially understood by looking at Kowalik's reply to Pesenti.

At the request of the editor of Kalecki's *Collected Works*, Kowalik wrote a rejoinder to Pesenti's critique (Kowalik, 1991), in which he made clear his limited role in contributing to Kalecki's positive arguments defining the 'crucial reform' (initially called the 'revolutionary reform'). He was more active in researching the earlier debates. Kowalik recognised the 'pessimism' of Kalecki's views on capitalism and testified that Kalecki liked to 'emphasise that his theory of developed capitalism went even further in its criticism than Marx's theory' (p. 614), while urging a revision of the classical theory of socialist revolution.

Kalecki's reflection in the article was not to be understood as a 'deviation', as in Pesenti. Confirming the intellectual path I have reconstructed, Kowalik claims in his rejoinder that

> When Kalecki wrote and spoke about a relative economic and social stabilization of capitalism, he had in mind *only* a comparison with capitalism between the First World War and the great crisis of the 1930s. (p. 615, my italics)

But he also adds that

> *in the light of the experiences of the 1970s*, Kalecki (and the undersigned as well) *failed to perceive, or underestimated, certain phenomena which limited the effectiveness of intervention even more than he had once foreseen.* (p. 615, my italics)

However, the 1970s crisis, the deepest since the 1930s, validates the idea that the crisis itself does not put the socialist revolution or the socialist system back on the agenda. We live in a contradiction without a guaranteed synthesis, as the old tradition loved to think: the way 'out' from capitalism has to be reconstructed anew.

Notes

1. I wish to thank Jan Toporowski for one of the most productive intellectual discussions I have had on political economy, and well beyond.
2. I would distinguish between the two: Roosevelt was not Keynesian and Keynes was not Rooseveltian, though a connection could be built, but this topic is outside the discussion I engage in this paper.
3. Cf. Bellofiore (2021).
4. The same point can easily be drawn from Luxemburg's chapter on the wage in *her Introduction to Political Economy*. See her law of the tendency of the relative wage to fall, which is compatible with higher monetary and real wages.
5. I have made the two entries known to Jan Toporowski a few years ago, and I know he will make them available to the English readers soon.
6. Although it is peripheral to this chapter, it is worth pointing out something that usually escapes the attention of interpreters, precisely with regard to armaments. Kalecki is certainly more sophisticated than Luxemburg on the subject of militarism. At the same time, he overlooks an important key element in Luxemburg, which is perhaps her key insight. In *Accumulation of capital*, the demand which must solve the problem of realisation must be capitalistically *productive*; that is, it must be capitalist investment. That is why militarism is the solution she proposes in a closed economy. The rush to armaments activates capitalist productive processes: but they are not *re-productive*; that is, the demand in this period does not increase productive capacity in the next period. Armaments temporarily solve the problem of demand without increasing potential supply: and this demand may be insatiable.

References

Bellofiore, R. (2021). The winters of our discontent and the social production economy. *Review of Political Economy, 33*(3), 394–413.

Colletti, L. (1972). Bernstein and the Marxism of the second international. In *From Rousseau to Lenin*. NLB, 109-143.

D'Antonio, M. (1978). Kalecki e il marxismo. *Studi Storici, 19*(1), 17–43.

Kalecki, M. (1943). Political aspects of full employment. *Political Quarterly, 14*, 322–331. Reprinted in Kalecki 1990, 347–356.

Kalecki, M. (1956). La situazione economica negli Stati Uniti in confronto al periodo prebellico. In A. Chilosi (Ed.), *Sul capitalismo contemporaneo* (pp. 59–79). Editori Riuniti. English version in Kalecki 1997, 279–286.

Kalecki, M. (1962). La congiuntura economica negli Stati Uniti nel periodo 1951–1961. In In A. Chilosi (Ed.), *Sul capitalismo contemporaneo* (pp. 59–79). Editori Riuniti. English version in Kalecki 1991, 386–401.

Kalecki, M. (1975). *Sul capitalismo contemporaneo* [*On Contemporary Capitalism*] (A. Chilosi, Ed.). Editori Riuniti.

Kalecki, M. (1990). *Collected works of Michał Kalecki, Volume I: Capitalism – Business cycles and full employment* (J. Osiatyński, Ed.). Clarendon Press.

Kalecki, M. (1991). *Collected works of Michał Kalecki, Volume II: Capitalism – economic dynamics* (J. Osiatyński, Ed.). Clarendon Press.

Kalecki, M. (1997). *Collected works of Michał Kalecki, Volume VII: Studies in applied economics. Miscellanea. 1940–1967* (J. M. Osiatyński, Ed.). Clarendon Press.

Kalecki, M., & Kowalik, T. (1971). Osservazioni sulla 'riforma cruciale'. *Politica ed economia, 2/3*, 189–196. English version as "Observations on the Crucial Reform" in Kalecki 1991, 466–476.

Keynes, J. M. (1936). *The general theory of employment, interest, and money*. Vol. 7 of *The collected writings of John Maynard Keynes* (A. Robinson and D. Moggridge, Eds.). Cambridge University Press for the Royal Economic Society, 1973.

Keynes, J. M. (1979). *The general theory and after: A supplement*. Vol. 29 of *The collected writings of John Maynard Keynes* (A. Robinson and D. Moggridge, Eds.). Cambridge University Press for the Royal Economic Society.

Kowalik, T. (1991). Rejoinder to Pesenti. In J. Osiatyński (Ed.), *Collected works of Michał Kalecki, Volume II* (pp. 613–615). Clarendon Press.

Minsky, H. P. (1975). *John Maynard Keynes*. New York: McGraw-Hill, 1998.

Messori, M. (1991). Financing in Kalecki's Theory.*Cambridge Journal of Economics*, 15/3, 301–313.

Toporowski, J. (2023). Political aspects of full employment in retrospect. *Contributions to Political Economy, 42*(1), 1–16.

CHAPTER 3

Tadeusz Kowalik Between Oskar Lange and Michał Kalecki

Jan Toporowski

Introduction

Tadeusz Kowalik is best known today for his collaboration with Michał Kalecki in the final years of that latter's life, and for his blistering critique of the Polish 'transition' to capitalism in the 1990s (Kalecki & Kowalik, 1971; Kowalik, 2011). However, Kowalik's collaboration with Kalecki was much deeper than that final coda to Kalecki's work and needs to be integrated with his earlier collaboration with Oskar Lange. This should be obvious from the Kowalik's own professional curriculum: From 1965 until the 1990s Kowalik worked on editing the Collected Works of Lange. From the mid-1970s this work expanded to take in supervision of the editing of the Collected Works of Kalecki. Along with his earlier studies with Lange, this provided Kowalik an unrivalled scholarly foundation for his own work.

J. Toporowski (✉)
King's College London, London School of Economics, London, UK
e-mail: jan.toporowski@kcl.ac.uk

G. Konat, G. Rae (eds.), *Exploring the Ideas of Tadeusz Kowalik*,
https://doi.org/10.1007/978-3-032-09283-0_3

The Lange Connection

In his study on Aleja Niepodległości, in the flat that he took over from Włodzimierz Brus when Brus left Poland for Glasgow and then Oxford in 1970, Kowalik had two portraits, one of Michał Kalecki, and the other one of Oskar Lange, the two thinkers among whose work Kowalik lived, thought and wrote. Of the two, Oskar Lange undoubtedly had the earlier and longer influence on Kowalik, although later in life he considered Kalecki to have been the more original of the two.

Kowalik became personally associated with Lange after Kowalik had completed his graduate studies in economics at the University of Warsaw. During his studies at the University Kowalik had come across Włodzimierz Brus, the Professor of Political Economy, who was later to become, after Lange, the leading proponent of market socialism. Kowalik's interests were in the direction of the history of Polish economic thought, and specifically the influence of Marxism in Poland in the decades before the First World War. As a member of the ruling Communist Party, the Polish United Workers' Party, Kowalik was able to obtain the supervision of Oskar Lange at the Party school, Instytut Kształcenia Kadr Naukowych przy KC PZPR (IKKN, The Party School for training scientific cadres at the Central Committee of the Polish United Workers' Party). The subject of his thesis was the early Polish Marxist Ludwik Krzywicki. Shortly after Kowalik started his doctoral studies, Lange was appointed Rector of the Main School of Planning and Statistics (today the Szkoła Główna Handlowa or Warsaw School of Economics).

In 1952, Joseph Stalin's booklet *On the Economic Problems of Socialism in the USSR* was published. It was hailed by Lange as due recognition of the role of the price mechanism in the socialist economy, and by Brus as re-opening the discussion on market socialism as the remedy for the economic difficulties in which the countries of the Communist bloc found themselves, in particular the problems of shortages of food and raw materials, and bureaucratic economic coordination (Lange, 1954; Brus, 1993). These problems were to last virtually until the fall of Communism at the end of the 1980s, making market socialism the leading reform option within the political constraints of Poland's position within the Soviet bloc.

The economic reformers, led by Brus and Henryk Fiszel, argued that the question of 'rational' pricing was the foundation of economic efficiency, but had to be supported by consistent incentive structures within the socialist enterprise, and in the economy at large through markets. The rationale for such mechanisms was referred to as the 'Law of Value' to give a Marxist flavour to the concept of equilibrium pricing. The somewhat dry, even neo-classical, reasoning behind the arguments about efficiency, were given a strong political impetus by strikes and the election of workers' councils in factories, and the widespread discussion of Yugoslav models of workers self-management, made all the more attractive by Tito's defiance of Stalin in 1948.

Tadeusz Kowalik was a fluent writer who took easily to journalism. In 1956, as the Stalinist leadership of the PZPR ceded power to Władysław Gomułka, the former party leader who had been imprisoned for his 'nationalist deviation' from 1951 to 1955, Kowalik took over the editorship of the fortnightly *Życie Gospodarcze* (Economic Life). At this time of considerable political excitement, it seemed as if, for once, economic reform actually mattered for the working class and the future of socialism. Tadeusz Kowalik threw himself into the discussions criticising the 'errors and distortions' ('błędy i wypaczenia') of the Stalinist system. The fortnightly journal became a weekly in 1957, to accommodate the flow of critical articles and commentaries. However, Kowalik lasted only two years in this position, before being removed as the ruling party started to close down the discussion on reform and changed the editorial team to remove radical voices. He appealed for support to his doctoral supervisor. But Lange, who was in charge of the government's economic reform, had already once, in 1948, renounced his market socialism. Lange made clear to his doctoral student that he would help Kowalik if he got into political difficulty. But he could not keep him in his editorial job.

The loss of his editorial job coincided with Kowalik's completion of his doctorate. He continued lecturing in political economy at the party school, and commenced research for the *habilitacja*, the second doctorate that Polish academics need for advancement at university, on Rosa Luxemburg, with the support of Lange. Kowalik completed this in 1963.

In that same year Kowalik obtained a permanent position at the Department of the History of Science and Technology of the Polish Academy of Sciences, editing the Lange *Collected Works*. A more immediate duty was editing a volume of essays in honour of Lange, together with one for Poland's other internationally regarded economist, Michał Kalecki, to celebrate their respective 60th and 65th birthdays. To both he contributed biographical essays based on extensive interviews with their subject as well as an essay (Kowalik, 1964a, 1964b, 1964c, 1964d). For Lange he wrote an essay on 'Three Conceptions of Political Economy' which hailed

Lange's 'open Marxism' for his willingness to embrace the concepts of 'bourgeois' economics. He summed up the discussion on economic reform during the period when he was editor of *Życie Gospodarcze* as follows:

> In the years 1956–1958, there was a lot of lively discussion in Poland, new ideas were born and authors had ambitious plans. The most mature fruit of this discussion on the economy of socialism is, in my opinion, Professor Brus' book: *General Problems of the Functioning of the Socialist Economy*. Another expression of this discussion, of the social atmosphere of those years, is Lange book already referred to here [*Political Economy*] in several essential points connected with the political economy of socialism. (Kowalik, 1964b; Brus, 1961; Lange, 1959)

In October 1965, shortly after being presented with his *festschrift* Lange died. Even before his death, the economic strategy of the government had run into difficulties, in particular with serious shortages of food and articles of consumption, at the same time as demands for greater democracy, in the ruling party and the country at large, were growing. Senior academics, such as Brus, were using their party positions to protect dissidents within and outside the ruling party. At the end of 1967, the Gomułka government responded to growing unrest with a purge of Jews and 'revisionists'. Kowalik was expelled from the party. But the Polish Academy of Sciences had a degree of autonomy (it is not a teaching institution, so Kowalik could not be accused of stirring up student unrest) and he kept his job working on the Collected Works of Lange.

Kowalik's views on market socialism in the 1970s and 1980s are difficult to track. His publications were restricted by the system of censorship, some of which he got around by having other academics publish his work. This did not change after Gomułka was removed in 1970 and replaced by Edward Gierek. After a two-year stay in Cambridge, beginning in 1972 (see below) Kowalik returned to Poland on the eve of a foreign exchange crisis that Gierek tried to resolve in the usual fashion of raising consumer prices. A wave of strikes in 1976 led to the formation of the Workers' Defence Committee (*Komitet Obrony Robotników*) consisting of academics and intellectuals. The strikes eventually gave rise to the formation of the Solidarity trades union, independent of the ruling party.

Kowalik supported this dissident activity with his own seminars discussing the economic reform of socialism. The present author recalls lively discussions on the financing of new technology in capitalist countries. Kowalik himself did not doubt that it was possible to create a more open and democratic socialism. He was active in support of the Gdańsk workers in Solidarity and their eventual Round Table Agreement in 1989, bringing to an end the hegemony of the PZPR. But it also brought about the end of socialism in Poland.

The Kalecki Connection

It is likely that Kowalik was first introduced at the ideas of Kalecki by Lange himself. In a lecture on the 28 April 1953 'Bourgeois Polish economics in the inter-war period', given to the IKKN, Lange described Kalecki, along with his pre-war collaborators, Marek Breit and Ludwik Landau as 'Left Keynesians'. They had, he said, a dual role in Poland. 'On the one hand, in the circumstances of the time, the Left Keynesians formed a conduit by which a significant portion of the progressive intelligentsia found their way to a critique of capitalism and to the Popular Front. But, on the other hand, the specific form in which the critique of capitalism manifested itself in left Keynesian circles confused [basic] concepts and proved an obstacle to crystalizing ideology on the basis of Marxism' (Lange, 1986, p. 483.).[1]

At the time, Kalecki was in New York, working for the United Nations Secretariat. He did not return to Poland until 1955. One of his first engagements, in November that year, was in Lange's class at the Party school, where Kalecki had given three lectures on 'The Impact of Armaments on the Business Cycle after the Second World War'. The lectures were wide-ranging and include discussion of inflation, deficit financing, and credit. On the basis of a four-sector model of a capitalist economy (investment, workers' consumption, capitalists' consumption, and armaments) Kalecki showed how deficit financed military expenditure adds to profits (Kalecki, 1955).

It is likely that Kowalik attended that lecture. Certainly one of his fellow-students, Kazimierz Łaski, did, and reported later his doubts as to Kalecki's reasoning: To simplify his argument, Kalecki had introduced the assumption that each of his four sectors is vertically integrated, so that each sector produces its own inputs. This then allows each sector's income to be divided easily into wages and profits, avoiding all the complications of joint production and input-output relations between industries (Łaski, 2006; see also Konat & Smuga, 2019, pp. 291–292).

Kowalik would also have observed the dispute between Brus and Kalecki during the 1956 debates on economic reform (see next section). But he certainly obtained a deeper insight into Kalecki's thinking in the course of the interviews that Kowalik undertook in preparation for Kowalik's biographical essay on Kalecki that introduced the volume of essays in honour of Kalecki (Kowalik, 1964c). This did not mention the clash between Brus and Kalecki, but noted the importance in Kalecki's view of the 'basic proportions' (i.e., the share of investment) in the process of economic growth in a socialist economy.

Kowalik's other contribution to the Kalecki *festschrift* was an essay on 'R. Luxemburg's Theory of Accumulation and Imperialism (a suggested interpretation)' (Kowalik, 1964d). Kowalik had just completed his *habilitacja* thesis on Luxemburg, and it clearly shows the influence of his adviser, Oskar Lange. While the influence of Luxemburg's analysis on Kalecki's theory is referred to, the solution to the questions raised by Luxemburg were in the works of Lange as well as those of Kalecki 'taken together'. Kowalik was to revise his view for the published version of his thesis.

The events of 1967 and 1968 brought Kalecki and Kowalik together in a final collaboration to try to understand the changes that had occurred in capitalism after the Second World War, when the problem of unemployment in capitalism appeared to have been solved. The result of this was their joint paper on the 'Crucial Reform' of capitalism, a 'radical reform of the system that, without abolishing existing relations of production … may stabilize the system at least temporarily' (Kalecki & Kowalik, 1971. See also King, 2013). Kowalik later related that Kalecki was also reflecting on the 'crucial reform' that was clearly necessary in Poland and other countries of the Communist bloc.

In 1970, Kowalik left Poland to stay as a Visiting Fellow of Clare Hall in Cambridge. This was an opportunity to resume his increasingly close association with Kalecki's oldest friends at Cambridge, Maurice Dobb and Joan Robinson, as well as a new generation of Keynesians, such as Geoff Harcourt and John Eatwell. In Cambridge, Kowalik was joined by Jerzy Osiatyński. Two years later, on their return to Poland, Osiatyński joined to Kowalik's team working on the Collected Works of Lange at the Polish Academy of Sciences, to bring out an edition of Kalecki's Collected Works.

Compatibilities and Incompatibilities

Kowalik always emphasised his own good fortune in having as his teachers two great thinkers in economics, in the form of Lange and Kalecki. However, their ideas were by no means compatible with each other, even on a most general level: Lange combining an orthodox Marxism with neoclassical economics, and Kalecki being unorthodox in his Marxism, and author of ideas that were to inspire the Post-Keynesian rejection of neoclassical economics.

This section highlights the topics on which Lange and Kalecki disagreed and the possible effect on Kowalik's ideas of those disagreements.

The first concerns the 1956 debates about the functioning of the price mechanism in a socialist economy which exposed some of the differences between the two thinkers' views on prices and markets. As mentioned in Section "The Lange Connection" above, the leading proponent of market socialism in which prices would bring markets into equilibrium was Włodzimierz Brus. He took his inspiration from Lange's famous economic theory of socialism (Lange, 1938). There were differences as to the extent to which, in the original Lange version, the central planners set prices, and varied them in accordance with excess demands and supplies in individual markets, and in the more radical market reform view, the prices were fixed by markets and brought about equilibrium without intervention by the economic planners. Brus, in particular, emphasised the need for profit-related incentives in enterprises to induce management to minimise costs and maximise sales revenues (Brus, 1961; see also Osiatyński, 1988, pp. 14–16; Brus and Łaski 1989). But the setting of prices by central planners was generally viewed as an aspect of the 'over-centralisation' of economic decision-making which could only be effectively remedied by market-determined pricing.

Kalecki's view was fundamentally different. In his view of the socialist economy (and the capitalist one), the economy is brought into equilibrium not by price changes, but by the investment in the economy. His theory of growth in a socialist economy is widely perceived as a critique of the Dobb-Sen strategy of industrialisation, giving priority to the production of investment goods, or heavy industry, as a means of accelerating economic growth. Kalecki showed that such a strategy breaks down under the imbalance that it creates between the rise in wages and the supply of consumption goods in the short run, and between planned output and supplies of raw materials in the long run (Nuti, 1989).

Kalecki correctly viewed over-centralisation as an outcome of excessive investment, rather than a cause of such ambition. Investment was necessary to satisfy social needs. But, taken to excess, investment creates imbalances that start to act as a drag on economic growth. In this situation, it becomes necessary to scale down investment in order to concentrate resources on those projects that can be completed with the biggest output benefit. The rationale behind this was that market responses to price changes were much slower than the market models suggested. In such a situation, it made more sense to adjust quantities through administrative changes in production (Kalecki, 1956). Such a centralisation, in particular of investment, concluded the first economic reform period in Poland after 1956, and the subsequent one under Gierek. Kalecki also saw dangers of the recurrence of unemployment in any system in which profit incentives drove production. And the recurrence of meat crises, and workers' response to attempts to change prices of consumption goods, showed that the scope for price mechanisms in the socialist economies was very limited indeed.

We do not know what position Kowalik took in this dispute over economic reform in socialism. His proximity to, and dependence on, Lange would suggest that Kowalik was closer to the thinking of Brus and Lange, at least in the 1950s.

In the 1960s there is more obvious evidence of Kowalik's position and a much more fundamental shift towards Kalecki, in Kowalik's essay for the Kalecki *festschrift*. As mentioned above, the essay was on Rosa Luxemburg's theory of accumulation and imperialism. The greater part of the essay summarises Luxemburg's *Accumulation of Capital*. Kalecki's reference to Marx and Luxemburg in his 1939 *Essays in the Theory of Economic Fluctuations* is cited.

However, Kowalik also cites with approval Lange's criticism of Luxemburg on two points. One is Luxemburg's acceptance of Marx's assumption that capital accumulation inevitably involves a rising organic composition of capital (i.e., a rising share of capital to labour). The second, concerns her use of Marx's schemes of reproduction:

> Rosa Luxemburg suggested that the problem of the movement of total social capital and the laws of its accumulation should be studied and presented in a mathematical form and should be analysed in terms as precise as those in which Marx presented his proportions and inter-branch relation-

ships in social reproduction. Thus she overestimated Marx's theoretical construction, rather than underestimated it.

This is followed by a footnote in which he quoted Oscar Lange's conclusion concerning Marx's schemes of reproduction: 'The discussion led nowhere because, as it turned out, the schemata of equilibrium of reproduction do not suffice for solving the problem involved in this discussion', namely the reconciliation of the analysis with the theory of value.

Nevertheless, Kowalik noted that 'The analysis of capitalism and of its development in aggregative terms and the emphasis on the deficiency of demand are the characteristic features of the Keynesian revolution. The same applied to the pre-Keynesian theory of business cycles based on the Marxian principles and of the theory of the dynamics of capitalism developed later by M. Kalecki.'

Kowalik went on to recognise Luxemburg's efforts to include the monetary system in process of accumulation. In a footnote he noted that 'One of the ways of solving this problem was given by Lange in his work *Price Flexibility and Employment*... It seems that the book by Lange... and the studies published by Kalecki taken together provide a sufficient solution to the problem raised by Rosa Luxemburg' (Kowalik, 1964d).

Two striking features emerge from Kowalik's 1963 discussion. First of all there is his rejection (citing Lange) of Marx's and Luxemburg's schemes of reproduction as a framework for macroeconomic analysis. Second, there is his presentation of Lange's *Price Flexibility and Employment*, one of the founding documents of the 'neo-classical synthesis' of Keynes and neo-classical analysis, alongside Kalecki's. Kowalik could not have known at that time that eight years later, inspired by Kalecki's 'more coherent version of the General Theory' Joan Robinson would launch Post-Keynesian economics with an attack on the neo-classical synthesis hailed by Lange (Robinson, 1971).

Kowalik's *habilitacja* was finally published in 1971, at around the same time as Joan Robinson was denouncing the neo-classical synthesis. In the published version, Kowalik modified substantially the view of Luxemburg's theory that he had taken in the festschrift essay. Whereas the 1963 essay considered that the schemes of reproduction are not a sound foundation for economic analysis, Kowalik's book on Luxemburg attempts to vindicate the schemes of reproduction, as monetary analysis showing flows, albeit incomplete without Marx's value theory.

In the book, Kowalik was also concerned to show how it provided foundations, in the Marxist discussion of the schemes of reproduction, for Kalecki's macroeconomics. Kowalik's work is nothing less than a Kaleckian interpretation of Luxemburg's theory of capital accumulation. Lange's neo-classical *Price Flexibility and Employment* is now more explicitly described as a Walrasian general equilibrium incorporating a Hicksian monetary analysis to arrive at a 'dynamic equilibrium' allowing Lange to reach 'similar conclusions to Kalecki, who used (modified) Marx's reproduction schemes' (Kowalik, 1971, p. 173). Kalecki was now more Marxist than Lange.

Kowalik's shift towards a Kaleckian interpretation of Luxemburg may even have happened before Lange died in 1965. In his book, Kowalik reported on the examination of his *habilitacja* thesis as follows. The two examiners were Lange and distinguished specialist in the political economy of agriculture, Jerzy Tepicht. In the examination, Lange stuck to his view that 'the problem of realisation ... is a problem of the confrontation of the equilibrium conditions of reproduction with the market processes. The impossibility of realisation is precisely the lack of coordination between the requirements of reproduction and the market mechanism' (Kowalik, 1971, p. 172).

The distance between Lange and Kalecki was remarked by Lange himself. Towards the end of his life, Lange asked Kowalik whether he thought Kalecki was a Marxist. Kowalik had reassured Lange that indeed Kalecki was (personal communication by Kowalik to this author).

Conclusion

Kowalik's work spanned the ideas of Oskar Lange and Michał Kalecki. Despite their common socialist sympathies, and interests in macroeconomics and development economics, the two theorists differed fundamentally in the way in which they viewed capitalism. These differences then seeped into their respective views of how socialism ought to function.

In Lange's case, capitalism can be analysed through an eclectic combination of Marxism and neo-classical economics, taking in some of Keynes's ideas. In Kalecki's case, capitalism is properly analysed through Marx's ideas taking in elements of the Keynesian revolution in a dynamic theory of business cycles. Lange came to believe that the market could generate equilibrium through a price mechanism. Kalecki concluded that it was investment, or capital accumulation, that generates a particular equilibrium in the system. This led on to Lange's belief in the efficacy of the price mechanism in the socialist economy, and Kalecki's scepticism about that mechanism.

Kowalik found himself in between the two theorists. Starting with Lange he moved to Kalecki and a renunciation of neo-classical economics. He retained Lange's scholarly range. But his embrace of Kalecki's ideas helped Kowalik to resist the free market capitalism that emerged in Poland after 1989.

Note

1. In citing this incident in my biography of Kalecki (Toporowski, 2018), I referred to Lange as Kalecki's 'friend'. I was later reproached for this by Kalecki's editor Jerzy Osiatyński, who told me that Lange was no friend of Kalecki's, although the two had worked together (but never collaborated) since the end of the 1920s.

References

Brus, W. (1961). *Ogólne problemy funkcjonowania gospodarki socjalistycznej (General problems in the functioning of the socialist economy)*. Państwowe Wydawnictwo Naukowe. English edition: *The Market in a Socialist Economy*. London: Routledge and Kegan Paul, 1972.

Brus, W. (1993). The Bane of reforming the socialist economic system. *BNL Quarterly Review, 187*(December), 363–405.

Brus, W., & Łaski, K. (1989). *From Marx to the Market: Socialism in search of an economic system*. Oxford University Press.

Kalecki, M. (1955). The impact of armaments on the business cycle after the Second World War. In J. Osiatyński (Ed.), *Collected works of Michal Kalecki, Volume II: Capitalism – Economic dynamics* (pp. 199–207). Clarendon Press, 1991.

Kalecki, M. (1956). Workers' councils and central planning. In *Selected essays on economic planning* (pp. 45–57). Cambridge University Press, 1986.

Kalecki, M., & Kowalik, T. (1971). Observations on the 'crucial reform'. In J. Osiatyński (Ed.), *Collected works of Michal Kalecki, Volume I: Capitalism – Business cycles and full employment* (pp. 466–476). Clarendon Press, 1990.

King, J. E. (2013). Whatever happened to the 'crucial reform'? In R. Bellofiore, E. Karwowski, & J. Toporowski (Eds.), *Economic crisis and political economy: Essays in honour of Tadeusz Kowalik, Vol. 2*. Palgrave Macmillan.

Konat, G., & Smuga, T. (2019). An interview with Professor Kazimierz Łaski. *European Journal of Economics and Economic Policies: Intervention, 16*(3),

291–301. Also in *Paradoksy ekonomii. Rozmowy z polskimi ekonomistami.* Warszawa: Wydawnictwo Naukowe PWN.

Kowalik, T. (1964a). Biography of Oskar Lange. In *On political economy and econometrics: Essays in Honour of Oskar Lange* (pp. 15–28). PWN – Polish Scientific Publishers.

Kowalik, T. (1964b). Three conceptions of the political economy of socialism. In *On political economy and econometrics: Essays in Honour of Oskar Lange* (pp. 85–112). PWN – Polish Scientific Publishers.

Kowalik, T. (1964c). Biography of Michał Kalecki. In *Problems of economic dynamics and planning: Essays in Honour of Michał Kalecki* (pp. 13–21). PWN – Polish Scientific Publishers.

Kowalik, T. (1964d). R. Luxemburg's theory of accumulation and imperialism (A suggested interpretation). In *Problems of economic dynamics and planning: Essays in honour of Michał Kalecki* (pp. 223–243). PWN – Polish Scientific Publishers.

Kowalik, T. (1971). *Róża Luksemburg: Teoria akumulacji i imperializmu.* Zakład Narodowy im. Ossolińskich. English edition: *Rosa Luxemburg: Theory of Accumulation and Imperialism.* Basingstoke: Palgrave Macmillan, 2014.

Kowalik, T. (2011). *From solidarity to sellout: The restoration of capitalism in Poland.* Monthly Review Press.

Lange, O. (1938). *On the economic theory of socialism.* In B. E. Lippincott (Ed.), *On the economic theory of socialism* (pp. 55–111). University of Minnesota Press.

Lange, O. (1954). The economic laws of socialist society in the light of Joseph Stalin's last work. *International Economic Papers, 4*, 145–180. London.

Lange, O. (1959). *Ekonomia polityczna, Tom 1: Zagadnienia ogólne.* Państwowe Wydawnictwo Naukowe. English edition: *Political Economy, Volume 1: General Problems.* New York: Macmillan.

Lange, O. (1986). *Dzieła, Tom 6: Działalność naukowa i społeczna 1904–1965 (Collected Works, Volume 8: Scholarly and Social Activities 1904–1965).* Państwowe Wydawnictwo Ekonomiczne.

Łaski, K. (2006). Kalecki's Place in My Career as an Economist. *Wiener Institut für Internationale Wirtschaftsvergleiche Monthly Report* 11.

Nuti, D. M. (1989). Michał Kalecki's contributions to the theory and practice of socialist planning. In M. Sebastiano (Ed.), *Kalecki's relevance today* (pp. 101–118). St. Martin's Press.

Osiatyński, J. (1988). *Michał Kalecki on a socialist economy.* Macmillan.

Robinson, J. V. (1971). The second crisis of economics. In *Collected economic papers, Volume IV* (pp. 123–132). Blackwell.

Toporowski, J. (2018). *Michał Kalecki: An intellectual biography, Volume II: By intellect alone, 1939–1970.* Palgrave Macmillan.

CHAPTER 4

The Wandering Intellectual: The Influence of Sociology on Tadeusz Kowalik

Gavin Rae

Introduction

Although Tadeusz Kowalik was a professor of both economics and humanities, who specialised in the history of economic ideas and comparative systems, he was increasingly drawn towards matters that have primarily concerned sociologists. Firstly, Kowalik emphasised how economic issues could not be separated from social matters and that the primary purpose of economic policy was to improve the population's living standards. Secondly, he sought to bridge the gap between different academic disciplines and was opposed to the positivisation of economics and the separation of social issues from economic analysis. He maintained such a stance throughout the socialist period in Poland and the transformation to capitalism from 1989, cooperating with sociologists throughout his academic career.

There are four main overlapping influences of sociology on Kowalik's work. Firstly, was the Polish Marxist and early sociologist, Ludwik

G. Rae (✉)
Department of Social Sciences, Kozminski University, Warsaw, Poland
e-mail: gavinrae@kozminski.edu.pl

G. Konat, G. Rae (eds.), *Exploring the Ideas of Tadeusz Kowalik*,
https://doi.org/10.1007/978-3-032-09283-0_4

Krzywicki, who was the subject of much of Kowalik's early intellectual work. Krzywicki also heavily influenced one of Kowalik's major intellectual and political mentors, Oskar Lange. Kowalik, partially via Lange, took from Krzywicki the understanding of how ideas can influence and shape socio-economic systems and their global uneven development. Secondly, Kowalik was interested in the question of (de)alienation and its particular form within 'really existing socialism'. Thirdly, Kowalik concerned himself with how economies are embedded within social relations and at how these can be destabilised when this connection is broken. Fourthly, Kowalik analysed how institutions are important in building and stabilising economies and how different institutional arrangements help to explain diversity in the global economic system.

These concerns of Kowalik were shaped by the changing social environment in which he lived, providing a sociological context for understanding his work. In this chapter I shall outline the main sociological themes in Kowalik's work, highlight the connections between them and consider how these reflected the changing social and political environment in which he lived.

Krzywicki and Lange

Explaining his interest in Ludwik Krzywicki, Kowalik wrote:

> Krzywicki attracted my attention for many years, both because we shared similar views and because he represented the model of a scholar who did not submit to the narrow confines of academic specialisation. He was simultaneously a historian, economist and sociologist. In dialogue with his views, I tried to form my ideas regarding the most important (as I understood them then) problems of our times. After studying Krzywicki's socio-economical views (in my doctoral dissertation), I began to reconstruct his meta-sociology (the general theory of social development). (Kowalik, 1981)

Kowalik's early writings on Krzywicki, which formed the basis of his doctoral dissertation, focused on Krzywicki's economic opinions (Kowalik, 1959). In this work, Kowalik originally recognised Krzywicki's early contribution to analysing monopoly capitalism and how he had foreseen many of the insights later developed by more internationally recognised figures such as Rudolf Hilferding (Konat, 2024). Krzywicki believed that a form of organised state monopoly capitalism may emerge that would eradicate many of capitalism's crisis tendencies and tame the anarchy of capitalist production. At this time, Kowalik was writing as an intellectual who belonged to the ruling Polish United Workers' Party (PZPR), seeking to defend Krzywicki as one of Poland's most significant Marxist thinkers, despite his partial move away from Marxism and revolutionary socialism towards the end of his life.

Kowalik returned to writing about Krzywicki during the 1970s. By this time, Kowalik had been expelled from the PZPR and rather than analysing his economic work and attempting to defend Krzywicki's reputation as a Marxist, he mainly focused on Krzywicki's broader sociological writings. Kowalik explained how Krzywicki had analysed social ties and how he believed that the strongest social bonds were family/ancestral bonds, similar to animal societies. Class societies developed through the weakening of these social bonds, with Krzywicki believing that human relations become dominated through relations to things rather than between people once private property dominates social relations. Furthermore, Kowalik explained, Krzywicki contended that class societies are by their very nature territorial societies, as they must exist within bounded geographical territories. Krzywicki believed that the territorial system provides a bond between people, embodying property relations and those arising from the division of labour. Kowalik wrote how Krzywicki was concerned with social relations in their broadest sense, including lifestyle, habits, and opinions, which are ultimately rooted in the social relations of production.

Kowalik also highlighted how the role of ideas played a prominent role in Krzywicki's work. For Krzywicki, a social idea can spread within society, gaining recognition and support, when it responds to real social needs. Some ideas, propounded by intellectuals, may not resonate within society as the economic conditions have not yet sufficiently matured to allow for their absorption. Therefore, Krzywicki saw how ideas and ideologies are closely connected to a country's economic base and, in alignment with Marxist thinking, that productive forces must be sufficiently advanced before certain ideas can take root within society. Kowalik wrote that one of Krzywicki's most influential theories was that of the 'wandering idea'. He explained how Krzywicki believed that external ideas could play an important role in advancing a country's economic and social progress, particularly when such ideas are imported from more advanced countries into less developed ones. However, the acceptance of some 'wandering ideas' is restricted by a country's 'historical base', when particular customs and traditions conflict with the idea imported by intellectuals.

The importance of Krzywicki to Kowalik's intellectual development was partially due to the profound influence that Krzywicki had on Oskar Lange. Lange wrote that Krzywicki had been one of the first scholars in Poland to systematically apply the Marxist method of historical materialism, including in his sociological work. Lange particularly praised Krzywicki for his analysis of early human societies and how ideas impact historical change (Lange, 1947). In a text written on the sociological dimension of Lange's economics (written at around the same time that he was analysing Krzywicki's sociological work), Kowalik explained that Lange was absorbed by sociological problems and that, before his death, he had planned to carry out wider research into socio-economic issues. Lange believed that many important issues of socio-economic life had been abandoned by economists and subsequently taken up by sociologists, suggesting the formation of a new subdiscipline of sociology: economic sociology (Kowalik, 1974).

The influence of Krzywicki on Lange is observable in Lange's first volume on political economy, described by Kowalik as 'one of the most ambitious undertakings in the social sciences in this century'[1] (Kowalik 1975). In this work, Lange tried to elaborate a historical materialist theory of social development alongside a model of rational behaviour. Lange began by citing Krzywicki's view that human societies are distinguished from animal societies, as humans act consciously and according to intent. He then adopted Krzywicki's historical materialist understanding of how relics from the past remain in the consciousness of a population and also that ideas from the past or outside interrelate with a society's historical base and shape its development. Lange believed that rational economic activity arises within individual capitalist enterprises. However, over time, a contradiction arises between the rational activity of these enterprises and the irrationalities and wastefulness of general capitalist production. Lange drew the conclusion that rational development of productive forces could only be ensured through the socialisation of the means of production.

(De)Alienation

During the Stalinist period of the early 1950s in Poland, the authorities banned sociology as an independent discipline, accusing it of being a 'bourgeois science'. Sociology only returned to some universities from 1956, becoming a centre for relatively free sociological thought and research in the Eastern Bloc. One of the leading sociologists of this time was Julian Hochfeld, who had cooperated closely with Lange in the left-wing current of the PPS before the Second World War. Thereafter, Hochfeld belonged to the group of 'Open Marxists' at Warsaw University, involving the likes of Zygmunt Bauman, Adam Schaff, and Jerzy Wiatr (Gdula, 2017).

He believed that sociologists should provide objective data and research on social processes, which would aid in the construction of socialism in Poland (Hirszowicz & Morawski, 1973). At Warsaw University, these sociologists (including notable figures such as Maria Hiszowicz, Witold Morawski, and Włodzimierz Wesołowski) considered such things as workers' participation and autonomy in the workplace as central to overcoming alienation in socialism. Kowalik also drew very close to the Polish sociologist, Jan Strzelecki, who also derived from the left-wing current of the pre-war PPS and during the socialist period moved between party and opposition circles. One of Strzelecki's most influential works was on the alienation of the 'market personality' in the United States, warning those in socialist countries against the dangers of consumerism. He believed that broad social and political pluralism and freedom should underpin the economic plan in a socialist economy (Grochowska, 2014).

Kowalik regularly participated in the seminars organised by the sociology department at Warsaw University, expanding his understanding of these topics which had been central to his thinking since the momentous events of 1956 and the attempts to forge an autonomous Polish road to socialism similar to that pursued in Yugoslavia. The issue of workers' self-management remained a dominant feature of Kowalik's work for the remainder of his life. The issue leapt from the pages of academic abstraction, during the momentous strikes that began in the Gdańsk shipyards in 1980, to which Kowalik helped organise a delegation of experts to mediate between the strikers and government representatives (Kowalik, 1998). Kowalik saw in these strikes a continuity of the movement of workers and intellectuals in 1956 and that they chimed with many of his own interests in issues such as de-alienation and workers' self-management.

Economy and Society

Kowalik's research on the nature of socialism and alternative models of socialism coalesced into a broader interest in relations between the economy and society and economics and sociology. In the 1970s, Kowalik wrote that economics in Poland was fixated on specialist technical issues and had become dehumanised in a similar manner to neoclassical economics in the West. Kowalik reviewed Winicjusz Narojek's book on sociology in a planned socialist economy (Narojek, 1973). Najorek's book criticised mainstream political economy in Poland for fixating on technical issues and the problems of optimising economic decision making and for following the western neoclassical trend of mathematising economic analysis. He followed Lange, in proposing the establishment of economic sociology as a distinct field of research He also countered the opinion that political economy in a planned socialist economy should be replaced by the scientific study of organising productive forces, believing that as people (producers, consumers, planners) make actual economic decisions, so the sociological study of social ties and relations remains essential. Kowalik noted how Najorek held similar opinions to sociologists such as Wesołowski and Wiatr, who believed that alienation occurs in socialism through the realm of politics and power, rather than private ownership and the market.

Kowalik wrote that Najorek had followed the likes of Wesołowski and Wiatr, in seeing alienation in socialism as occurring through politics and power, rather than via private ownership and the market. In socialism, large state organisations and their bureaucracies make decisions on such things as employment and wages, with power relations within these organisations shaping the form of alienation that people experienced in their everyday lives. The corresponding technicalisation and positivisation of economics, which to some degree replicates these power relations, had brought into question whether economics could still be regarded as a social science. Kowalik therefore reluctantly agreed with Najorek that sociologists were better placed to take up the social issues that economists had now neglected.

Planning and Freedom

The hope that a new era of reform would open in Poland, leading to a more decentralised and self-managed form of socialism, was finally dashed when the authorities introduced Martial Law in December 1981. This broke the back of the Solidarity trade union movement, a mass movement of the working class, paving the way for the eventual reintroduction of capitalism from the end of the 1980s. By the time Martial Law had been introduced, Kowalik was already working in the United States, as a research fellow at the Woodrow Wilson International Center for Scholars in Washington (DC). During the next decade Kowalik spent time working at a number of universities abroad, including in the UK, Austria and Canada, as well as in the United States. He was researching the views of Lange on a socialist economy and trying to develop his own proposals for reforming the socialist system in Poland.

Throughout the 1980s, Kowalik regularly returned to some of the themes that he had developed during his engagement with sociologists throughout the previous decade. He wrote some of his most critical evaluations of Lange's praxeological vision of rationalising economics, questioning Lange's view that socialism could realise the rationalist aspirations of capitalism, by rejecting the very idea of a rational capitalist economy. He believed that Lange had effectively separated social issues from the task of constructing a socialist economy, believing that planning could not be treated as a technical issue but as one embedded in social relations. Kowalik criticised Lange's view that socialist industrialisation (and the subsequent growth of a conscious working class and intelligentsia) would result in socialist economies overtaking their capitalist rivals, thus proving the rational superiority of the socialist system. The failure of the socialist economies to supersede the developed capitalist economies had resulted in some left-wing intellectuals reflecting on the nature of socialism and how it may be reformed.

During the 1980s, Kowalik's writing moved away from the Marxist-inspired political economy of his earlier work towards a more subjective and institutionalist comparative analysis of economic systems. He postulated that economic systems can have a range of organisational and institutional structures. Socialism could have different subsystems, such as central planning, regulated markets, workers' self-management, and cooperatives. Kowalik drafted proposals for a 'crucial reform' of socialism, which would leave the core economic system intact, but allow for the transformation towards more decentralised and democratic subsystems. Kowalik's interest in the plurality of economic (sub)systems was partially derived from his work on Krzywicki, who had believed that economic systems could overlap and be transformed through the import of ideas. The role of ideas and institutions on economic change also came to Kowalik through his previous research into the German historical school and Max Weber, which Kowalik had also been drawn to through his engagement with Lange.[2]

Although Kowalik wrote more critically about 'really existing socialism' in Poland during the 1980s and proposed far-reaching reforms, he remained a critical supporter of the Polish socialist system until its final collapse in 1989. He dismissed those in Poland and abroad who advocated the dismantling of socialism in Poland, deploying, in the defence of socialism, evidence from empirical sociological research. He cited the research conducted by a leading Polish sociologist, Stefan Nowak, which had revealed that although most Poles rejected the official ideology of Marxism, they still remained deeply entwined with the foundational values of the socialist system. The vast majority of Poles supported the nationalisation of industry, land reform, economic planning, and the principle of building a more egalitarian society (Kowalik, n.d.).

A New Capitalist Environment

The neoliberal reforms that ushered in the return of capitalism brought new meaning to many of the themes that Kowalik had developed through his earlier engagement with sociology. The dominant neoliberal narrative included the view that market forces should be free from political interference and that social welfare spending hindered the development of a rational and efficient capitalist economy. Connected to this perspective was the view that economics and social issues should remain separated and that neoclassical economics was the one form of scientific economic thought (Kowalik, 2000). From the onset of the 'post-socialist' transformation in Poland, Kowalik argued that social concerns such as growing poverty and unemployment should be of primary concern for economists. He argued that in order for markets and their accompanying institutions to develop efficiently, they must be embedded within society. Kowalik drew on Karl Polanyi's theory of the double movement, arguing that a 'market economy' must be built carefully and gradually in order for it to be sufficiently embedded in society (Kowalik, 1996).

Kowalik opposed the view that there exists only one form of capitalism and that Poland should choose its own specific institutional combination that reflected its particular historical circumstances. He adopted a more subjectivist approach to the 'post-socialist' transformation, in which the lingering influence of Krzywicki and Lange is evident. Both Krzywicki and Lange had placed great emphasis on the role of ideas, with the concept of the 'wandering idea' used to analyse how the import of ideas could shape the course of a country's socio-economic development. The dominant neoliberal ideology, brought to Poland from the outside, were unquestionably accepted and applied by the country's elites. Kowalik rather urged Poland to consider alternative models of capitalism, such as the German social market economy and Scandinavian welfare state (Kowalik, 2000). Kowalik had moved away from the critical political economy, influenced by Marxism, of his early years and more towards a subjectivist and institutionalist analysis of the emerging capitalist system and what alternatives may exist to it. This may well have partially been due to the *realpolitik* of the time, where class analysis and criticisms of capitalism were virtually excluded from mainstream political and academic discussions.

Kowalik also countered the tendency within Polish economics to narrow the field of analysis and discussion. Neoclassical economics dominated in Poland during the 1990s and 2000s, with many associated with the discipline seeking to naturalise markets and present the neoliberal jump to capitalism as a 'return to normality' (Kowalik, 1999). Economics was presented as an objective science, based upon abstract models of market equilibrium. In order for markets to function effectively and economic equilibrium achieved, they should be free from both social and state interference. Kowalik rejected these equilibrium assumptions, returning to his criticism of the economics mainstream during socialism, by arguing that social issues should be at the centre of any economic research and analysis. Kowalik retained a deep concern and interest in social questions, continually pointing out how high unemployment and poverty were both morally reprehensible and economically damaging. According to Kowalik, Poland was one of the most unequal societies in Europe and the task of economists, alongside other social scientists, was to work out how to reduce unemployment and poverty and raise the living standards of the most socially excluded (Kabaj & Kowalik, 1995).

A Public Intellectual

Tadeusz Kowalik was an intellectual of his time. The division between the academic disciplines was less defined than nowadays, with intellectuals able to take a more fluid and pluralistic approach in their work. Although intellectuals such as Kowalik had to endure political censorship and repression, during the period of the Polish People's Republic, they were also at times closely connected to mass workers' and social movements. They were thus more organically bonded to different layers of society and had to respond more directly to their concerns than many intellectuals are obliged to today.

Kowalik's concern for social equality and reducing poverty remained with him throughout his life, partially drawn from the impoverished environment in eastern Poland where he had been raised. He opposed trends to both separate economics from social concerns and move it in a more positivistic direction. He drew inspiration from sociologists and sociology, often regarding this discipline as having been less infected by positivist tendencies. Following in the footsteps of Lange, he believed that sociology was often better placed to take up the most important socio-economic issues of the time, which economists had disregarded. Despite the huge changes that Poland underwent after its transformation from socialism to capitalism, Kowalik continued to engage in this intellectual struggle as mainstream economics acted as the ideological mouthpiece of the governing authorities. This pushed Kowalik closer towards sociology and deepened his intellectual engagement with sociologists.

Notes

1. Kowalik explained: 'Lange was able to finish only the first volume. It was published in 1959. Published posthumously as the second volume (1966) the first four chapters were written in 1961–1964. The remaining chapters of this volume were to comprise the problems of commodity production and a comparative economic analysis of different social formations. The third volume was to be devoted to a detailed analysis of the capitalist and socialist formations' (Kowalik, 1975).
2. This included Kowalik's research made during his participation during the 1960s in a UNESCO-funded research project in which the likes of Oskar Lange, Włodzimierz Brus, and Ignacy Sachs participated. Kowalik's section in this report looked at modern economics in the broader context of the human sciences and at the main schools of economic thought, including Marxism, Keynesianism, and the German Historicism (Kowalik et al., 1967).

References

Gdula, M. (2017). Warsaw School of Marxism. *Stan Rzeczy, 2*(13), 197–225.

Grochowska, M. (2014). *Strzelecki: Śladem nadziei*. Świat Książki.

Hirszowicz, M., & Morawski, W. (1973). *Samorząd robotniczy w gospodarce socjalistycznej*. Książka i Wiedza.

Kabaj, M., & Kowalik, T. (1995). Who is responsible for post-communist successes in eastern Europe? *Transition: The Newsletter About Reforming Economics, 6*(7–8), 7–8.

Konat, G. (2024). *The polish transformation: Tadeusz Kowalik on the epigonic bourgeois revolution of 1989*. Brill.

Kowalik, T. (1959). *O Ludwiku Krzywickim: Studium społeczno-ekonomiczne*. Państwowe Wydawnictwo Naukowe.

Kowalik, T. (1974). Socjologiczny obszar w ekonomii Oskara Langego. *Studia Socjologiczne, 3*, 5–37.

Kowalik, T. (1975). Economics and praxiology: O. Lange's political economy. *Organon, 11*, 303–324.

Kowalik, T. (1981). Scientific Curriculum Vitae. Tadeusz Kowalik's Archive, File 32, Polish Academy of Sciences, Warsaw.

Kowalik, T. (1996). On the transformation of post-communist societies: The inefficiency of primitive capital accumulation. *International Political Science Review, 17*(3), 289–296.

Kowalik, T. (1998). Inteligenci jadą do Stoczni Gdańskiej (jak powstała grupa „ekspertów" MKS). *Przegląd Społeczny*, 3–4, 16–23.

Kowalik, T. (1999). *Jaką cywilizację Polacy tworzą? In Indywidualizm a kolektywizm*. Instytut Filozofii i Socjologii PAN.

Kowalik, T. (2000). *Współczesne systemy ekonomiczne: Powstawanie, ewolucja, kryzys*. Wydawnictwo Wyższej Szkoły Przedsiębiorczości i Zarządzania im. Leona Koźmińskiego.

Kowalik, T. (n.d.). The systemic presuppositions of the Polish August: Self-governing socialism or the restoration of capitalism. Draft. Tadeusz Kowalik's Archive, File 72, Polish Academy of Sciences, Warsaw.

Kowalik, T., Sachs, I., & Brus, W. (1967). *New trends in contemporary economic thought*. Szkoła Główna Planowania i Statystyki.

Lange, O. (1947). *Ludwik Krzywicki jako teoretyk materializmu historycznego*. Spółdzielnia Wydawnicza.

Narojek, W. (1973). *Społeczeństwo planujące: Próba socjologii gospodarki socjalistycznej*. PWE.

CHAPTER 5

Tadeusz Kowalik vs. "Western Marxism": Two Attempts to Conceptualise the Post-1989 Changes in East Central Europe as "Bourgeois Revolutions"

Grzegorz Konat

Introduction

In my earlier works (Konat, 2022, 2024), I subjected to a detailed examination a fragment of the work of the prominent Polish historian of economic thought and economist, Tadeusz Kowalik, in which he postulated treating the post-1989 systemic transition in Poland in terms of a "bourgeois revolution" (an "epigonic bourgeois revolution", as he called it). I pointed out that although this thesis—which he put forward in his 1996 article titled "Sierpień—epigońska rewolucja mieszczańska" ["August—the Epigonic Bourgeois Revolution"] (Kowalik, 1996)—is characterised by a high degree of originality, its justification seems rather superficial and unconvincing. I have also pointed out, although without developing this argument more extensively, that the aforementioned article may appear

G. Konat (✉)
SGH Warsaw School of Economics, Warsaw, Poland
e-mail: gkonat@sgh.waw.pl

G. Konat, G. Rae (eds.), *Exploring the Ideas of Tadeusz Kowalik*,
https://doi.org/10.1007/978-3-032-09283-0_5

theoretically tenuous in particular when juxtaposed with a not much later text by two Marxist authors, a British sociologist and historian Colin Barker and Canadian political scientist Colin Mooers ("Theories of Revolution in the Light of 1989 in Eastern Europe" (Barker & Mooers, 1997)), who not only extensively justify the analogous hypothesis, but also generalise it for the entire region of East Central Europe (ECE).[1] However, I have not conducted an in-depth comparative analysis and, to the best of my knowledge, no one else has done so to date.

The aim of this chapter is therefore to thoroughly compare these two articles treating the systemic transformation in ECE in the late 1980s and early 1990s in terms of a "bourgeois revolution". This comparative analysis is intended to help determine to what extent my earlier impression of the superiority of Barker and Mooers' article over Kowalik's work is justified by actual differences between the two texts.

In order to make this comparison, I will reconstruct the arguments of Kowalik and Barker and Mooers in their respective works, attempting in each case to answer the following questions: Where (in a geographical sense) do the authors locate the revolution(s) they describe?; Do they explain what they mean by "bourgeois revolution"?; Do the works contain any references to theories of bourgeois revolutions?; Or perhaps references to theories of revolution in general?; Do the authors use other terms from revolution theory (e.g. "political revolution", "social revolution" etc.) and do they explain which ones and why they consider applicable?; What are the main features of the revolutions described (what did they consist of)?; Which classes/social groups are considered agents of revolutions?; Finally: what conclusions (if any) do the authors draw from their analyses? These reconstructions will therefore be clearly different from my previous attempts in this regard (Konat, 2022, 2024).

In the remainder of this chapter I will in turn: reconstruct the content of Tadeusz Kowalik's article, outline a discussion of Barker's and Mooers' work, present a comparative analysis of these two texts, and then summarise my reflections with conclusions and inferences.

Tadeusz Kowalik's "August—the Epigonic Bourgeois Revolution"[2]

Although in his article Kowalik showed awareness of the fact that in the past bourgeois revolutions had taken place throughout Europe (this is clear from the very first sentence of the article—"The assertion that the workers played the key role in the bourgeois revolutions of continental

Europe is a banal historical truth" (Kowalik, 1997a, p. 49)[3])—his text is devoted exclusively to one country: the bourgeois revolution "made" by the workers "... was repeated in almost classic form in Poland in 1980–82 [sic!]"[4] (p. 50). Let us just add in passing that Kowalik did not actually describe in terms of a bourgeois revolution either August 1980, as one might infer from the title of the text (he most probably used an unfortunate mental shortcut there), or the period before the changes initiated in 1988–1989 in general. I have explained this at length in (Konat, 2024, pp. 39–41).

Although he uses the term "bourgeois revolution", in the article Kowalik did not present a *precise* definition of it. Perhaps the closest he came to defining what he meant by such a revolution is in the passages where he listed its characteristics: it was, according to Kowalik, "... a revolution dependent on mass unemployment, impoverishment and glaring inequality ..." (p. 52), or, as he wrote elsewhere, characterised by "... the appearance of mass unemployment[,] ... the precipitate fall in real wages by at least a third, ... the increase several times over in poverty, ... [and] the massive speculation, corruption, sudden appearance of huge fortunes ..." (p. 55). However, he did not explain whether, in his view, these were to be features of all bourgeois revolutions or only of this particular one.

Nevertheless, Kowalik did use a particular specification. Namely, he wrote of an "epigonic" bourgeois revolution. He explained this "epigonism" as follows:

> This type of bourgeois revolution has already become increasingly a relic of the past. In many countries modern private market economies have been established without the primitive accumulation of capital on the American, English, or even German model. On the one hand, this makes possible the association of (equity) capital; on the other, the fact that these new revolutions took place in countries in which big industry (often too big) already existed meant that the accumulation of the proverbial first million through speculation, theft, or fraud was not necessary to assist the transition from manufacture to industrial production. For the same reason, the impoverishment of some to increase the capital of others was entirely unnecessary. (pp. 51–52)

This is all the more important because in Kowalik's use of the term "epigponic" there appears perhaps the only overt reference to Marxist terminology: the use of the category of "primitive accumulation" evident in the above quotation.

What we do *not* find in the article are any comprehensive references to theories of bourgeois revolutions, or theories of revolution in general. One of the only two observations that, in a last resort, can be considered theorising (the other will be discussed later) is that "The greatest, most massive workers' movement in Europe carried out a social revolution from which emerged one of the most unjust social systems that history has known on this continent this century" (p. 50). Or, as Kowalik puts it elsewhere in the text, that there was a "peaceful transformation of a workers' revolution into a bourgeois one" (p. 51).[5]

The former quote also contains the answer to another of my questions outlined in the Introduction of this chapter: in it, Kowalik made the only reference in the entire article to a type of revolution other than the "bourgeois" one, namely the "social revolution". Any other mentions are not theoretical but merely journalistic. An example would be the term coined by Czesław Bywalec and frequently cited by Kowalik, that in Poland at the beginning of the transformation (certainly before 1993, when Bywalec proposed this phrase) there was a "revolution in incomes" (p. 50).

However, it is not the case that Kowalik's thesis of a "bourgeois revolution" in Poland is completely devoid of literature references that would point to this type of revolution. Already at the very beginning of his article, Kowalik quoted the following passage from Oskar Lange's 1931 paper (Lange, 1990):

> When, after the war in all the countries of central Europe, in Germany, Austria, Hungary, Poland, the remains of the ancien regime collapsed and, on the wreckage of the Hohenzollern, Habsburg and Romanov monarchies, bourgeois democratic republics were created, it was the workers' movement which was the creator of these republics. Since the workers' movement did not have the strength to endow the newly created republics with a proletarian class character, it was unable to avoid the republics it had created becoming bourgeois states. This created … the tragi-comic situation in which workers' parties created republics which were in their sociological content bourgeois states. (Lange, 1990, p. 93; quoted in Kowalik, 1997a, pp. 49–50)

Importantly, as I argue elsewhere (Konat, 2022), it was Kowalik's (re-) reading of this text by Lange that most likely inspired the former's use of the term "bourgeois revolution".[6]

Apart from stating that the revolution was, in his opinion, epigonic, Kowalik wrote only in passing and in very general terms about what he thought it was characterised by. In particular, it is striking that the article tells us virtually nothing about the course of the revolution. Rather, Kowalik's description focuses on the causes and especially the consequences of the events described.

As for the causes of this revolution, he argued, as we have seen, that it occurred as a consequence of the workers' revolution. However, the most important element in Kowalik's explanation of how the "epigonic" bourgeois revolution in Poland came about was his adoption of the thesis of the "betrayal of the elites". Among the first manifestations of this treachery—which later resulted in Solidarity's tacit consent to the neoliberal shape of the systemic changes—were "the exodus of the intelligentsia" (p. 53) / "a huge exodus of its intellectuals" (p. 54) from the trade union camp to the new career opportunities, which had begun beforehand, in pre-transformation times. While drawing attention to the anti-worker propaganda of the new capitalist elites in Poland, Kowalik elaborated on this as follows:

> A large, perhaps preponderant part of its former advisers and activists went into an opposing anti-working class ideological camp, misrepresenting the history of Solidarity and even slandering it. The most insidious effect was the widespread presentation of the mass movement of 1980–81 as exclusively oriented to anticommunism, civil rights and national independence. The working class character of its demands and the social content of the movement were systematically passed over in silence. ... Sometimes maybe this is "only" an unintended bias. What is worse, perhaps, is that a persistently repeated myth of a "Second Solidarity" is being created; it is simply presented as an irresponsible, populist opponent of market reforms. (p. 54)

The above is a part of Kowalik's more general reflection on what he calls the "ideology of legitimation" (p. 50) of the new social and political order:

> Here we are not concerned—at least not first and foremost—with the inevitable tendency for the class employed in heavy industry in the "socialist mammoths" to lose out, because the modern industrial structure, to which we aspire, is entirely different. Such assertions are part of the new ideology of legitimation. (p. 50)

Kowalik alluded to the thesis of the "betrayal of the elites" even more indirectly in those parts of the article where he referred to the figure of Jacek Kuroń. Firstly, attention is drawn to the quotation from Kuroń quoted by Kowalik with approval, from which it follows quite unambiguously that in constructing the new social order the "elites" acted "above society":

> The catastrophe of Solidarity took place because the government which had emerged from it, instead of leading a mass movement for reform, acted over people's heads. It carried out a statist technocratic programme over people's heads, which pushed the majority towards ultra-left attitudes, which were the more radical because of the painful costs associated with the collapse of communism. (Kuroń, 1994, p. 6; quoted in Kowalik, 1997a, p. 55)

Secondly—and here let us return to the words of Kowalik himself—he pointed out that this betrayal concerned not only the ideals of the workers' movement (Solidarity), but even the Round Table Agreements, which were thrown into the dustbin the same year in which they were signed through the adoption of the Balcerowicz Plan. Such, it seems, were the motivations behind the following excerpt:

> In retrospect, unfortunately, Kuroń appreciated, as he himself recalls, that Solidarity was a reform movement, which could have been a great source of support for reform, only it opted for other reforms. It had them, it thought, in the form of guaranteed agreements. (p. 55)

As far as the consequences of the "epigonic bourgeois revolution" in Poland are concerned, for Kowalik these were mainly negative and primarily of an economic nature:

> The new social system above all meant the institutionalisation of very high and stable unemployment, a several fold increase in poverty and "a real revolution in incomes" (the term is Czesław Bywalec's). … All these three features will however remain with us as constitutive features of the new order … (p. 50)

However, the consequences of the "epigonic bourgeois revolution" in Kowalik's views can also be quite easily recounted using the division into "winners" and "losers". For him, the losers were much more important, and this will be the leitmotif of probably the majority of his works written after the transition (see e.g. (Rae, 2025)). In the text under discussion here, Kowalik even listed—using the form of rhetorical questions—the social and professional groups that, in his opinion, lost out on the revolutionary leap into capitalism:

> Have workers employed in the private sector not lost out, when they are very often denied the most elementary workers' rights, including the right to join a trade union? [And what about small farmers?[7]] And what about nurses and teachers? (p. 50)

Finally, in Kowalik's article we find some attempts at historical generalisation (which also constitute the second of the previously mentioned statements that can be considered somewhat theoretical). He distinguished between two categories of revolutionary effects—social and political—and stated that

> ... the revolution in Central Europe, which Lange was writing about, was lost by the workers' parties in a political sense. But not in a social sense. They achieved the first breakthroughs in the employment legislation of these countries. Polish workers won the eight hour day and many other rights. Some said the workers had been bought off in the face of the revolution knocking on the door. In Poland today a wild capitalism of a nineteenth century character has emerged. (p. 51)

For Kowalik, it is therefore obvious that the "epigonic bourgeois revolution" was a defeat for the workers in the sense of not even just economic, but even "social". At one point in the text, almost in passing, he even wrote about "the great defeat of the workers" (p. 51). But was it also a defeat for them in the political sense? This is not entirely clear from the content of the article, for, on the one hand, we read in it that

> Certainly, both in material terms and surprisingly in terms of prestige, these categories of people [wage workers, small farmers etc.] have lost much as the price of gaining freedom. This is a great prize. (p. 50)

However, Kowalik immediately, in the very next sentence, discounted this indication of the "regaining of [political] freedom" as the great achievement of the revolution in Poland:

> But for other social groups such an assertion of freedom has little significance. The shaken foundations of material welfare make it impossible for them to benefit from it. (p. 50)

Moreover, elsewhere in the article Kowalik complained that this freedom, acquired with so much difficulty, was imperfect and he pointed to freedom of speech as an example: "Such is our freedom of speech, [subjected to] an unprecedentedly subtle process of control" (pp. 55–56).

The question of the "regaining freedom"—which, according to Kowalik, different groups could benefit from to varying degrees—brings us straight to the question of the "beneficiaries" of the revolution. In the article we find the following remark: "Opportunity beckoned in the new system for economists and lawyers" (p. 51). This statement is easy to generalise: in it Kowalik referred to the professionals, intellectuals-specialists, that is, as one might say, not strictly bourgeois elements within the broadly understood bourgeoisie. However, this remark should probably also be read in conjunction with another statement from the article: that, as a result of the revolution in Poland, a "new political elite" emerged (p. 51). These observations seem to be complementary.

Since we are on the subject of social groups that won and/or lost, it is worth noting a certain paradox that occurs in Kowalik's work. On the one hand, according to Kowalik (who took this from Lange), the agent of the revolution—the class thanks to which these events were made possible at all—was, as we have seen, the working class. And yet, when it came to the climactic moment, to this "peaceful transformation of a workers' revolution into a bourgeois one" (p. 51), what guaranteed the success of the "shock therapy" in Poland was nothing other than the *passivity* of the working class, above all under the influence of the impulses coming from the Solidarity movement. Kowalik expressed his astonishment at this situation, writing: "… if the scale of the attack on labour is taken into account, the restraint shown [by the working class] in terms of collective action is quite amazing" (p. 54).

Finally, a discussion of the characteristics of this "epigonic bourgeois revolution" would not be complete without one more observation. As is evident from the very use of the term "epigonic", this revolution was, according to Kowalik, above all unnecessary. This was so not only for the "obsolescence" of the prescriptions used (I mentioned this view of Kowalik's above), but also because "there were alternatives" and they were, in his view, much better than the path actually taken: "But it could have been otherwise. Another programme for development existed in Poland—that of the Round Table" (p. 52). However, Kowalik also honestly admitted that the alternatives he wrote about still meant a transition to capitalism, only perhaps less abrupt and of a somewhat gentler type:

> [The Round Table Agreement] ... was not an agreement aiming to give a dramatic advantage to speculative entrepreneurship. Indeed the principle of equal rights for different forms of ownership was upheld. The radical reform which was projected did not specify exactly how the "new economic order" was to be constituted. Nothing however was put forward which would have been in contradiction with—let us say—the Nordic-Austrian model. (p. 53)

This is important because, among other reasons, such voluntarism[8] will remain a characteristic feature of Kowalik's approach to the Polish transformation, and will even develop significantly, probably reaching its apogee in his most important work devoted to this issue (Kowalik, 2012). However, both there and in the article discussed here, Kowalik soberly admitted that perhaps—under the given conditions—the actual shape of transformations and the pace of their implementation had been the only possible (which does not mean desirable) ones:

> Given certain assumptions, it is a basic premise that the Solidarity vision of a new order was nothing more than a utopia. It can also be taken (again, I stress, on the basis of certain assumptions) that we were destined to shock-change. (p. 56)

So what conclusions did Kowalik draw from his analysis? In this respect, a reading of his text is truly striking. After introducing the completely original concept (at least in the Polish literature) of an "epigonic bourgeois revolution" into the discussion on the restoration of capitalism in Poland, he does not actually end the article with any specific conclusions, and certainly none concerning the revolution itself. The text wraps up with Kowalik complaining about the Solidarity trade union that, instead of joining forces with left-wing or even centre-right groupings (even of Christian Democrat provenance), falls into the arms of the extreme right. That showed, according to Kowalik, that the union was not learning from its own, quite fresh, mistakes. One can only suspect that this abrupt break in the narrative at the end of the work was due, at least in part, to its journalistic nature (more on this in the Conclusions of this chapter).

Colin Barker and Colin Mooers' "Theories of Revolution in the Light of 1989 in Eastern Europe"

Unlike Kowalik, Barker and Mooers wrote about "revolutions" (plural). In the very first sentence of the article, the authors also precisely indicated where, in their opinion, such events took place: "The 1989 revolutions in Eastern Europe (defined here as Poland, Hungary, former Czechoslovakia and the GDR, Bulgaria and Romania) have a number of significant characteristics" (Barker & Mooers, 1997, p. 17).

Also unlike Kowalik, when it comes to defining what a "bourgeois revolution" is, Barker and Mooers presented a clear and comprehensive explanation of their position:

> What gives a revolution its "bourgeois" character is that it creates the conditions for capitalist development. This definition says nothing about the social background of those who carry out the reconstitution of the state. Bourgeois revolutions need not be carried out by actors who are capitalists or who are consciously acting in the interests of capitalism, though they may be. (p. 36)

This is a de facto *consequentialist* approach to "bourgeois revolutions"—the position according to which "outcomes, not causes or agents, matter" (Teschke, 2005, p. 6)[9]—and it is followed by some further clarifications:

> "Bourgeois revolution" as a category is sufficiently broad to include "revolutions from below" involving varying degrees of popular mobilization as in the "classic" bourgeois revolutions in England and France, "revolutions from above" such as that initiated by the samurai-bureaucrats of Japan in the 1860s, and the "anti-colonial revolutions" of the 20th century. (p. 36)

The authors thus presented an approach that is not only consequentialist, but also very inclusive. This is followed by further theorising of fundamental importance:

> The classic bourgeois revolutions were *initiators* of capitalist development. In other words, they were political revolutions coupled with a deeper social revolution in the relations of production. But bourgeois revolutions may also occur *within* already constituted capitalist relations. Because capitalist

> development is both "uneven and combined", nations not only leap over stages of development, they also fall backward. Capitalism not only revolutionizes the means of production, it also revolutionizes the political conditions of its own existence. Specific state and regime forms become impediments to further capitalist advance. On occasion crises of capitalist reproduction produce revolutions that accomplish a shift "sideways" from one path of capitalist accumulation to another. Such were the 19th century revolutions in France, the German political transformations of 1918–19, 1933 and 1945, the Iberian revolutions of the 1970s and the Latin American "democratic transitions" of the 1980s. Such, we suggest, were the 1989 revolutions. (p. 36)

Let us observe that the passage quoted above uses the terms "political revolution" and "social revolution", which immediately addresses another of our questions: whether the authors utilise terms other than "bourgeois revolution" (even if, as here, not necessarily in the context of post-1989 events). Secondly, the authors clearly support the concept of "uneven and combined development", which in itself would place them in a specific strand of Trotskyist thought. Finally, it follows from the above passage that, according to these authors, the revolutions of 1989 were bourgeois in the sense that they transferred the countries they affected from one (exhausted, dead-end) path of capitalist accumulation to another, more effective one (neoliberal, "openly" capitalist). This is already obvious in the light of the statement made at the very beginning of the article ("… the 1989 revolutions should be seen as a form of 'bourgeois revolution' within capitalism" (p. 17)) and it indicates that we are dealing with authors who subscribed to the concept of "state capitalism".

Indeed, the authors directly posed a fundamental theoretical question: "Did the transition in 1989 represent a qualitative shift in systems—from communism to capitalism—or might it not be more accurately described as a move from one form of capitalism to another …?" (p. 34), and in attempting to answer it, they presented and summarised the theory of "state capitalism" mentioned above, which they clearly favour:

> On this view, "communism" was simply the most complete form of state control of capital accumulation. The state was both the mechanism through which production was organized and the appropriator of economic surpluses. It was the key agent of competition with other ruling classes in a world system dominated by the logic of competitive accumulation. For the

Eastern bloc states the form of this competition was initially military but increasingly involved market competition as well. (p. 34)

Barker and Mooers then developed this argument by presenting a specific version of the "convergence thesis". First, they approvingly quoted Narayanswamy, who, referring to Ellman (1988), argued that "in reality, pure market economies or pure centralised economies simply do not exist. Not only are they invariably impure, but they are also necessarily mixed" (Narayanswamy, 1992, p. 365; quoted in Barker & Mooers, 1997, p. 34). They then also approvingly quoted Haynes, who stated that "if we placed all the economies of the world on a scale of state control measured from 0 to 100 per cent, virtually all economies would fall in the middle third" (Haynes, 1992, p. 56; cited in Barker & Mooers, 1997, p. 34).

Furthermore, regarding the similarities between countries in the "East" and "West", including in terms of revolutionary movements, Barker and Mooers write that: "In a number of countries in Europe and elsewhere, similar regime transformations [to those in Eastern Europe] have taken place, both on the basis of convulsive popular rebellions and through 'negotiated transitions'" (p. 35). In this context, the authors mention Portugal, Spain, Brazil, Argentina, Chile, and the Philippines, referring to the period since the 1970s. They then point out that "All these examples, no one disputes, were cases of regime changes within capitalism. Whatever the particularities of 1989 in Eastern Europe, the differences look more like ones of degree than of kind" (p. 35).

It is on this "pillar"—their disagreement that "...the pre-1989 regimes were qualitatively different than those which emerged afterwards" (p. 38) and thus belief that "real socialism" was in fact a form of "state capitalism"—that the authors based the assertion that "The East European revolutions ... make sense as a species of 'bourgeois revolution'" (p. 35).[10]

As can be seen above, the article contains numerous references to revolutionary theory in general and to the literature on the subject. The work even includes an entire section entitled "Theorizations" (p. 28 et seq.). In it, Barker and Mooers attempted to answer the following question: "how should we categorize the 1989 revolutions and what common features do they share with revolutions of the past?" (p. 28). Addressing this issue, they immediately rejected the narrative of a "surge to freedom", but also the attempts to apply modernisation theory, civil society theory or postmodernism to the events of 1989 (pp. 29–32).

Moreover, Barker and Mooers began the core content of the article by considering an even more general question: "What should we mean by the term 'revolution'? Indeed, were these events [of 1989] 'revolutions' at all?" (p. 18). In response to this, they presented various definitions of what a revolution is (according to Petras, Huntington, or Aya, among others) and seemed to agree most with the latter and his "defining revolution in parsimonious and strictly political terms … [as] a set of events with two distinguishable parts: a 'revolutionary situation' and a 'revolutionary outcome'" (p. 19).

When it comes to explaining what exactly these revolutions were supposed to consist of, already in the second paragraph of the paper, the authors listed their most important features, in a very abbreviated and yet exhaustive way:

> They occurred in relatively advanced urban-industrial societies, and their main protagonists came from urban classes. Oppositional demands were "political" rather than "social". There was little internal political struggle among the oppositional forces along "moderate/radical" lines. The revolutions involved only limited popular mobilization. Romania apart, they were accomplished with less violence than, say, the British miners' strike of 1984–5. The armed forces did little to defend the old regimes, and in some cases military chiefs urged concessions to the opposition. The existing rulers, mostly, gave up power quickly and with comparatively little resistance. Generally political change occurred within the provisions of existing constitutions. Although each specific national pattern of events was different, there was a "domino effect" as the wave of revolt spread swiftly across the whole region toppling one regime after another. Despite differences in local detail, the political outcomes were similar: communist party political monopolies were broken, elected parliamentary regimes emerged, committed to dismantling the command economies, to privatization and subjection of national economies to market forces. (pp. 17–18)

The above is also a—extremely condensed and with inevitable generalisations—description of the course of the revolutions discussed by the authors. Not the only one, although others are equally or even more perfunctory, such as the statement that "The new governments brought in market reform programmes which were, as Ost … remarks of the Polish 'shock treatment', decidedly anti-working class in character" (p. 36). And elsewhere Barker and Mooers briefly referred to the course of specific events (let us conventionally call them "revolutionary outbursts"; see

(Konat, 2024, chapter 2)) which were to be regarded as landmark events for the Eastern European revolutions:

> In Poland, two waves of strikes in April and August 1988 finally impelled the regime and Solidarity towards talks. Solidarity had not called these strikes, even if Wałęsa still had the authority to end them. Thereafter strikes and demonstrations played little part in the political process. … All the population was asked to do, in practice, was to watch the talks on TV, and then vote for the Solidarity list in the June elections. The Hungarian negotiated transition was accomplished with even less public mobilization. The few street demonstrations that occurred enjoyed semi-official blessing. The "revolution" in Hungary was, as Ash … remarked, largely a "media event" so far as the majority of the population were concerned. They were never called into action. It was of course different in the GDR, Czechoslovakia and Romania. Here mass demonstrations swelled in the streets. The great demonstrations in Leipzig, Berlin and Prague eventually precipitated the regime collapses. Romania had days of actual street-fighting. (p. 27)

These claims are also important in the context of the role of the "passivity of the masses" in the Eastern European revolutions, about which more later. Here, let us note what (structural) causes of these revolutionary events Barker and Mooers pointed to:

> The Eastern bloc countries offer prime examples of how the competitive pressures of the world system can result in economic failure. … the exigencies of military competition undermined the [Eastern European] rulers' ability to meet their populations' basic economic demands …. Competition in its political-military form dominated the original Stalinist autarchic model. The powerful drive to accumulation was focused on the state's needs for military goods. But world conditions of military competition altered, away from simple mass production models, at the same time that the costs of economic autarchy in an increasingly interdependent world economy grew. More purely market axes of competition became of ever greater significance, and with them the need to adopt more complex measures of productive efficiency. Further growth now depended increasingly on "intensive" rather than "extensive" factors. Faltering growth and moves towards economic integration with world markets and multinational capital all combined to loosen and reconfigure party control. The formerly homogenized elements of the "one-party" system showed marked tendencies to separation into distinctive "interests". (p. 33)

Regardless of how exhaustive the above description may seem, Barker and Mooers devoted even more attention to the effects of the revolution than to its causes. First and foremost, they focused on the effects on labour:

> With the IMF and a host of western advisers pressing them forward, the new governments disclosed a less-remarked feature of "civil society": new disciplines on labour. Unemployment and official poverty levels rocketed .... Social inequalities widened, as avid marketeers had hoped. (p. 36)

This argument is further developed in a description of a strongly "macroeconomic" character:

> Growth was difficult or negative. The world economy was entering its most serious postwar recession. Despite price reform, closures, loss of jobs, falling real wages, the promised boom did not materialize. The main new growth was in small business, especially commerce rather than manufacturing. ... Up to 1993 some 55,000 enterprises had been taken over by foreign multinationals ... However, privatization proved slower than had been expected, and state enterprises proved to have a staying power—and a variety of allies—that even "shock treatments" did not overcome. The death of the state has been much exaggerated. (p. 37)

Following the above discussion of the socio-economic effects of the revolutions at the level of nation states, the authors also highlighted the consequences at the level of the global economy: "... the states and economies of Eastern Europe have been more fully integrated into the world economy. But their status is that of junior partners, not neo-colonies of western imperialism" (p. 38). The last sentence indicates that, although Barker and Mooers were highly critical of the effects of the transformations, they were nevertheless careful to remain scientifically objective and not to exaggerate. Perhaps the most visible proof of this they provided by pointing out the positive effects of the Eastern European revolutions:

> ... 1989 brought three unqualified gains. First, if popular self-mobilization was not the basis of these revolutions, nonetheless the political conditions they achieved—rights to freedom of speech, assembly and organization, and to vote—are precious victories in themselves. Second, the 200th anniversary of the French Revolution saw a thousand pundits, including numerous miserabilist ex-leftists, proclaim the impossibility and undesirability of revo-

> lution. History replied: European revolutions were celebrated. Third, Stalinism was dealt a death-blow. (p. 38)

This combination—in Barker and Mooers' analysis—of a discussion of the positive and negative effects of the revolutions with a class analysis inevitably resulted in an indication (albeit very perfunctory) of the "winners" and "losers" of these transformations. Regarding the former, the article states that "… those who benefited were as often as not members of the former nomenklatura, converting into a new 'priviligentsia'", with the generalising comment that "The degree of personnel change within the ruling classes was lower than many had expected, or feared" (p. 36).

For Barker and Mooers, an important part of painting the picture of the "winners" was to draw attention to the phenomenon of "enfranchisement of the nomenklatura", progressing "apace" in Eastern European countries since 1989 (p. 34). They claimed that the "[e]ntire sections of the old ruling class, especially in Poland and Hungary, have shifted fairly painlessly into positions of authority in both denationalized firms and in western multinationals setting up operations in the former Eastern bloc countries" (p. 34). And elsewhere in the article they added that the "… local Communist Party officials and nomenklatura were themselves the beneficiaries of privatisation and the turn to the market" (p. 38).

However, at a slightly different level of analysis, in the passage cited above we find the following sentence: "The main new growth was in small business, especially commerce rather than manufacturing" (p. 37), pointing to yet other beneficiaries of the revolutions, namely: the petty bourgeoisie, rapidly emerging at the time and carrying out the primitive accumulation.

As for the "losers" of the 1989 revolutions, Barker and Mooers pointed in this context, albeit indirectly, to the "mass of the population": "For the mass of the population, the outcome of the revolutions was not quite the joyous leap into freedom and democracy many had imagined. Disaffection had various expressions" (p. 37). This, it seems, is also closely related to the descriptions quoted above concerning, for example, the drastic increase in unemployment or social inequality.

Unlike the issue of "winners" and "losers" of the revolutions, the question of "agency" is discussed at length in Barker and Mooers' article. The authors begun by identifying three social groups which, in their view, "played significant parts": "the old ruling class", "the opposition" (or "the democratic intelligentsia" (p. 25)) and finally: "the wider (mostly urban) populations" (p. 21), a little further on in the text described more precisely as "the urban crowds (manual and white-collar) who constituted the majority of the populations" (p. 25). The authors then moved on to discuss the role of each of these groups separately, first noting that the vast majority of groups "'at the top' of the social ladder remained after the transition more or less where they had been before it, with their 'privileged position … never seriously threatened'" (p. 23).

This, in the authors' argument, was no coincidence: Barker and Mooers explicitly suggested that this was the outcome that the nomenklatura had been aiming for even before the transition and that they had agreed to co-shape these changes in order to influence exactly this course of change. In this context, the authors approvingly quote Elmer Hankiss stating that:

> When in the late 1980s they [the communists] discovered the possibility of transferring their power into a new and more efficient socio-economic system and of becoming part of an emerging new and legitimate ruling class or *grande bourgeoisie*, they lost their interest in keeping the Communist Party as their instrument of power and protection. (Hankiss, 1990, p. 31; quoted in Barker & Mooers, 1997, p. 23)[11]

According to Barker and Mooers, this was the result of an evolution within this social group that had been ongoing since at least the 1970s:

> By the early 1970s, the Kremlin encouraged East European governments to look west for investment and technological assistance. The strategy failed, but produced new relationships between eastern enterprise heads and western business. Worsening growth weakened the ideological appeal of the old economic models, and the parties became less effective mechanisms of ruling-class unification. Pragmatic, self-seeking elements in party membership increased. … [Subsequently, in the 1980s] [t]he pressure for economic reform increased. … Increasingly loudly, regime spokesmen promoted the virtues of "the market", often with the same utopian accents as the Adam Smith Institute and their own oppositions. Further marketization involved a new spurt of "nomenklatura privatization". Party members with connections, sometimes with dubious legality, converted profitable segments of state industries into private businesses. (p. 22)

Moving on to the two other social groups whose role in the 1989 revolutions was, in their opinion, crucial, Barker and Mooers stated that it was "their alliance that completed the 'collapse of communism'" (p. 25). The authors seem to consider it essential to determine how all these social groups positioned themselves politically in relation to each other. In this context, we first read that "Leadership [in the arrangement of "democratic opposition" and "the wider populations"] came from the intelligentsia, their organisations and their ideas" (p. 25). The authors also pointed out that "Even in opposition, the intelligentsia in Eastern Europe enjoyed a political importance, and a sense of self-importance, unmatched by their western confreres", and that "Their ideas had undergone a significant evolution, varying in tempo in different countries" (p. 25).[12]

As a consequence of the evolution of dominant attitudes and ideas as described by Barker and Mooers, which took place both among the party bureaucracy and the opposition intelligentsia, according to the authors, an alliance of common (potential) interests was formed:

> The evolution of their [democratic intelligentsia's] thought from top-down "socialism" (Stalinist or revisionist) to top-down "market liberalism" was matched … by a convergent evolution within the Hungarian and Polish ruling parties. Official and oppositional discussions cross-fertilized each other. It was not that one stole the other's clothes; both came to share the same wardrobe. (p. 26)

As a result:

> By the end of the 1980s, the thinking of Solidarity intellectuals had been so transformed that their ideas on the relationship between the market and the state were virtually indistinguishable from those of the Communist Party. For both party and opposition, transition to the market was seen as the only possible salvation for the Polish economy. By 1990, leading figures in the former workers' organization, Solidarity, were presiding over a "shock therapy" to Polish society that shoved unemployment up and living standards down. (p. 31)

There is no doubt that, in the opinion of Barker and Mooers, it was this alliance of two proto-bourgeois segments of society that fulfilled, at least in the case of Poland, taken here as a model example, the role of agent of revolution—a social force shaping change and at the same time the main beneficiary of that change.[13] This view, however, raises a fundamental question: What about other social forces, especially the revolutionary workers' movement, which had around 10 million members at its peak in 1980–81?[14] Barker and Mooers attempted, albeit indirectly, to address this issue by presenting the evolution of the Solidarity movement from the introduction of martial law in Poland in 1981, with particular emphasis (again) on the role of the intelligentsia:

> [In Poland] ... underground debates about the causes of Solidarity's defeat were dominated by the right. Solidarity, it was argued, had lost because of its "leftism", an over-emphasis on its "trade union" and working-class side. It had been too militant, insufficiently moderate. Conservative ideas about workers flourished, along with open hostility to working-class activity and demands. Solidarity's left was notably silent ... one reason was that they had nothing coherent to say. In the years of illegality, Solidarity's working-class base decayed. Impulses from below subsided. Its membership decline, shift in social com position and rightward evolution all made Solidarity an increasingly suit able "partner" for accommodation with the party's reform wing. (p. 26)

These considerations seamlessly lead us to the part of their analysis where Barker and Mooers discussed the dialectic of activity and passivity of different social groups in Eastern European revolutions. Such considerations are based on the observation that

> ... the 1989 revolutions were popular, in the sense that the majority of the population approved ... the fall of the one-party regimes. But the part the majority played was more complex than many commentators recognize. (p. 27)

Particularly noteworthy is the issue of passivity among the vast majority of society (which also serves as a discussion of the role of the third of the social groups mentioned earlier). Apart from the above comments on the evolution of Solidarity, which also apply here, we read in Barker and Mooers that "... what was notably absent from the 1989 revolutions was anything significant by way of independent working-class forms of contention" (p. 27) and that "In some countries the level of popular struggle was simply low, in others it never acquired autonomous self-organisation. No lasting counter-institutions of popular power emerged" (p. 32). These important observations, especially with regard to the activity of the working class, were then elaborated as follows:

> The year of 1989 was characterized by an "absence": any significant element of independent grass-roots institution-building. No strike committees or

> workers' councils emerged, no peasant committees, to enunciate specific class demands. Certainly nothing appeared in 1989 comparable to the workers' councils and civic committees of the 1956 revolution in Hungary, or the inter-factory strike committees and the like of Solidarity's birth in Poland during 1980. Specifically "social" demands were not directly posed by organizations created by representatives of particular classes. There was little in the way of a "moderate-radical" split. Habermas ..., Petras ... and others have pointed to the notable absence of "new ideas" in 1989. That ideational gap cannot be dissociated from the relative brevity at best of popular involvement in the process of regime change, and its actual non-appearance in Poland and Hungary. The mass of the population of these countries were not active participants in these revolutions. These were not simply the first "TV-revolutions", but also the first "TV-watchers' revolutions". (p. 28)

However, it is very important to note that in the "model" case of Poland, such passivity, especially among the working class, which only a few years earlier had been well organised and combative, was not solely "internal"—resulting from processes taking place exclusively within the class itself—but, as Barker and Mooers argued (on more than one occasion), at the crucial moment for the revolution it was "assisted" by the intelligentsia, which, although formally part of the working-class (or perhaps "working-class") opposition camp of Solidarity, had been, as we have already seen, striving quite openly for an alliance with the businessmen-in-the-making from the Communist Party:

> ... one thing was required: Solidarity must contain any radical tendencies on its own side. This it was willing and able to do. The leadership under Wałęsa drew the teeth of the 1988 strike movements, and systematically excluded former "radicals" from decision-making during the Round Table process. Once the June [1989] elections were decided, a selected "Citizens Committee" chose all the Solidarity candidates without any open election procedures .... It was something of a come-down from the direct democracy of August 1980. (pp. 26–27)

Finally, as regards the conclusions drawn by the authors from their analyses (apart from everything that has already been discussed in sufficient detail above in this reconstruction), three are particularly noteworthy.

Firstly, Barker and Mooers spoke quite categorically against all concepts according to which the Eastern European revolutions, and especially their extremely neoliberal economic shape, were supposedly imposed on the region from the outside. For example, after the already quoted passage on "local Communist Party officials and nomenklatura ... themselves [being] the beneficiaries of privatisation and the turn to the market", the authors emphasised that "These groups were not 'local Quislings' of foreign powers ... Neo-Liberal policies were as much welcomed and actively encouraged by local ruling groups as they were imposed from the outside" (p. 38).

Secondly, the following excerpt from the article is striking:

> ... most East European intellectuals revealed few qualms but multiple illusions about the "how" and the "whom": the market would provide the framework for "securing the social rights of citizens" and a reinvigorated petty bourgeoisie—"the traditional carriers of liberal values of self-reliance, small businessmen and middle-class people" ...—would be the social force to underpin the new "civil society". If that social force did not yet exist, it would have to be invented, or the conditions for its flourishing created, and only bodies like the IMF and a host of western advisers on expenses could help with that job. (p. 32)

It may follow that Barker and Mooers favoured the thesis of "social constructivism" of revolutionary/transformative elites, which was also pointed out by other authors including, in his other works, Tadeusz Kowalik (see e.g. (Kowalik, 1991)).

Finally, thirdly, the authors wrote that "The 1989 revolutions were also marked by, and reflected, the weakness of the Left", supplementing this with an indication that "The limits of capitalist 'freedom' and 'democracy' and 'wealth' were not criticized [and] [a]lternatives to the hegemony of the right were not offered" (pp. 38–39). They then attempted to explain this trend:

> For Eastern Europe, this is not so surprising. Stalinism's "conceptual embezzlement" ... of the language of socialism necessarily played a part. But the Left's weakness also reflected wider world processes. The 1980s also saw the Left in Western Europe and beyond drifting right, adopting "market" arguments and abandoning socialist language for "new realism", post-modernism, and the like. Few impulses from the West contradicted the rightward flow of oppositional thought, indeed East and West reinforced each other. The Left internationally paid in the 1980s for its insufficiently critical view of Stalinist politics, for its underdeveloped theory of world capitalism, and its lack of clarity about working-class self-emancipation. Its cen-

> tral error was its notion of working-class disappearance, which it misread from a downturn in working-class struggle—to which the Left's own flaws contributed not a little. It transmuted a conjunctural, political phenomenon into a depressive image of structural decline. The oddity is that the 1980s probably marked the occasion when world proletarianization gave the working class its first global majority. (p. 39)

Comparative Analysis

In the introduction to this chapter, I pointed to a number of questions concerning the content of works under analysis, the answers to which I sought in reconstructions of both texts. Already in the case of the first of these questions, namely where (in a geographical sense) do the authors locate the 1989 revolution(s), we see a fundamental difference between Kowalik and Barker and Mooers. The former referred exclusively to Poland, while "Western Marxists", although they devoted a lot (perhaps even the most) space to the events in this country, discussed the transformations in the entire region.

The same applies to the definition of "bourgeois revolutions". While Kowalik limited himself to a brief list of several characteristics of the "epigonic bourgeois revolution" (such as mass unemployment, impoverishment, and inequalities), Barker and Mooers presented a theoretically grounded definition which, as I showed, not only represents the authors' adoption of one of the important theoretical positions on bourgeois revolutions (consequentialism) but also demonstrates their ability to apply this concept in an innovative way (inclusiveness combined with the use of the notions of "state capitalism" and "uneven and combined development", resulting in the application of the term to the events of the late twentieth century).

Closely related to this is another difference between the two texts: while Kowalik made no theoretical considerations about bourgeois revolutions (even stretching the definition of "theoretical" to its limits, it would be difficult to consider as such Kowalik's reference to Lange's 1931 paper discussed above), the article by Barker and Mooers, as we have seen, presents a detailed discussion in this regard.

Furthermore, in Kowalik's text, only with difficulty can one find references to theories of revolution in general, like in his really brief attempts to distinguish between two categories of revolutionary effects: social and political. In Barker and Mooers, on the other hand, such considerations constitute, as we have seen, a large part of their work.

However, when it comes to the use of other terms from the theory of revolution ("political revolution", "social revolution", etc.), we can see some similarities between the works analysed. In his article, Tadeusz Kowalik, apart from certain "journalistic" terms such as "revolution in incomes", referred to a "social revolution". Barker and Mooers used the same term, also employing "political revolution". And in both texts, these are merely mentions, not elaborated upon and essentially not part of the core argument.

The result of the comparative analysis is much less clear on the issue of the overview of the main features of the "bourgeois revolutions" described in both texts: the analysis of their causes and effects (as well as the winners and losers).

When it comes to the causes, we again find a difference between Kowalik, who saw them primarily in the failure of the earlier workers' revolution, and especially in the "betrayal of the elites", while Barker and Mooers pointed to what I refer to as "structural" causes: in their opinion, it was the competitive pressures of the capitalist world system that resulted in the economic failure of the Eastern bloc.

On the other hand, when we look at the effects of the "bourgeois revolutions", similarities between the two works become apparent. In both accounts, we find references to the emergence of unemployment and growing inequalities as the most important socio-economic consequences of the changes, particularly acute for the workers (Kowalik referred to a "revolution in incomes", while Barker and Mooers spoke of "new disciplines on labour"). Interestingly, in both texts, the authors also pointed to the same positive effects of the revolutions: Kowalik wrote in this context about the "regaining of freedom" (and mentioned one particular example: the freedom of speech), while Barker and Mooers, somewhat more extensively, drew attention not only to the latter, but also to "freedom of assembly and organisation, and to vote" as "precious victories in themselves".

However, there are differences also in this respect. Kowalik pointed out that the success in regaining political freedoms has been somewhat offset by the defeat of workers in the social sense. Meanwhile, Barker and Mooers referred to macroeconomic issues (economic "growth was difficult or negative") and pointed out that "the states and economies of Eastern Europe have been more fully integrated into the world economy", and in terms of positive results: that the Eastern European revolutions brought an end to "Stalinism" and showed that even at the end of the twentieth century, revolutions are still possible.

The authors of both texts also approached the issue of the "winners" of the "bourgeois revolutions" in Eastern Europe in a slightly different way. Tadeusz Kowalik, as we have seen, pointed in this context to the "new political elite", intellectuals and professionals (economists, lawyers). Meanwhile, for Barker and Mooers, those who benefitted from the revolutions were "as often as not members of the former nomenklatura, converting into a new 'priviligentsia'". In this context, they also described the "enfranchisement of the nomenklatura", using this term to refer to entire sections of the ruling class. They also pointed to the growth in small business, which can be interpreted as an indication of the emergence of the petty bourgeoisie.

Finally, the similarity between the two articles can be seen in the issue of the "losers" of the revolutions. Kowalik drew attention to wage earners, including those in the public sector (teachers, nurses), as well as farmers, while Barker and Mooers wrote simply about the "mass of the population", but it seems that they meant, if not entirely, then at least to a large extent, precisely the same as Tadeusz Kowalik.

As regards the question of agency in "bourgeois revolutions" of 1989, despite the different emphasis in both works, it can be claimed that their authors, at least to some extent, presented a similar point of view.

Firstly, both Kowalik and Barker and Mooers emphasised the importance of the "democratic intelligentsia" in the transformations they wrote about. Kowalik pointed out that it was this social group that Solidarity entrusted with programmatic issues, and that it was its representatives who ended up in the government ("the exodus of the intelligentsia"), acting—as the workers naively believed—on their behalf ("the betrayal of the elites"). Barker and Mooers, on the other hand, wrote explicitly that "Leadership came from the intelligentsia, their organisations and their ideas". The only difference in this regard is that Kowalik did not mention the role of the party nomenklatura in this process and its emerging alliance with this "democratic intelligentsia", as pointed out by Barker and Mooers.[15]

The second dimension in which the authors of both texts agree is the role played by the passivity of the broad masses of the population in the "bourgeois revolutions" of Eastern Europe. Kowalik wrote about this explicitly, pointing to the astonishing restraint of workers in expressing their anger at the effects of the restoration of capitalism in Poland. And Barker and Mooers seem to agree with this entirely when they stated that "... what was notably absent from the 1989 revolutions was anything significant by way of independent working-class forms of contention". Moreover, as we have seen, they pointed out that this "passivity" was not solely "internal", resulting from processes taking place exclusively within the class itself, but "assisted" by the intelligentsia. Here, too, there is a clear parallel with Kowalik's argument, with the only difference being that Barker and Mooers did not describe this phenomenon—as Kowalik did—in terms of "betrayal".

The effect of our comparative analysis, in terms of what conclusions (if any) the authors drew from their investigations, is ambiguous. On the one hand, there is a certain similarity between the two texts in the sense that in both the authors do not seem to present any elaborate conclusions in their summaries.

On the other hand, however, it cannot be ignored that they wrote completely different things. And so Kowalik, as we have seen, ended his article by complaining about the state of the Solidarity trade union in the mid-1990s (the fact that the union, instead of joining forces with left-wing or even centre-right groupings fell into the arms of the extreme right). And Barker and Mooers, firstly, spoke quite categorically against all concepts according to which the Eastern European revolutions were supposedly imposed on the region from the outside. Secondly, it seems that they favoured the thesis of "social constructivism" of revolutionary elites. And lastly, they pointed to "the weakness of the Left" in 1989 revolutions.

Finally, it is impossible not to notice two other elements of the argumentation presented in both texts that are not included in the list of issues I have adopted as the framework for my reconstructions, but which show a noticeable similarity. The first is the influence of "international financial organisations" (as Kowalik writes; Barker and Mooers mentioned the IMF) on the shape of the "revolutions". On the other hand, when Barker and Mooers wrote that "Habermas ... Petras ... and others have pointed to the notable absence of 'new ideas'" in 1989, it can be said that in a sense they drew attention to the "epigonism" of the revolutions that took place at that time, a similarity with Kowalik that I have already pointed out in (Konat, 2024, p. 160).

In summary, in the comparative analysis above we have two fairly clear similarities, four noticeable differences and two issues (answers to our questions) where it is difficult to reach a clear conclusion.

Conclusions

As we have seen in the previous section, the two articles have significantly more differences than similarities, at least if we accept the criteria for reconstruction that I outlined in the Introduction to this chapter. To this list of discrepancies, we can add a general impression: Barker and Mooers' work seems to be much better thought out, with clear and consistent arguments, supported by appropriate explanations, including numerous definitions (revolution, revolutionary situation, etc.).

It should be noted here that a fundamental reason why such an impression of differences between the two texts may arise is that while Barker and Mooers' piece was a scholarly article published in a scientific journal, Kowalik's work was largely polemical and journalistic in nature. Furthermore, we should remember that Kowalik originally published his text in Polish, in a Polish journal and for an audience that may not have been widespread, but was nevertheless broader than just academics. Moreover, he wrote about current situation which had been ongoing for only a few years at the time of publication. It is, therefore, quite obvious that he did not see the need to describe, for example, the course of the revolution, since these events must have been perceived by readers as current and well known.

However, referring here solely to the nature of the works under examination, their style and volume, would be a gross oversimplification. In my opinion, the reasons for the differences between the authors and their texts should also (if not primarily) be sought in their ideological affiliations. Therefore, based on my earlier studies of Tadeusz Kowalik's work, I believe it is worth considering the hypothesis that a certain brevity and theoretical superficiality in Kowalik's text might not have been so much a conscious choice as a natural, but unintended, consequence of his theoretical awareness and ideological affiliations at the time he wrote his piece.

Yet before moving on to the evaluation of this suggestion for interpretation, it must first be emphasised that the concept of "bourgeois revolution" is thoroughly Marxist, as convincingly demonstrated, for example, by Neil Davidson's entire book (2012), as well as by the disputes surrounding this term, which, it seems, are only seriously debated among Marxists (see e.g. (Davidson, 2025)). In such a case, it can be assumed that any application of this concept to historical events requires the use of a Marxist research apparatus, and in particular: the use and discussion of notions such as mode of production or mode of exploitation, and their application to specific historical situations in a materialist-historical manner (regardless of the conclusions this may lead to). This is exactly what, in my opinion, Barker and Mooers did. Although they did not explicitly use the categories mentioned above, their knowledge of them, as a basis for the article's arguments, is clearly visible. Their use of the idea of "state capitalism", on which the authors base their thesis of a "sideways movement"—from one regime of capital accumulation to another—also speaks volumes, showing that the use of the term "bourgeois revolution" does indeed have Marxist foundations here, giving their article the impression of an exhaustive and well-founded analysis (which is not to say: theoretically justified).

In Kowalik's work, as we have seen, such elements of analysis are largely absent. One could, of course, try to point out (and probably not entirely without grounds) that he, as a scholar primarily concerned with economic issues, simply lacked the tools to discuss issues in the field of the theory of revolution at an advanced level. However, this would again be only a partial truth, certainly not applicable to the issue of Kowalik's lack of a *Marxist* research apparatus. After all, from the 1950s to at least the 1970s, he was an outstanding *Marxist* historian of economic ideas (Konat, 2024, pp. 1–3; Rae, 2025, pp. 5, 103).

In my opinion, the answer to the question of the shortcomings of his article (especially compared to Barker and Mooers' work) should therefore be sought in Kowalik's changed attitude towards Marx and Marxism in the mid-1990s. This issue has already been discussed elsewhere: it is largely the subject of Gavin Rae's (2025) intellectual biography of Tadeusz Kowalik. In it, the author points out that towards the end of his life, Kowalik succumbed to increasing subjectivism (pp. 72–72, 167). In my opinion, this is not inconsistent with Paweł Kozłowski's (2013, p. 255) comment on Kowalik's "idealism" and my discussion of what I have termed his "voluntarism" (Konat, 2024, pp. 176–180).

To repeat or expand on these considerations is beyond the scope of this chapter, especially since this would inevitably require more in-depth research on Kowalik's Marxism in general. I will therefore limit myself to a few comments on the "state of Marxism" in Kowalik at that time, based on another text of his, which I consider emblematic of his views from that period: the 1997 article (Kowalik, 1997b), in which he critically and polemically refers to the content of Andrzej Walicki's book entitled *Marxism and the Leap to the Kingdom of Freedom* (Walicki, 1995). Indeed, it is one of the few texts by Kowalik from the aftermath of 1989 in which he refers directly to Marx and Marxism, because, as Rae (2025) rightly points out, these topics had largely disappeared from his work during this period.

Generally speaking, in his polemic with Walicki, in which he claimed that "[his] aim is not to lose sight of what Marx gave to social sciences" (Kowalik, 1997b, p. 64), Kowalik comes across as quite convincing, although this seems to be for two reasons. Firstly, because he focused on issues with which he was very familiar and in which he felt proficient: "comparative economic systems". Secondly, because (or perhaps even primarily because) he was responding to Walicki's exceptionally unsophisticated and incompetent attack on Marx and Marxism. In doing so, however, Kowalik revealed his state of knowledge about Marxism at the time and his attitude towards it.

Leaving aside even fairly simple errors, such as attributing to Marx the authorship and support of absolute impoverishment thesis (p. 62),[16] Kowalik criticised and completely rejected Marxian labour theory of value in a rather astonishing way:

> I believe that the [Marxian] labour theory of value, uncritically adopted from Ricardo, played a disastrous role … in the fate of real socialism. This concerns both the disregard for capital expenditures[17] and the fatal distinction between productive and unproductive labour. Admittedly, Marx slowly freed himself from this theory, stating, for example, that "science becomes a direct productive force" (*Grundrisse*), or began to attach much greater importance to the use value of commodities (Vol. III of *Capital*). However, the changes were hardly noticeable. (p. 63)

And in other parts of the text, Kowalik seems to present a ***moderantist*** vision of Marx (and Engels): creating an image of a sharp rift in their legacy and siding with the "late" Marx (and Engels) as he perceived them, however, going in a completely different direction than, for example, Louis Althusser with his "epistemological break" (see (Althusser, 1969)). For example, Kowalik claimed that

> … in his later works, Marx recognised … two new forms of ownership – joint-stock companies and cooperatives, which changed his previously rigid dichotomy: state or private ownership, with nothing in between. There are also many statements about participation and organised labour, which, after all, give a different meaning to social ownership. It can therefore be argued that Marx was moving towards a pluralism of forms of ownership. That he

somehow took into account the warnings of critics (e.g. [Franz] Mehring) not to destroy "individual determination of needs", as total planning would inevitably lead to the enslavement of consumers. (Kowalik, 1997b, pp. 62–63)

On the other hand, regarding the position of Marx and Engels in *Critique of the Gotha Programme* and of Engels in *Anti-Dühring*, Kowalik wrote that "This is already a position very distant from the original fundamentalism of the years of *The Communist Manifesto.* In general, when confronted with the texts of the young Marx, *Capital* gives the impression of a positivist work ..." (p. 63).

In my book, I pointed out that perhaps Kowalik's was from the outset "a very specific form of Marxism" (Konat, 2024, p. 170n), which would result from, among other things, his ideological formation: a strange mixture of the writings of Ludwik Krzywicki and Edward Abramowski, overlaid with Stalinism, followed by a rapid leap into revisionism. However, the above excerpts show us an author whom we could only with great difficulty classify as belonging to this current. It is not the aim of this chapter to discuss the reasons for Tadeusz Kowalik's ideological evolution, so I will focus on just one of them. In the same polemic with Walicki, we read:

> I simply believe that Walicki has much less to say on the confrontation between utopia and life. ... Perhaps this stems from the fact that economists and economic historians have much more to say about the foundations of totalitarianism and the collapse of real socialism than philosophers or historians of ideas. (Kowalik, 1997b, p. 64)

In this division, Kowalik, who, as I mentioned, had been a historian of (economic) ideas for many decades, seemingly considered himself part of the broadly understood group of economists.[18] And therein lies the problem. In my opinion, his departure from Marxism, probably beginning at least in the 1980s, is largely due to his growing association with economics rather than the history of (economic) ideas, in this case especially *revisionist* economists, which at that time had already largely shifted—like the opposition intelligentsia, which he criticised for the very same thing in the article discussed here—to pro-market, marginalist, neoliberal positions.[19]

This is also evident in his polemic with Walicki. In it, Kowalik treated Marxism in terms of economics: he engaged with "macroeconomic" problems and with considerations about economic systems, while ignoring or outright rejecting other fundamental matters (such as the labour theory of value). Meanwhile, if we are to consider it in such terms at all, Marxism is not economics, it is an entire social science (see e.g. the discussions in (Wright, 1989) and (Tant, 1999)).

Kowalik's misunderstanding of this is evident in the mid-1990s, in his first article on the "epigonic bourgeois revolution" discussed here in detail, but also in all subsequent texts in which he mentions it. According to my findings, Kowalik mentioned this thesis in more than a dozen works, including many academic ones (some of which were published in English), but in none of them did he present any additional arguments to support it. Although he had the opportunity to develop such an argument and, over the years, the time to study the issue more thoroughly, he apparently never did so. This contradicts the claim that the shortcomings of the 1996 text in comparison with the work of Barker and Mooers—which I have demonstrated in the above comparative analysis—were due to the journalistic character of Kowalik's work, or to his lack of tools from the field of the theory of revolution,[20] or from the fact that he was writing for a Polish audience. He did not do so, I believe, because it was too far outside his academic and political affiliations and interests at the time.

Acknowledgement The author gratefully acknowledges the financial support from the Polish Minister of Science and Higher Education under the "Regional Excellence Initiative" Programme.

SGH

Regionalna Inicjatywa Doskonałości

Ministry of Science and Higher Education
Republic of Poland

Financed by the Minister of Science and Higher Education under the "Regional Excellence Initiative" Programme

Notes

1. The fact that Barker and Mooers' work falls into the category that in the title of this chapter is referred to as "Western Marxism" (or at least "Western" thought) is indirectly acknowledged by the authors themselves at the end of their text, where we read that "… the forces behind the Eastern bloc's crises were not peculiar to that region. *Our news in the 'advanced West'*, too, is about declining growth rates, pollution, waste, bureaucratic government, falling living standards, and loss of belief in an improving future" (p. 39, my emphasis). My use of the term "Western

Marxism" in this chapter is not, of course, intended to suggest that Kowalik was in any particular opposition to this (however understood) strand of Marxism, but rather, on the one hand, to avoid an overly broad reference to the opposition between Tadeusz Kowalik and Marxism in general, and on the other hand, to distance myself from attempts to define the views of Colin Barker and Colin Mooers more specifically, which goes beyond the scope and possibilities of this chapter.

2. In the remainder of this chapter, I will refer to the English translation of Kowalik's (1996) article by David Holland, which appeared in 1997 in *Labour Focus on Eastern Europe* (Kowalik, 1997a). However, I have made one systematic change in my references: unlike Holland, I translate the Polish term *epigońska rewolucja mieszczańska* as "epigonic bourgeois revolution" rather than "bourgeois epigone revolution", following Emil Tchorek and Gavin Rae's convincing translator's decision in (Konat, 2024). This also applies to the title of that article.
3. In the original version of the text in Polish, Kowalik consistently used the term *rewolucja mieszczańska*, which literally translates as "burghers' revolution". Elsewhere (Konat, 2024, pp. 47–49) I have discussed this problem and explained that it is quite clear from the context of his other works that by using such a term Kowalik nevertheless actually meant "bourgeois revolution".
4. In the Polish version, as well as in its reprint in the collection of texts which was selected and edited by Kowalik himself, we have "1980–1992"; see (Kowalik, 1996, 2013).
5. "The temporary alliance of the workers with the intelligentsia, which was entrusted with programmatic matters, the highly important support of the Church, together with international financial organisations, made possible the peaceful transformation of a workers' revolution into a bourgeois one" (p. 51).
6. It may be worth adding here that for Lange—who was not an expert in the theory of revolution—bourgeois revolutions were not a primary area of interest. He dealt with them only because, as he claimed, the attitude towards such events was the first tactical problem faced by an independent workers movement (Lange, 1990, p. 91). Moreover, in these theoretical matters, he seems to have relied entirely on findings of other thinkers, especially Rosa Luxemburg and Austro-Marxists. Since I have already discussed Lange's inspiration from Luxemburg's work in this regard in (Konat, 2022, p. 192), here I will only briefly refer to Austro-Marxism. As one of the most important representatives of this current, Otto Bauer, who was highly regarded by Lange, put it: "The victory of the Western Powers over the Central Powers was the victory of bourgeois democracy over the oligarchical, military monarchies. It was the greatest and bloodiest bour-

geois revolution in the history of the world" (Bauer, 1925, p. 71). Lange's adoption of Bauer's position was not unusual at the time. As Jean-Numa Ducange convincingly explains: "... many social democrats saw [after World War I] the defeat of the Central Powers as a new stage in the 'bourgeois revolution', in a sense continuing the sequence that began in France in 1789. According to this vision, in 1918 it was the 'bourgeois democracies' of the West that crushed the autocratic empires of the East. The losers of history were the great dynasties, not the French Republic and the British constitutional monarchy. ... Was 1918 not, in a sense, a belated 1789, long awaited by the workers' parties now elevated to power? In many circles, the idea was spread that 'defeat is irrelevant if it brings about a republic and pushes history forward'" (Ducange, 2024, pp. 92–93). This is significant here because—if we accept my suggestion that Lange's paper was most likely the sole inspiration for Kowalik's thesis about "epigonic bourgeois revolution" in Poland—it indicates that this thesis was based on a series of successive theoretical borrowings, which were, moreover, very distant in time and thus from completely different historical and political realities.

7. A sentence that appears in the Polish original (Kowalik, 2013, pp. 520–521) but is missing from David Holland's translation.
8. I write about it in more detail in (Konat, 2024, pp. 176–180).
9. An extensive discussion of consequentialism and a detailed argument in its favour can be found in (Davidson, 2012).
10. Although with the proviso that "This claim requires several assumptions about the nature of bourgeois revolutions" (p. 35).
11. The authors of the article repeat opinions along these lines several times. We read, for example, that "For many [in the party apparatus] 'communism' had become a sentimental nuisance", that "... ruling-class consumption and even political tastes shifted sideways across the political divide" and that "Most could hope to survive a lateral jump into a new, less state-centred, regime of accumulation" (p. 33).
12. This evolution, again with the necessary level of generalisation, was described as follows: "Into the 1970s, their main axis of criticism was 'revisionist'. Accepting the claims of 'socialism', they looked for reforms from above which would better match reality to the regimes' professed ideals. But revisionism's attractions weakened by the 1980s. The intelligentsia became increasingly critical of the failings of the command economies and looked for alternatives in a new direction: to the revival of classical liberal themes. The conviction spread that freedom was inherently connected to market institutions. Still assuming that what existed in the East was 'socialism', they now desired its replacement with capitalism—perhaps, some mused hopefully, 'with a human face'. Dissident celebrations of the market and capitalism took on some of the mystical air that previously character-

ized Stalinist invocations to 'socialism'. Both positions shared an elitist assumption: the intelligentsia knew what was in society's interest, and had a duty to introduce a brave new world" (pp. 25–26).

13. Although pointing out this particular similarity is beyond the scope of this chapter, it is perhaps worth mentioning that Tadeusz Kowalik expressed essentially similar opinions in his later works, especially in (Kowalik, 2012).
14. An excellent description of the Solidarity movement in Poland in 1980–81 in terms of a workers' revolution can be found in (Siermiński, 2020).
15. Interestingly, Kowalik's (1996) article appeared in 1997 not only in David Holland's precise translation in *Labour Focus on Eastern Europe*, which we discuss here. In a different translation and slightly modified version (with only a few paragraphs of difference), it was also published in the same year in the American magazine *Dissent* (Kowalik, 1997c). One of the differences was that *The Polish Revolution*, as Kowalik published his text in the US, included comments on the role of the nomenklatura in the "epigonic bourgeois revolution" in Poland, which were exactly in line with those of Barker and Mooers: "... the former rulers [of Poland, from the communist party] became the willing agents of an imitative bourgeois revolution. ... It was impossible ... for anyone to have illusions about the nature of the social system that was to emerge. ... It seems incontrovertible that shifting perceptions of self-interest among the nomenklatura, many of whom had already begun to enrich themselves through the acquisition of state assets [in the 1980s], provided a major impetus for approval of the Balcerowicz programme" (Kowalik, 1997c, p. 29).
16. On the fact that Marx actually never put forward such a thesis, see e.g. (Foster & McChesney, 2012, pp. 130–132).
17. Kowalik thus moves towards the neoclassical theory of production factors.
18. Undoubtedly, Tadeusz Kowalik's respect and intellectual authority enjoyed by one of his two most important mentors (alongside Michał Kalecki), Oskar Lange, were very important in this regard. Lange clearly suffered from a tension between Marxism and marginalist economics much earlier than Kowalik. A detailed examination of this particular influence on Kowalik has already been written about by Rae (2025), whose conclusions I generally agree with, and by Toporowski in this volume, whose conclusions I question, but this goes far beyond the scope of this chapter.
19. A figure who perhaps deserves special mention here is one of the undisputed authorities of Kowalik and a large part of his generation of thinkers belonging to what Gavin Rae (2025) calls the "Polish School": Włodzimierz Brus (whom I therefore refer to as the "Leszek Kołakowski of economics"). Let us just note in this context the highly valued by Kowalik book co-authored by Brus: *From Marx to the Market* (Brus & Łaski, 1989), in which, among other things, the strong influence of Joseph Schumpeter's

thought—especially his cult of "entrepreneurship"—is clearly visible. For more on the effect of this study on Kowalik's views, see (Konat, 2024, pp. 173–174).

20. Interestingly, in his polemic with Walicki, Kowalik casually mentions some theoretical reflections on revolutions by Alexis de Tocqueville.

References

Althusser, L. (1969). *For Marx*. Verso.

Barker, C., & Mooers, C. (1997). Theories of Revolution in the Light of 1989 in Eastern Europe. *Cultural Dynamics, 9*(1), 17–43.

Bauer, O. (1925). *The Austrian Revolution*. Leonard Parsons.

Brus, W., & Łaski, K. (1989). *From Marx to the market: Socialism in search of an economic system*. Clarendon Press.

Davidson, N. (2012). *How revolutionary were the Bourgeois revolutions?* Haymarket Books.

Davidson, N. (2025). *The Davidson debate: Bourgeois revolutions in historical perspective* (S. Edwards, Ed.). Brill.

Ducange, J.-N. (2024). *Republika we krwi. Berlin, Wiedeń: u źródeł nazizmu*. Instytut Wydawniczy Książka i Prasa.

Ellman, M. (1988). *Socialist planning* (2nd ed.). Cambridge University Press.

Foster, J. B., & McChesney, R. W. (2012). *The endless crisis: How monopoly-finance capital produces Stagnation and Upheaval from the U.S.A. to China*. Montly Review Press.

Hankiss, E. (1990). What the Hungarians saw first. In G. Prins (Ed.), *Spring in Winter: The 1989 Revolutions* (pp. 13–38). Manchester University Press.

Haynes, M. (1992). Class and crisis: The transition in Eastern Europe. *International Socialism, 54*, 45–104.

Konat, G. (2022). Oskar Lange and Tadeusz Kowalik on the Bourgeois revolutions in twentieth-century Poland: A note on two papers. In J. Toporowski (Ed.), *Polish Marxism after Luxemburg* (pp. 187–201). Bingley.

Konat, G. (2024). *The Polish Transformation: Tadeusz Kowalik on the Epigonic Bourgeois Revolution of 1989*. Brill.

Kowalik, T. (1991). Zmiana ustroju—wielka operacja czy proces społeczny? In R. Gortat (Ed.), *Społeczeństwo uczestniczące, gospodarka rynkowa, sprawiedliwość społeczna* (pp. 29–50). Instytut Nauk Politycznych PAN.

Kowalik, T. (1996). Sierpień—epigońska rewolucja mieszczańska. *Nowe Życie Gospodarcze, 37*, 22–24.

Kowalik, T. (1997a). August—A Bourgeois epigone revolution. *Labour Focus on Eastern Europe, 57*, 49–57.

Kowalik, T. (1997b). Spór o Marksa i ZSRR ciągle otwarty: dwóch Marksów, wiele marksizmów. *Zdanie, 1*(2), 62–65.

Kowalik, T. (1997c). The Polish Revolution. *Dissent*, Spring, 26–30.
Kowalik, T. (2012). *From solidarity to sellout: The restoration of capitalism in Poland*. Montly Review Press.
Kowalik, T. (2013). *O lepszy ład społeczno-ekonomiczny*. Polskie Towarzystwo Ekonomiczne & Instytut Nauk Ekonomicznych PAN.
Kozłowski, P. (2013). Tadeusz Kowalik (1926–2012) –Krytyczne spojrzenie na transformację. *Kwartalnik Historii Nauki i Techniki, 58*(2), 255–261.
Kuroń, J. (1994). *Rzeczpospolita dla każdego. Życie Gospodarcze, 21*, 2.
Lange, O. (1990). Kryzys socjalizmu. In O. Lange (Ed.), *Wybór pism* (Vol. 1, pp. 89–103). Państwowe Wydawnictwo Naukowe.
Narayanswamy, R. (1992, February 15). Causes and Consequences of the East European Revolutions of 1989. *Economic and Political Weekly*, 365–371.
Rae, G. (2025). *Tadeusz Kowalik and Poland's return to capitalism through socialism: Full circle*. Manchester University Press.
Siermiński, M. (2020). *Pęknięta Solidarność. Inteligencja opozycyjna a robotnicy 1964–1981*. Instytut Wydawniczy Książka i Prasa.
Tant, T. (1999). Marxism as social science: Celebration or nonchalance? In A. Gamble, D. Marsh, & T. Tant (Eds.), *Marxism and social science* (pp. 104–125). Palgrave.
Teschke, B. (2005). Bourgeois revolution, state formation and the absence of the international. *Historical Materialism, 13*(2), 3–26.
Walicki, A. (1995). *Marxism and the leap to the Kingdom of Freedom: The rise and fall of the communist Utopia*. Stanford University Press.
Wright, E. O. (1989). Marxism as social science. *Berkeley Journal of Sociology, 34*, 209–222.

CHAPTER 6

Tadeusz Kowalik: Personality and Living Ideas

Paweł Kozłowski

There are some people we keep asking about things that matter. We talk to them; they are part of our dialogue and an essential ingredient in the exchange of ideas and in forming our own judgements. Many of them are no longer alive, their vital records are now sealed, but their presence still accompanies us. Two types of people can be distinguished within this group. Each of them is the foundation of life and is a fertile ground of culture. It is special when these two types meet and are embodied in one person. Anyone who consciously witnesses such an encounter with their own eyes is very fortunate.

Two types of extraordinarily valuable and irreplaceable presence are: love and classicism. Friendship implies a unique relationship linking people. It does not result from unity of blood, but from choice. It requires reciprocity and permanent readiness. It is not inherited, but personally achieved. It takes place not in a single act, but in a continuous existence. It need not be a corporeal, physically tangible presence, because it is realised through the existence of a deeper, spiritual relationship. It does not require complete

P. Kozłowski (✉)
Centre for Europe, University of Warsaw, Warsaw, Poland
e-mail: p.kozlowski@uw.edu.pl

G. Konat, G. Rae (eds.), *Exploring the Ideas of Tadeusz Kowalik*,
https://doi.org/10.1007/978-3-032-09283-0_6

homogeneity of views and interests, but has at its core uninterrupted communication, trust and understanding. It presupposes purity of intention and clarity of words. Friendship cannot be faked, contracted, or turned into a game with roles attached to it. One is a whole person in it; friendship builds us up. It is perhaps the only such relationship that binds people together.

The second account is not personified. Its world is culture and its protagonist is the classic. Just as a friend constantly—even after death—accompanies a friend, so the classic creates our culture. He invariably has a say in it, his opinion must be reckoned with. That is why we talk to the classics all the time, and they are by our side in the most important decision-making situations.

Tadeusz Kowalik belongs to these two types simultaneously: he was and is a friend, and he is also a classic. He always behaved like a friend, but he never stood on a pedestal in a monumental pose. He disliked distance, formalities annoyed him, haughtiness was alien to him, and he tolerated commemorations only as a brief prelude to a content-saturated conversation connecting people. The latter usually concerned current events, although he also talked about his fundamental views and their relationship to the present. It would be the same if he were alive today as he did not change his personality.

One can apply to him what Jan Strzelecki wrote about Emanuel Mounier: 'there was a visible resemblance in him to the best pages of his work' (Strzelecki, 1969, p. 119). Strzelecki, a Polish socialist personalist from Warsaw's Żoliborz district (an important place in the world)[1] and the author of *Próby świadectwa* (Attempts at testimony), was close to the French philosopher, and both of them—to Tadeusz Kowalik. I don't know if Kowalik came into personal contact with Mounier, but he knew his thoughts. We had all read him, Strzelecki and Kowalik before me. What is known, on the other hand, is that Kowalik not only knew but was friends with Strzelecki. There was much that brought them together, and if anything divided them, it was the perspective in which they recognised the same reality. They were also united by the unity of their thoughts and deeds, their way of life and the ideas they proclaimed, the responsibility of choices made in proximity and in the wider circle. Also the attitude to, as Strzelecki called it, 'small and great history'. Both Kowalik and Strzelecki were positive towards the former, created by people and dependent on them, and negative towards the latter: Strzelecki from the start, and Kowalik, one might say, achieved this position gradually. Strzelecki promoted the idea of socialist humanism, while Kowalik proudly emphasised that, although he was an economist, he was a 'professor of humanities'. The last word of the title was important to him, the first was irrelevant. Both were strangers to treating 'great history' as a planetary mechanism subordinated to necessity, about which self-anointed chosen ones tell 'historical tales'. Jan Strzelecki was primarily concerned with human individuality and the irreplaceable value of close, fraternal contact with others, that builds it up, while Tadeusz Kowalik focused on the qualities of individual societies, creating a space in which concrete, corporeal, personality-endowed individuals live, situating themselves among other, equally worthy, though not the same people. This perspective reveals not the mass of the human species or the leadership exercised by God (often called History), but the importance of fraternity. Now we can affirm that for each of them the most important thing was subjectivity and resistance to the enslavement flowing from outside, as well as the even more dangerous self-slavery. Jan Strzelecki defended the human being with the help of personalism against socialism (as did Zygmunt Bauman in *Modernity and the Holocaust* and his later books), while Tadeusz Kowalik saw in the peculiarities of societies an answer to economic simplification and a refuge from the waltz towards the universalisation of a single economic system. For one and the other, sociology and the history of social thought were essential to understanding the world and discovering its diversity. They did not succumb to the limitations of applying the perspective of only one scientific discipline.

Kowalik belonged to a special, the last intellectually prolific, Polish generation until today. It was made up of people who were born before 1939, and so at home, in the backyard, at school, in the family and in their circle of friends, they experienced the tragedy brought by fate. They felt it; they saw the symbols and the victims. Before 1939, let us recall, a capitalist system prevailed, in which there was more feudalism than industrialisation and urbanisation. Large cities were very different from small towns, while there was a gulf between both of them and the countryside. It was a time of deep social divisions, with conflicts along both national and class lines. It was a period of political authoritarianism and another attempt at modernisation. Then and later, the intelligentsia played a huge role; it had, by its own impulse and national expectations, a great responsibility: to open a pathway for millions out of poverty and lack of independence. To bring them closer to the world. To make the state an organism that is strong, close to the people and protective of them. To provide their own, safe, non-oppressive, and friendly home. The intelligentsia set the course for the modernisation of culture and the modern form of all its components: education, art, science, institutions, customs. Changing the conditions of existence for the much better and broadening everyone's outlook on life.

The generation have lived through upheavals: intra-national social conflicts, the Great Depression, difficult tests of the elite's ability to govern. And the greatest of these: The Second World War. The years of the Age of Furnaces. During it and the occupation, and afterwards, this generation had to make choices and decisions that only accompany boundary situations. It was authentic because it was filled with death. The choices that its representatives were forced to make shaped this entire generation. They even created it. And the generation in turn created Polish culture, which after the end of the war took on (of course, apart from the Stalinist period and the aesthetics of Socialist Realism) a world status. Film, theatre, posters, and modern music co-formed the face of the West and the European East. Elementary education was developing at a very fast pace. The popular classes were learning to read and write. Top-level education and science were also growing. Intense development also extended to the social sciences, where Marxism clashed with neo-positivism and local achievements met global trends.

Tadeusz Kowalik belonged to this exceptional generation, or at least had direct contact with it. He was part of the generation that performed the last (so far) tasks ascribed to the Polish intelligentsia. He worked alongside our greatest scholars. Although younger than them, according to demographic classifications by one 'phase', he lived in the aura created by them. He had teachers from this group. He was their student, protégé, and collaborator, and participated in the process of the flourishing of normal science. He cited Oskar Lange, Michał Kalecki, Czesław Bobrowski, and Włodzimierz Brus as his masters. The latter also played an additional, and sometimes the main, role in Kowalik's life: that of a friend. So did Kazimierz Łaski. Each of them belonged to an elite (though always accessible to others) circle of first-rate economists, and all contributed to the Polish left-wing intelligentsia. Along with an entire generation, they experienced a trauma that became a constitutive factor, or at least a factor that influenced their formation.

But Tadeusz Kowalik had a special life story. Not only did he want a just and open world for all. He came from the popular classes, and so his identification first with Marxist socialism—and later simply with socialism—stemmed directly from his life experiences (Chołosiński, 1958). He did not have to justify his path or his expressed convictions to anyone or anything strenuously. In his case they were class-rooted (as a Marxist would say) and then enriched by an intellectual sensibility. The cognitive perspective he adopted derived not only from his position in the social structure, the significance of which we know well from Karl Mannheim's sociology of knowledge. It also stemmed from Kowalik's life. Here, as rarely before, the individual biography is linked to the collective history, the individual subject becomes a representation of the collective subject. The French drama of this intertwining has recently been shown by Annie Ernaux in her novel *The Years* (Ernaux, 2008). Perhaps this is why Kowalik was never overtaken by either the virus of neophytism or the plague of apostasy. He did not interrupt his life story and orient it anew. There was in him neither the heroism of the builder nor the heroism accompanying expiation. There was, on the other hand, a sense of defeat (especially after 1990), but this did not turn into resignation and withdrawal. Continuity of conviction and continuity of biography were accompanied by unity of words and deeds. Intellectual activity became social activity, and the work effort united the substantive charge with the ideological and physical one. He personally confirmed Norwid's and Brzozowski's convictions about the primary role of socially useful work. He was neither a quietist nor a clerk, isolated somewhere higher. The importance of work was determined by its social utility and, unfortunately, its necessity for individual survival.

Stability of beliefs did not mean the staticity of thought. Kowalik would change them, but never the most important ones. He had to establish early on which the core ones were. First and foremost there was socialism. Marxism was for Kowalik only one of a rich set of arguments favourable to its establishment. Continuity was fostered by the link between experience and reflection. He knew how to draw strength from this link. He found himself in the culture of a society in which social affiliations and community ties are sometimes stronger than the importance of ideological unities. Political courage and struggle come at a higher price than civil courage. The tyranny of the prevailing regime and opinion unifies the content of the community, but destroys intellectual independence and annihilates inner freedom (Mill, 1859). Kowalik was not subject to the tyranny of the collective. He greatly valued friendships and was devoted to them, but he derived them, among other things, from meetings of thought. Not the other way around. External control, small or large in scale, was completely alien to him.

Sociologically, having attained the relevant degrees and developed an intellectual output, he belonged to the elite. But psychologically and personally, he did not subscribe to it. This was because he believed that while elites could generate new ideas and express them discursively or artistically, the embodiment and implementation of these ideas was determined by large social groups. That is why he held John Maynard Keynes in such high esteem, arguably the highest of all foreign economists. But it is also why he chose Karl Polanyi as a guide for the transformation of free-market-corporate capitalism and the construction of a new society. For although they were both concerned with the same thing, according to the former, the project of a system in which the state takes care of all its citizens, distributes goods fairly and opens up many paths of life was a gift to the public brought by the academic elite. Meanwhile, according to the latter, only the continued involvement and attentiveness of the popular classes makes it possible to realise this supra-economic grand idea. Without the activity of the relevant social classes, such an idea will wane and fail to gain strength. It was no coincidence that Kowalik looked in rapt attention at the role played by legal associations in various systems, and considered their levelling in Poland after 1990 not only as a failure of Solidarity and its self-degradation, but also as a defeat of his own ideological programme. However, this did not cause him to give up; he never stopped looking. We, however, see no reason to regard Tadeusz Kowalik's guiding ideas as withered. On the contrary, today, at the end of the first quarter of the twenty-first century, they remain relevant. They are gaining vitality like few others. There is a whole bundle of these guiding ideas and it is worth looking at them individually. Not only do they show Kowalik, but they can also represent us, set the stage for the movement of our convictions.

Our country was to be a People's Poland. This is how the Freedom, Equality, Independence party (PPS-WRN) called it in August 1941, and this is how it was seen by all those in exile and at home who did not want a return to the state before the outbreak of the Second World War. They rejected the restoration of the Second Republic; 1939 was not the funeral of Poland, but it marked the burial of the system that had hitherto prevailed. The new one was to be an economy serving the needs of all. Both individual and collective needs. The process of satisfying these needs determines the development of individuals, and creates the social bond that is essential to the life of each. We know this not only from Aristotle and Marx. The economy as a whole cannot be driven by profit, although the economic calculus is necessary so that desire and noble impulses do not supersede the role of the mind and rationality.

The economy is to grow out of diverse forms of ownership. To benefit from private, cooperative, community, local government, and state initiatives. Czesław Bobrowski called this a three-sector system and Tadeusz Kowalik: a mixed system (Bobrowski, 1985, pp. 176–186; Kowalik, 2005).

The economy should be dynamic and grow. It is driven by two engines: the plan and the market, the prospect of the future and ad hoc action. This dynamic is expressed by the coexistence of two currents: constructivist (designed and incorporated by a powerful authority) and spontaneous (running organically and emerging from below). The relationship between these two processes and the formal and informal institutions that constitute them is neither fixed nor given in advance. It depends on place and time, the stage of economic development, the resources available, and the socio-cultural characteristics of the surroundings. There is nothing universal here, except the very principle of plurality of paths and possibilities. The state is not excluded from the economy and the economy is not separated from society.

This is a model system, empirically present and proven. It has, of course, its weaknesses. Some are immanent to it, and some arise from its poor practice, that is, politics, or as a result of environmental pressures.

All the better that these weaknesses exists, because the preoccupation with the system does not aim at the world of Platonic ideas, and is not limited to an Aristotelian perspective of facts. Tadeusz Kowalik quotes Włodzimierz Brus in this connection, identifying with his statements. They briefly characterise the evolution of economists leading from hopes located in a centrally planned economy to a mixed system of market socialism. The former, historically linked in practice to Stalinism, was overseen by a monoparty referring to the schemes of Marxism cultivated in the USSR. The latter: to the work of Oskar Lange, among others. Brus presented the course of thought of an important circle of Polish economists: 'The target model of the socio-economic system for those among the reformers who emphasise their commitment to socialist values is usually the "Swedish model". In other words, they give up their aspirations to overthrow the institutions of the capitalist system ... and are ready to limit themselves to complementing them with policies ... supporting structural change with as little deviation from full employment as possible, mitigating income inequalities, guaranteeing a minimum of social security, caring for free access to education and culture.... This approach—let us call it social democratic in the broadest sense of the word—preserves from the socialist idea the conviction that there is an interest of society as a whole, not reducible simply to a plane of individual self-interest' (Kowalik, 2013, p. 598).

The Swedish model or, to use a similar name, the Scandinavian system, was permanently present in the last period of socio-economic research conducted by Kowalik (2005). The Polish road leading to it, however, was to be different from the original. Sweden, it should be recalled, chose it as a way out of the backwardness of the country of incipient capitalism and the feudalism that still existed there. The nascent Scandinavian system was a thoroughgoing reform of capitalism, linked in economic theory to the achievements of Keynes (although Sweden had its own intellectually original school of economics), in ideological practice—to Eduard Bernstein's revision of Marx, and in the organisation of the state—to the social liberalism of J.S. Mill and a group of similar thinkers (Walicki, 2013, pp. 319–424).

Poland and countries like it, at the time of the implosion of the USSR and the disintegration of its empire, were in a different situation. Here, the Swedish model and the road leading to it were to begin not in capitalism but in state socialism. This road opposed the repetition of primitive accumulation deemed necessary by the enthusiasts of 'pure', that is, laissez-faire capitalism. It was an oasis for socialist values, which were being surrounded and trapped from the outside by a new form of Social-Darwinism (calling itself exceptional individualism) and from the inside by the compromises of the last decades of local 'real socialism'.[2] It also provided a constructive alternative protecting against the pressures of the neoliberalism particularly touted by the United States (Ronald Reagan) and Great Britain (Margaret Thatcher).

Tadeusz Kowalik, and the members of the circle to which he belonged, proposed the Scandinavian system as a goal marking the path out of a system that was collapsing, inefficient and turning into chaos. A creation that was ceasing to be a system and therefore a balanced, coherent whole. This was not the only path out of disaster. The liberal (propagated by, inter alia, A. Walicki, M. Dzielski or B. Łagowski) and Christian Democratic (W. Trzeciakowski) paths were also proposed, as well as others related to those. Among them, the neo-conservative entanglement of political institutions referring to the principles of religious integrism with a fully free market and full private property giving it dynamism (S. Kisielewski, J. Korwin-Mikke). Pointing to the model of the Scandinavian system was therefore not only based on realist premises. It was also a manifestation of concern to prevent social regression and the creation of a breeding ground for major destructive social conflicts. Moreover, it testified to the continuity of Kowalik's thought and ideological clarity. It represented a development of the reform attempts in the era of Polish October 1956, to which Brus often referred and to which Łaski was faithful (Brus & Łaski, 1989). Kowalik referred to Bobrowski's multi-sectoral economy programme of the immediate post war years, and continued the line of reasoning contained in the pre-war works of Oskar Lange and Mark Breit. He was true to himself and others.

Kowalik, as a historian of economic thought and researcher of economic and social systems, did not shy away from value judgements. He knew that one cannot escape from them, and that, unlike camouflaging, revealing axiology allows for scrutiny by readers and listeners. As a form of organisation of the human collective, he preferred the welfare state. Born and enacted in the twentieth century, this was, perhaps, the greatest invention of mankind. He did not regard it as outmoded and was convinced that its reduction implemented in the last decades of the twentieth century need not lead to the annihilation of the whole. He was against any fatalism in history, and was on the antipodes of the historicist ethic that Karl Popper accused Marxists of using. He defended the values that form the foundation of the welfare state. He was genuinely attached to them and appreciated the meeting of socialist, liberal, and Christian ideas that took place on their basis. As a socialist, he found allies all the more easily, as he was not a maximalist in his social actions and expectations. He was, one might say, an integral gradualist. He could—as with Andrzej Walicki—argue about the proportional merits of liberalism and socialism in the Great Reform, but he did not negate the contributions of others. He enjoyed such encounters.

Once, in the 'Introduction' to the last book prepared by Tadeusz Kowalik personally and thus a creation of his in the truest sense of the word, I wrote: 'Tadeusz Kowalik emphasised that he had nothing in common with neoliberalism and neoclassical economics. He regarded neoliberalism as the most dangerous and deceptive ideological current of the late twentieth and early twenty-first century. He saw a difference between philosophical and social liberalism and contemporary economic liberalism. He identified with the former and rejected the latter' (Kozłowski, 2013, p. 12).

He looked to others for thoughts close to his own and found them. More often in criticism of the present world, less often in pointing out the sources of its ills and identifying ways to remedy them. He was an open socialist by conviction (like the aforementioned Jan Strzelecki).

He remained principled when someone practised something different from the words he preached. Or when one succumbed to the pressures of the new spirit of the times. That is why Kowalik did not succumb to the programme of the Third Way as proposed by Anthony Giddens and (even less so) Tony Blair. In this and similar cases, however, he remained hopeful for a long time, since 'the concept of the New Third Way should not be regarded as definitively formed' (Kowalik, 2013, p. 104). For the same reasons, he did not identify with the Polish party presenting itself as social democratic after 1990.[3]

Among its many features, the welfare state best flattens the social extremes of wealth and poverty. It expands to the greatest extent the centre of the social structure—that deep foundation of democracy. We know this from the classics: Aristotle and Tocqueville, and from our contemporaries: Piketty and many others. Kowalik also found evidence of this in the economic history he studied. He always confronted thoughts with their object; the perspective of the history of ideas belonged to his cognitive equipment. He felt personally and morally responsible for the areas of misery and backwardness in his society. That is why he became an economist; he did not want his attitude to express mere intimate indignation. He was genuinely convinced that it was possible to change the world for the better, and he believed that this should be done. As a Polish intellectual, he felt guilty for the fate of the underprivileged classes. He rejected all privileges if those less fortunate were not granted at least the same. He justified this theoretically and pointed to John Rawls' *maxmin* principle (maximisation of the minimum), which was close to his heart. He said: 'Daniel Bell has written, with obvious exaggeration, that Rawls's theory is the best justification of socialism to date. But I see no exaggeration in other authors who argue that if socialism is identified with public ownership and equality, it is reconcilable with liberalism. From Rawls's theory comes, among other things, the concept of the so-called "liberal socialism"' (Kowalik, 2013, p. 263).

Kowalik was also outraged by the role and size of wealth. Not only because of the norms derived from the principle of social justice, but also for the same reasons as with poverty, that is, those arising from the commitment to democracy. In the latter, every citizen is equal. Replacing the principle of 'one citizen—one vote' with 'one dollar—one vote' leaves democracy with nothing more than a name, stripping away the ornamental substance of the word. Tadeusz Kowalik did not like hypocrisy.

Moreover, he emphasised (among other things, in many conversations with Kazimierz Łaski and myself) that modern capitalism has a rentier form. This is the other face of financialisation. It is devoid of the virtues that excited Marx and Engels, as expressed by them in the *Communist Manifesto* (Marx & Engels, 2004). Fortunes today are rentier in origin, they reproduce themselves and are now not necessarily linked to entrepreneurship, investment, employing others, risk-taking and innovation. They are a negation of that capitalism, not its higher phase. Hence, we might add, the term 'neo-feudal system' is now sometimes used and taken as a basic category for describing modernity (see e.g. Mazzucato, 2018).

Minimising distances between parts of the community and promoting social justice are among the first-rate principles cultivated by Tadeusz Kowalik. Both as a citizen and as an economist. Contrary to Robert Lucas and other neoclassical economists from the time of neoliberalism's dominance, he believed that the issue of distribution of the national wealth was one of the primary tasks of economics and economic policy. Today distribution and redistribution determine the direction of change, and the path is development, not growth. This distinction has been present in economics for a long time and its exponents close to Kowalik recognise it well.

The means by which to achieve a 'better socio-economic order' (Kowalik, 2013) were also important to Kowalik A viable choice included the set of already existing systems, emerging from the critique of the unregulated capitalist economy—that Keynes, Polanyi, Kalecki, and Lange had warned about—and from the practical rejection of state socialism and the millenarian idea of Marxist communism (Walicki, 1996). Kowalik advocated, as I have mentioned, an economic programme grounded in Keynesian theory, but he looked for the engines of its implementation not so much in the power of ideas as in the power of social movements, although he always took into account the relationship of the latter to ideological elites. Solidarity was always close to him for this reason, and he was therefore was particularly pained by betrayal of this movement committed by those who drew their power from it. He would admit that contemporary leftists, especially Marxists, who believe that today there is a 'populist moment', are right. They are on the antipodes of the critique of populism situated in circles of political and symbolic power. It is the popular classes that are the driving force. During his lifetime, Kowalik expressed understanding for the actions of 'Samoobrona' (Self-Defence Party), and the style of its leader, Andrzej Lepper, was as unrepulsive to him as that of Lech Wałęsa, the chairman of 'Solidarity'. Kowalik took seriously the reasons for the emergence of these movements and approved of the rationale for their existence. He did not consider them to be amorphous and merely manifesting a pre-rational mood. Even less did he regard them as expressions of collective obscurantism or conspiratorial initiative.

He could echo Chantal Mouffe pointing out that '[i]n the next few years … the central axis of the political conflict will be between right-wing populism and left-wing populism' (Mouffe, 2018, p. 6). The Belgian philosopher sees this as a reaction to a situation in which '[w]e have a vote but we do not have a voice' (Mouffe, 2018, p. 41). So, in the dispute waged (indirectly) within Marxism between Gramsci and Lenin over whether it is more important to have power in the hands of the new elites or the power derived from cultural hegemony, she argues in favour of Gramsci (although she does not completely reject Hegelian elite constructivism). Populism is therefore, or at any rate can be, a radicalisation of democracy rather than its annihilating opposite (Kozłowski, 2022, pp. 29–34; see also Mouffe, 2018; Eatwell & Goodwin, 2018).

It was after Tadeusz Kowalik's death that the Women's Strike movement swept Poland. When I participated in its mass demonstrations in Warsaw, I talked to Tadeusz. Many times. I tried to listen carefully to his words and recall what he used to say. I am convinced that he would have been part of the Women's Strike. After all, he had previously stressed that women were now playing a particularly significant role. He was moved by a book: an interview with Danuta Wałęsa, Lech's wife. He described himself as a feminist (we both used this term) and he had reasons for this. They came from his loyalty to the leftist demands of emancipation and from always standing by the socially disadvantaged. But also from liberal reasons: women's rights are human rights.

Tadeusz Kowalik was a pluralist. Without the existence of diversity, there is no possibility of choice. There is no space for the realisation of freedom. He thought not only like a socialist (although he drew much of his love of freedom and pluralism from the writings of his early heroes: Krzywicki and Luxemburg), but also as a socially sensitive liberal who valued open paths to development for all. For this reason, he was against economic primitivism and, for these reasons, did not accept a levelled [*zglajszachtowany*] world. He did not succumb to sentiments that accepted its quasi-naturalness. He demolished it. He therefore opposed globalisation, discovering in it a contemporary manifestation of US neoliberal expansion. He was wary of the current form of the European Union, opposed to William Beveridge's project: of making the EU more like the

United States, subject to the economic and political domination of the United States, seeking to nullify the diversity of systems. A region that does not form a consciously alternative part of the modern, developed world in relation to the United States. It was for these reasons that Kowalik was interested in the Asian path, first that of Japan and later that of China. In the second case, he was cautious, but there was more hope than fear. China, he insisted, had proved that a move out of central planning could take place without the imposed, supposedly Schumpeterian 'creative destruction' and without triggering a 'transformational recession'. He regarded the latter term as taken from the contemporary repertoire of economic newspeak, obscuring the enforced costs borne by a large part of society and falsely explaining the benefits captured by the new beneficiaries. He denounced this expression of neoliberal quasi-historical necessity.

Tadeusz Kowalik aimed at signposting development with 'realistic utopias'. He used this term eight years before Rutger Bregman, a Dutch social writer two generations younger than the Polish intellectual (Bregman, 2017). Nor is Kowalik's thought alone today. The phrase 'realistic utopia' only seemingly creates an oxymoron and is not merely an expression of poetic spirit. This would be a misleading trope of perception. For utopia is not characterised by a lack of realism, but by a rejection of what is now. Another reality may be no less real than the present one. The work of ethnologists provides numerous examples of this. When we think of it, the present ceases to be self-evident and becomes the consequence of choices that depend on us. Utopia, by targeting fatalism, empowers and activates people. It is not only for these reasons that Kowalik promoted it. Also because, as Friedrich Hayek said, 'what we lack is ... utopia' (Hayek, 1949, p. 432). This is one of the very few thoughts linking him to Kowalik. But let us add: the creation of utopia is one of the constitutional features of communist and socialist ideas; it is even a duty of the leftist intellectual circle. Its withering away in Poland testifies to the left's neglect of this peculiar imperative.

The limiting addition of 'real' alludes not only to the accusation of a mental detachment from reality, a flight from intellectual responsibility in favour of an imbibing of dreaminess and the establishment of certainties in place of, by their very nature, uncertain resolutions. A charge well known from the texts of many authors, including Engels' book *The Development of Socialism from Utopia to Science* (Engels, 2022), and supposedly overcome by them. This addition also points to the importance of the experiences that some of Kowalik's teachers, Polish (and especially Russian) society, and Marxism went through in preaching the programme of building communism.

Kowalik learnt his lesson. Utopia should be real, not top-down imposed and proclaimed in an unobjectionable way. Interactive and not all-encompassing. It is a moving target, the achievement of which by no means justifies the means. The multifaceted criticism of the Polish transformation conducted by Kowalik was accompanied by his pointing to other solutions. Had they been adopted, Poland would have been a different country and not the society it is today. The criticism of this transformation—carried out especially in the name of the necessity of 'shock therapy' and consequently, as he emphasised, 'introducing the worst form of capitalism into Poland' (e.g. in Kowalik, 2013, p. 520)—is also indirectly a criticism of unrealistic utopianism, of the detachment of illusory simplicity of thoughts from their place of application. It always produces effects far from the intended ones, or at least different from those heralded by its advocates. Weberian ethics of responsibility was the basis of Tadeusz Kowalik's public statements and actions. It was also the source of his constant activity.

Today he would be with people of left-wing criticality, with a generation of his grandchildren walking the streets, working as wage labourers in the countryside and lending a helping hand to others in the forest.[4] He did not succumb to the wave of 'fluid personalities', as Zygmunt Bauman, equally stable, would say. He remained loyal to ideas and faithful to friendships.

Translated from Polish by Grzegorz Konat and Gavin Rae

Notes

1. Żoliborz is a district of Warsaw that in the twentieth century was often associated with the intelligentsia elite.
2. A term for the existing state that was used by Leonid Brezhnev, who gave up on achieving communism quickly.
3. In a long conversation published in 2004, he asked rhetorically: 'But you do not assume that President Kwaśniewski is a leftist, I hope … He believes that the welfare state should be abandoned, that the scope of the state should be reduced, although there is no evidence that any country on the European continent is doing this effectively. That the question of "tenure" [*etat*]—work, employment, unemployment—is a matter of individual responsibility. That the state has nothing to do with it. If only he had at least preached the

views of Western European liberalism' (see chapter "Three on One: Mustard After Dinner" in this volume).

4. The author refers here to the ongoing migration crisis on the Polish–Belarusian border, where people fleeing countries in Asia and Africa are attempting, often at risk to their health and lives, to cross the green border into the country (editors' note).

References

Bobrowski, C. (1985). *Wspomnienia ze stulecia.* Wydawnictwo Lubelskie.

Bregman, R. (2017). *Utopia for realists: How we can build the ideal world.* Bloomsbury.

Brus, W., & Łaski, K. (1989). *From Marx to the market: Socialism in search of an economic system.* Clarendon Press.

Chołosiński, J. (1958). *Przeszłość i przyszłość inteligencji polskiej.* Ludowa Spółdzielnia Wydawnicza.

Eatwell, R., & Goodwin, M. (2018). *National populism: The revolt against liberal democracy.* Pelican.

Engels, F. (2022). *The development of socialism from utopia to science.* Legare Street Press.

Ernaux, A. (2008). *Les années.* Gallimard.

Hayek, F. A. (1949). The intellectuals and socialism. *University of Chicago Law Review, 16*(3), 417-433.

Kowalik, T. (2005). *Systemy gospodarcze: Efekty i defekty reform i zmian ustrojowych.* Fundacja Innowacja.

Kowalik, T. (2013). *O lepszy ład społeczno-ekonomiczny.* Polskie Towarzystwo Ekonomiczne & Instytut Nauk Ekonomicznych PAN.

Kozłowski, P. (2013). Wprowadzenie. In T. Kowalik, *O lepszy ład społeczno-ekonomiczny* (pp. 11-12). Polskie Towarzystwo Ekonomiczne & Instytut Nauk Ekonomicznych PAN.

Kozłowski, P. (2022). *Przeciw systemowi 2. Rozmowy nie tylko o książkach.* Instytut Wydawniczy Książka i Prasa.

Marx, K., & Engels, F. (2004). *The communist manifesto.* Broadview Press.

Mazzucato, M. (2018). *The value of everything: Making and taking in the global economy.* Penguin Allen Lane.

Mill, J. S. (1859). *On liberty.* John W. Parker and Son.

Mouffe, C. (2018). *For a left populism.* Verso.

Strzelecki, J. (1969). *Kontynuacje (1).* Państwowy Instytut Wydawniczy.

Walicki, A. (1996). *Marksizm i skok do królestwa wolności.* Wydawnictwo Naukowe PWN.

Walicki, A. (2013). *Od projektu komunistycznego do neoliberalnej utopii.* Universitas.

PART II

Contemporary Socio-Economic Problems Viewed Through the Lens of Tadeusz Kowalik's Thought

CHAPTER 7

How Neoliberalism Undermines the Health of the Polish Population

Hanna Szymborska and Janusz Szymborski

Introduction

The political and economic transition in Poland since the late 1980s has fundamentally changed the relations of production within the Polish society and economy. While there are undisputable benefits of these changes that are enormous and quite widely shared, the negative social consequences of some political decisions are noticed both in government reports and in scientific debates. Prepared in the twentieth year of political transformation, in the fifth year since Poland's accession to the European Union, the report of the Team of Strategic Advisors to the Prime Minister (the so-called "Boni Report") on Poland's development challenges until 2030 confirmed that "the reform effort of the transformation period, focusing on successful reconstruction of democratic institutions, building the foundations of a market economy and creating the basis for

H. Szymborska (✉)
The Edward Lipinski Foundation for Promoting Economic Pluralism,
Poznań, Poland

J. Szymborski
Institute–European Observatory of Health Inequalities, Calisia University,
Kalisz, Poland

G. Konat, G. Rae (eds.), *Exploring the Ideas of Tadeusz Kowalik*,
https://doi.org/10.1007/978-3-032-09283-0_7

self-government and civil society, only to a small extent eliminated the deficits related to the unequal opportunities and possibilities of people with less education, poor health, low income or advanced age" (Boni, 2009, p. 373). Prof Tadeusz Kowalik (1926–2012)—a perceptive scholar and supportive mentor—one of the most famous critics of the Polish transformation model, spoke more clearly: "…Poland has created one of the most unjust social and economic systems of the second half of the twentieth century …" (Kowalik, 2012, p. 10).

In this work, we focus on the part of social policy that covers health issues. The immediate reason for our interest was the scale of the health catastrophe during the COVID-19 pandemic in 2020–2022, when 332,000 additional deaths were recorded compared to the average for the last 50 years (Table 7.1).

The research question is: What explains such deep public health disaster in the aftermath of the COVID-19 pandemic in Poland? Our research hypothesis is as follows: The scale of the pandemic health disaster in Poland is determined, on the one hand, by the deteriorating health of the population since the early 2000s and, on the other hand, by the dysfunctional health system adopted in 1997 and implemented in 1999 and modified in 2002–2004. The COVID-19 pandemic exacerbated the already acute crisis of public health in Poland which emerged as a result of the neoliberal character of the health system transition since the 2000s. The causes of the existent public health crisis are thus systemic and as such require solutions that go beyond addressing market failures (Szymborska, 2024; Szymborski and Szymborska, 2025).The scholarship of Tadeusz Kowalik is a source of inspiration for identifying alternatives to economic neoliberalism present in the Polish health system.

The structure of this study includes the issue of the health condition of the Polish population in the years 1990–2022, and the transformation of

Table 7.1 Number of excess deaths in Poland compared to the average over the last 50 years

Years	*Total number of deaths*	*Number of excess deaths*
2020	477,355	100,000
2021	519,517	154,000
2022	448,400	78,000
Total	1,445,272	332,000

Source: Own calculations based on data from the Central Statistical Office

the health system in the corresponding period. The discussion concerns possible connections between the state of health and the implementation of market solutions in the health system.

The analyses were carried out on the basis of data from the Central Statistical Office, Eurostat, UE, OECD, publications of the Ministry of Health and its subordinate scientific and research institutes, scientific reports, and own observations. An exceptionally rich source of knowledge about the health situation of society and the functioning of the health system in the second half of the first decade of the twenty-first century was the institution of the Commissioner for Human Rights, headed by Dr J. Kochanowski (1940–2010). The 844-page White Paper documents a wide and diverse range of health issues, both individual and systemic. A common feature of the interventions undertaken by the Commissioner was their reference to human rights—as a patient and as a subject of public health policy. Most of the cases undertaken by the Ombudsman related directly to the problems and difficulties experienced by citizens using health care (Commissioner for Human Rights, 2009). Other important sources are materials and positions signed by the chairman of the Government Population Council (RRL), Prof Zbigniew Strzelecki (1949–2016) (Szymborski & Zatoński, 2017), and publications of the Supreme Audit Office.

Health Status of the Polish Population in the Years 1990–2022

The research results of the team led by Prof Witold Zatoński, a leading Polish epidemiologist, showed that in the first decade of political transformation in Poland, mortality due to ischemic heart disease decreased significantly, which contributed to a constant increase in average life expectancy. Between 1990 and 2002 Poland experienced one of the steepest rates of health gain in Europe. Catching up and implementation of health policy programs and lifestyle changes contributed to this phenomenon (Zatoński, 2004). It should be noted, however, that health programs regarding cardiology, oncology, and mother and childcare were a continuation of the programs from the previous decade. The undoubted achievement of the 1990s was the spectacular development of civil society campaigns, including the anti-tobacco movement. Since 2002, the rate of health growth in Poland has slowed down, and since 2014 for men and

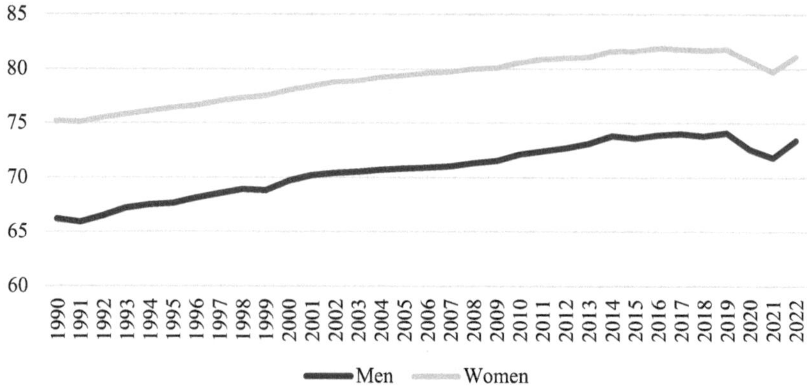

Fig. 7.1 Average life expectancy at birth between 1990 and 2022 in Poland. (Source: own calculations based on data from the Central Statistical Office)

2016 for women, the increase in life expectancy has stopped (Zatoński et al., 2021). This is confirmed by data from the Central Statistical Office (Fig. 7.1).

Using data from the Central Statistical Office, Zatoński et al. (2022) show an increase in deaths due to diseases related to alcohol consumption. In the years 2002–2019, the cumulative number of deaths from this cause was 130,000 for both sexes combined. The main cause of death among people who died from alcohol-related diseases was alcoholic cirrhosis (50% of deaths in men and 69% of deaths in women). In the years 2002–2019, the cumulative number of deaths due to alcoholic cirrhosis was 57,000 for both sexes combined (Zatoński et al., 2022).

Alcohol-related diseases were the main, but not the only, cause leading to the pre-pandemic health recession in Poland. Despite the officially declared, relatively stable epidemic situation, in the middle of the second decade of the twenty-first century, the threat of infectious diseases aroused justified concern. In the course of preparations for the 2nd Demographic Congress in 2012, during congress debates and discussions at conferences organised by the Government Population Council, the issue of infectious diseases was raised as an important factor influencing morbidity, hospitalisation and mortality rates. As a result, the issue of "Prevention and combating infectious diseases and cross-border threats" was included in the last version of the Assumptions of Poland's population policy prepared in

2016—five years before the COVID-19 pandemic—as one of the seven priorities of the population policy goal entitled "Improving the health of the population and reducing mortality" (Government Population Council, 2016), an in-depth diagnosis of the epidemiological situation of infectious diseases was then made and directional recommendations were made, including those regarding epidemiological surveillance. It was emphasised that, contrary to various optimistic predictions, infectious diseases still constitute and will constitute an important element of the "epidemiological landscape" of Poland. This is due to the fact that old, well-known diseases are replaced by new threats, including SARS and MERS CoV. The document also includes a number of recommendations for improving epidemiological surveillance, including: introducing an electronic surveillance system, increasing the reliability of epidemiological data from disease registration, using appropriate laboratory diagnostic methods performed for epidemiological purposes for public health, improving the quality of data on the causes of death in Poland, the need to conduct educational activities to raise public awareness of the ways in which infections spread and the importance preventive actions in the field of public health, including preventive vaccinations (Government Population Council, 2016). In turn, according to the report of the Institute of Tuberculosis and Lung Diseases, since 2000 the number of deaths due to pneumonia has doubled, mainly in people aged 70 and older. This problem increased in 2016–2018, when 13,323, 15,974, and 17,889 deaths due to pneumonia were registered, respectively (Korzeniewska-Koseła, 2020). There is no doubt that in the five years before the pandemic, Poland was already undergoing a health recession.

As reported by OECD (2021), although on the health catastrophe caused by the pandemic spread worldwide, an analysis of individual health indicators shows significant differences in the health situation between countries. Excess mortality in 2020 was highest in Mexico and Colombia, which saw 52% and 28% increases in overall mortality, respectively, compared to the previous five years. Among European countries, the highest percentage of excess deaths was recorded in Poland (22%), while in the Scandinavian countries this percentage did not exceed 5 (Fig. 7.2).

As another analysis covering 31 countries shows, the percentage increase in mortality in 2020 compared to years 2015–2019 was the highest in Poland and amounted to 14.4 (Parildar et al., 2021). During this time, a decrease in mortality was recorded in Finland (−3.1%), Norway (−3.6%), and Denmark (−4.3%). In turn, most countries showed a

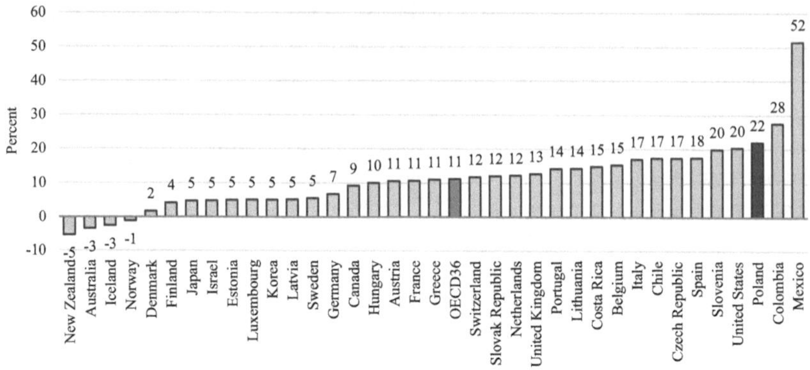

Fig. 7.2 Total number of deaths in 2020 as a share of the 2015–19 average, adjusted for population. (Source: OECD, 2021)

reduction in life expectancy in 2020, with the largest overall reduction in life expectancy at birth (in years) in Russia (−2.32), the United States (1.98), Bulgaria (−1.75), Lithuania (−1.61), and Poland (−1.36). Among European countries, Denmark and Norway have not recorded significant changes in life expectancy (Islam et al., 2021).

According to data, the percentage of additional deaths compared with average monthly deaths in 2016–2019 in Poland was much higher than the European Union average in November 2020 (97.0% vs. 40.0%), in April 2021 (65.4% vs. 20.9%), and in December 2021 (69.1% vs. 23.8%) (Fig. 7.3).

An analysis of life expectancy and mortality data for the Polish population in 2020 and 2021, performed by the National Institute of Public Health, indicates that there was a fundamental deterioration in the health of Poles, particularly older people, during the years of the COVID-19 pandemic. In 2021, life expectancy for men was 71.75 years, 2.3 years shorter than in the pre-pandemic year 2019 and for men aged 65 years, 1.9 years shorter. Life expectancy for women was 79.68 years, 2.1 years shorter than in 2019 (at age 65, it was reduced by 1.7 years). The reduction in life expectancy caused by the pandemic showed a significant inter-regional and inter-county variation (National Institute of Public Health, 2022, p. 16). The life expectancy of the Polish population changed more during the pandemic than in most EU countries. The shortening was greater than the average for EU countries by 1.1 years for all men and by

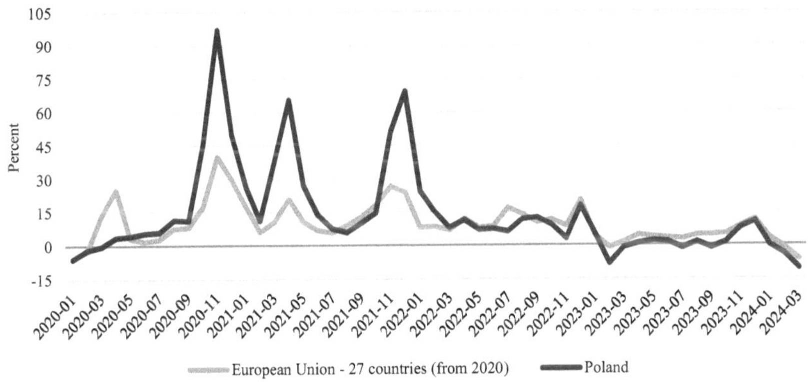

Fig. 7.3 Excess mortality by month as a share of additional deaths compared with average monthly deaths in 2016–19. (Source: Eurostat (n.d.) Excess mortality by month *demo_mexrt*)

1 year for those aged 65, while for women it was shorter by 1 year and 1.1 years, respectively. The authors point out that "The greater reduction in life expectancy of the Polish population than that of the EU population as a whole because of the COVID-19 pandemic has further widened our unfavourable deficit in this basic indicator of population health in relation to the EU countries as a whole" (National Institute of Public Health, 2022, p. 17).

EU and OECD data provide an overall summary of the health crisis in Poland. European Commission (2023) reports that the COVID-19 pandemic had a greater impact on mortality in Poland than in most other EU countries, with life expectancy at birth falling by 2.5 years in 2020–21. Excess deaths surpassed COVID-19 deaths reported in 2020 and 2021, which may be an indication of underreporting of COVID-19 deaths or of other challenges, such as delayed access to healthcare services during the pandemic. OECD (2023) provides the most recent comparable data and trends on population health and health system performance at the time of writing. It shows that health crisis in the time of the pandemic has further widened the gap in population health in Poland in relation to the OECD average:

Health status 2021: Life expectancy was 75.5 years, 4.8 years below the OECD average. Preventable mortality was 227 per 100,000 (higher than the OECD average of 158); with treatable mortality at 117 per 100,000 (higher than the OECD average of 79). 10.3% of people rated their health as bad or very bad (OECD average 7.9%).

Risk factors 2021: Smoking prevalence, at 17.1%, was higher than the OECD average of 16.0%. Alcohol consumption was higher than the OECD average; at 11.0 litres per capita versus 8.6. There were 73.3 deaths from air pollution per 100,000 population (OECD average 28.9).

Access to care 2021: 94% of the population is covered for a core set of services. 51% of people were satisfied with the availability of quality healthcare (OECD average 67%). Doctor spending enough time with patient during consultation 65% (OECD average 82%). Doctor providing easy-to-understand explanations 82% (OECD average 91%). Doctor involving patient in decisions about care and treatment 64% (OECD average 84%). 2.6% of the population reported unmet needs (OECD average 2.3%). Financial coverage, with 72% of spending covered by mandatory prepayment, was lower than the OECD average of 76%. Out-of-pocket spending, at 20% of health expenditure, was higher than the OECD average of 18%.

Quality of care 2021: Primary care: There were 663 avoidable hospital admissions per 100,000 population, more than the OECD average of 463. Preventive care: 33% of women were screened for breast cancer, less than the OECD average of 55%. Acute care: 30-day mortality after AMI was 5.2% (OECD average 6.8%) and 11.8% after stroke (OECD average 7.8%).

Health System in Poland in the Years 1990–2022

Among the 21 demands of "Solidarity" of August 17, 1980, number 16 stated: "To improve the working conditions of the health service, which will ensure full medical care for working people." Changes in the health system did not turn out to be a priority for the experts of the underground structures of Solidarity in the years 1982–1988. During the Round Table in 1989, the health sub-team led by Prof Zofia Kuratowska (1931–1999) and the government representative Prof Andrzej Wojtczak (1933–) did not even present an outline of a coherent concept of reform of the "health care and social assistance system." The final decisions of the Round Table included only "universal awareness of the need for a radical reform of the Polish health care system" (Woźniak, 2009).

In discussions after 1989, it was assumed that the costs of operating health care facilities would be fully marketised. The new model of medical care was to be built on commercial foundations (Golinowska, 2000). On August 30, 1991, during the government of Jan Krzysztof Bielecki, the Act on Health Care Facilities was passed, which granted state hospitals significant autonomy and imposed responsibility for managing their own budget (Sejm, 1991). This was supposed to lead to a partial rationalisation of expenses and create an appropriate basis for future reforms, in which an efficient internal market for medical services was to be an important aspect. During the process of commercialising the health system, there were unsuccessful attempts to solve the many existent problems (Golinowska et al., 2002). Free specialist care was now to be available on a very limited basis, that is only by a referral from family doctors, who provided it to a small number of patients. Patients who obtained such referrals were forced to wait a long time for advice. People who did not want or could not wait, began to use (according to their financial possibilities) the services of private offices and specialist clinics, which began to be established at a rapid pace in the 1990s (Tymowska, 1999). Although private medical practice was common before 1989, after 1990 almost all doctors practiced it—in their own offices and clinics, or employed by others. This type of activity was regulated by an ordinance of Izabela Płaneta-Małecka, Minister of Health and Social Welfare in the government of Mieczysław Rakowski, issued just after the June 1989 elections. Over time, a network of small private hospitals, private analytical laboratories and imaging diagnostic facilities began to emerge. The financial success of some of these facilities or the accumulation of large capital by partners led to the creation of larger commercial hospitals with a wide range of activities in academic centres and surrounding areas. This situation had a serious impact on the relations between various professional groups employed in public hospitals, as it led to increasing income inequality. In the case of university research workers, the pursuit of quick financial advancement was associated with a decline in interest in scientific work (Płonka-Syroka, 2022). Multi-stage work also became a phenomenon that had a negative impact on the effectiveness of scientific work in medical universities and in hospitals across the country in the entire country. Doctors were employed by several employers, therefore limiting the time devoted to research, improving qualifications or recreation. Multi-job employment concerned mainly younger doctors, which hampered their scientific development. The economic emigration of those doctors who did not accept the organisational situation also had an unfavourable impact on the staffing situation of the entire health system.

Only for two years after 1995, did the Polish Parliament (Sejm) deal with draft bills reforming the health system, and on February 6, 1997, the Act on Universal Health Insurance was passed by the left-wing majority followed British models (Sejm, 1997). The Act of July 18, 1998, amending the Act on Universal Health Insurance, introduced approximately 200 amendments to the original act (Sejm, 1998). The changes introduced after the parliamentary elections by the new solidarity-liberal majority administration referred to pre-war Polish experiences modelled on the German health insurance system. The functioning of the decentralised insurance model in the health system began on January 1, 1999, in the new political reality (Włodarczyk & Koprowska, 2000).The introduced insurance system of financing health care particularly declared the principles of: social solidarity, self-government, self-financing, the right to freely choose a doctor and a sickness fund, ensuring equal access to services, non-profit operation of sickness funds, economy, and purposefulness of action. Sixteen health insurance funds were established, one in each voivodeship, and one industry health insurance fund covering employees of the police, army, and other uniformed services. The health insurance contribution was set at 7.5% of the assessment basis. However, the reform was introduced along with three other costly social reforms: pension, educational, and administrative, during the economic slowdown, which resulted in a permanent shortage of financial resources. As a result of the insufficient preparation of the reform, numerous problems appeared in the everyday functioning of health care facilities, including from insufficient and—above all—very large diversification in the valuation of services provided to patients. There were significant differences between voivodeships in access to good quality health services, especially specialised ones. The prevention of diseases and health threats suffered the most (Ćwiąkała-Małys & Łagowski, 2013). It must be admitted that these problems were noticed by the National Association of Sickness Funds and gradually solved, especially during the period when Franciszka Cegielska (1946–2020) headed the Ministry of Health and Social Welfare (from March 26, 1999), and then the Ministry of Health (from October 19, 1999).

At that time, the phenomenon of using health problems in support of a political agenda and the lack of cross-party cooperation to improve the health of citizens emerged with full force, thus undermining an elementary condition for agreeing on a common, coherent concept of the health system. The coalition of the SLD, the Labour Union and, until March 3, 2003, the Polish People's Party (PSL), following the 2001 parliamentary elections, under the premiership of Leszek Miller, abolished health insurance funds, replacing it with the National Health Fund (NFZ). The Constitutional Tribunal, in its judgment of January 7, 2004, reference number no. K 14/0354, found most of the provisions of this act inconsistent with the Constitution of the Republic of Poland, which resulted in the adoption by the Sejm of the Republic of Poland of a new act on health care services financed from public funds (Sejm, 2004).The Act retained the National Health Fund as the main entity responsible for collecting and spending funds for medical services.

Discussions and decisions made on health matters since 1999 should be seen in the context of Poland's planned accession to the European Union (Frączkiewicz-Wronka, 2001). It was time for a thorough analysis of the theoretical foundations and practice of functioning of very diverse health systems in the 15 countries forming the EU before May 1, 2004. More or less consciously, the then ruling coalition, which rightly boasts of implementing Poland's EU accession on May 1, 2004, also introduced a health system modelled on British solutions. The UK society has been experiencing their negative effects for 20 years (Bourdieu & Wacquant, 2001). Prime Minister Margaret Thatcher claimed that "there is no alternative" (TINA) to deregulation of economic activity, market liberalisation, and privatisation of many public services. The role of the state in the economy was limited to actively supporting market mechanisms. The "TINA" approach flourished in socio-economic life in the 1990s and at the beginning of the twenty-first century (Szymborska, 2021). "Thatcherism" and then "Blairism" (only seemingly different from the previous one but in fact perpetuating the neoliberal order) presented the country with two major socio-economic problems: persistent income and wealth disparities and the collapse of the public sector, including the health and care system, permanently underinvested and poorly managed (an example of Blair's idea is subletting private companies to provide services for the public sector, for example, cleaning hospitals, as a result of which private companies began to employ former hospital employees on much worse conditions) (Marsh, 2023). The failure of the British, strictly neoliberal approach to social issues, was well realised and documented not only in the UK, but also recognised in Poland (Szczeklik, 2003).

The key features of neoliberalism include a cult of individual choice; representative agent models; emphasis on the behaviour of individual firms and consumers; limiting the tools and scope of economic policy; accepting there is no alternative to market mechanisms; believing "free" markets allocate economic resources more efficiently; shifting to private ownership; and the state actively promoting its withdrawal from the production and distribution of goods and services (regardless of its political stance). Professor Kowalik drew attention to the perverse understanding of the role of the state in neoliberal economics: "the paradoxical fact that under the banner of efforts to create a minimal state … a bloated state machinery has evolved, incapable of or unwilling to fulfil the social obligations imposed on it by the constitution" (Kowalik, 2012, p. 277). In the neoliberal reality, market mechanisms are activated through privatisation; deregulation (internal and external), suppression of labour movements in the name of greater market flexibility; direct market creation; outsourcing and reregulation (management of the public sector according to private sector principles) (Karwowski, 2019).

In countries implementing a neoliberal model of the health system, certain common features can be seen:

Privatisation of care: Dealing with inefficiencies, reducing costs, accommodating rising demand; a purchaser-provider split; creation of internal markets; shift from vertical (state-determined) to upward-sloping (market-determined) supply of healthcare; healthcare spending becomes a function of production costs (wages of nurses, doctors, costs of machinery, equipment, etc.).

Adoption of market logic in healthcare provision and financing: Assigning monetary value to care by using Quality Adjusted Life Years (QALYs) and cost-benefit analysis to determine spending; a shift in approach from "doctor knows best" to patients becoming consumers with the right and responsibility to make informed choices about services they consume; acceptance by the health establishment; prioritising cost-saving over patient well-being and access and quality of care (Lancet, 2018; Horton, 2018).

Each of these components raises serious concerns. We take assigning monetary value to care by using Quality Adjusted Life Years (QALYs) and cost-benefit analysis to determine spending as an example. The biggest limitation for QALY is choosing the appropriate utility values (Sawhney et al., 2023). They may not fully reflect patients' preferences with regard to their health status and therefore may distort the resulting cost per QALY. The strength of health status preferences may depend on factors such as age and lifestyle, and thus may differ from person to person with similar health status; for example, it is very difficult to compare health of a potential Olympic champion who suffered a tendon injury during a warm-up session with a person in the elderly who have had some mobility restored. The QALY index is less appropriate for groups of patients with specific diseases. In the case of diseases with a high risk of death, mainly oncological or haematological diseases, overall survival is the most important parameter. On the other hand, adopting a rigid threshold value profitability, determined on the basis of GDP data from several years ago, seems to be unacceptable and discriminatory for rare and ultra-rare diseases. Another limitation for the QALY index is the insufficient consideration of emotional and mental problems, as well as the complete failure to take into account the impact of health conditions on the quality of life of caregivers and family members of sick people. It is also worth noting that by hypothetically increasing the utility of a given health state while reducing life expectancy, a higher QALY can be obtained. The concept of putting quality of life above life expectancy is controversial in the medical world and raises ethical questions among many people (Browne et al., 2021).

Discussion: What Caused the Public Health Recession in Poland?

According to the logic of economic neoliberalism, the public health recession has been caused by unfavourable demographics and market failures:

Excess demand: Due to the growing number of elderly and dependent people (rising costs of healthcare).

Insufficient financing: Low financial outlays on health in Poland compared to most EU countries: 7% of GDP per capita in 2019 vs. 10% EU27 average.

Constrained supply: Shortages of medical and nursing staff in Poland compared to most EU countries.

Imperfect information: Health crises are caused by low health awareness of people.

These arguments obscure systemic factors and have limited evidence.

Is ageing population responsible? Central Statistical Office data from 2021 show that the percentage of the population aged 65 and over in Poland (18.7) is lower compared to Italy (23.5), Greece (22.5), Germany (22.0), France (20.7), Sweden (20.1), Hungary (20.3), and the Czech Republic (20.2). Forecasts concerning the impact of demographic changes in Poland on health status and health needs demonstrate that the proportion of the population burdened with disability and chronic diseases would increase only because of the ageing process, which would increase both the need for and the cost of medical and nursing services; the share of patients treated in hospitals would consequently increase (Szymborski & Marciniak, 2015). However, there is limited empirical evidence for the positive relationship between an ageing population and health expenditures. The belief that the ageing of the population plays a major role in the rapid increase of medical care costs and pertaining problems in the functioning of the health care is questionable (Norton, 2013). In the United States, since 2000, expenditures unrelated to an increase in the number of benefits or an ageing population have accounted for as much as 91% increase in costs. Hospitalisation costs increased by 4.2% per year, costs professional medical care by 3.6%, costs of medicines, medical equipment and devices by 4.0%, and administrative costs by 5.6% per year. Chronic diseases were consuming 84% of health care spending for the entire American population—and the more elderly population. These diseases in the population under 65 years of age generated two-thirds of health care expenditure (Moses III et al., 2013). Thus, the challenges resulting from the development of demographic processes should be accompanied by an appropriate health policy aimed at systematic actions addressed to all age groups of the population and concerning health promotion, prevention of risks and diseases and restoration of health, on the rationalisation of medicines, medical equipment and apparatus, and the optimisation of administrative costs (Szymborski & Marciniak, 2015).

Is low spending responsible? While expenditure on the health system in Poland is relatively low relative to GDP, the rapid increases in healthcare spending (particularly public) in 2015–2019 were not met with improvements in life expectancy and in stopping the pre-pandemic health recession. About 72% of spending on health care in Poland is covered from public funds, but expenses for non-reimbursed health services—mainly for pharmacy drugs—are high and account for over 20% of current healthcare spending (OECD, 2021). The consequence of the incorrect composition of healthcare spending in Poland (only 2% for prevention in 2019; see Fig. 7.4) is a high mortality rate from preventable causes (Fig. 7.5) Therefore, a necessary increase in health expenditure should be associated with fundamental changes in the health system.

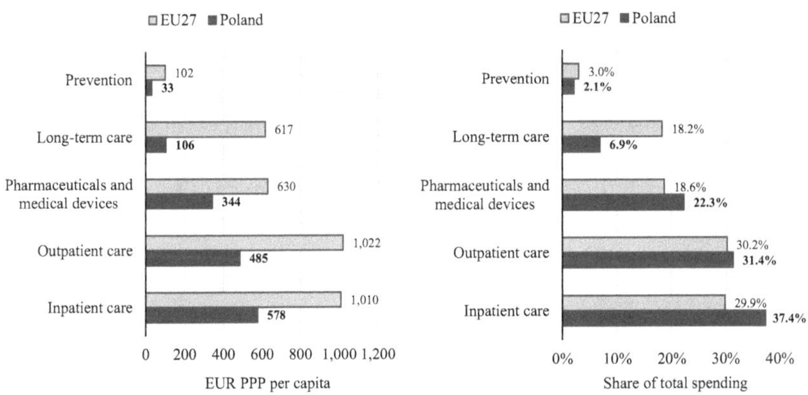

Fig. 7.4 Composition of health spending, 2019. (Source: European Commission, 2021)

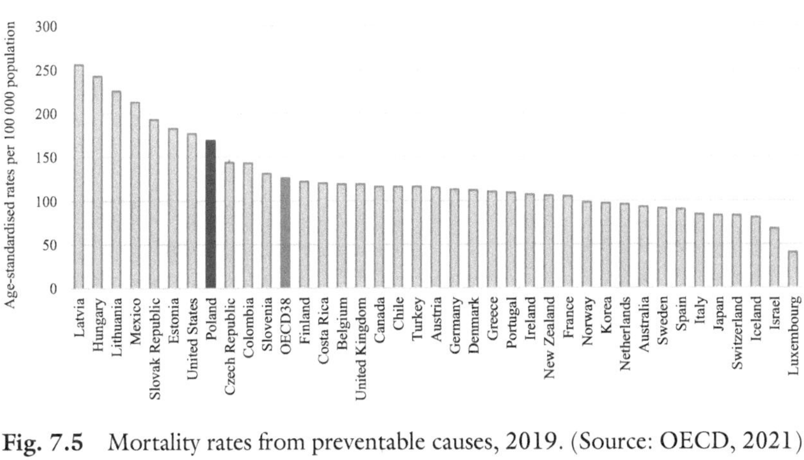

Fig. 7.5 Mortality rates from preventable causes, 2019. (Source: OECD, 2021)

Are staff shortages responsible? In the EU, Poland is among the countries with the lowest number of doctors and nurses per inhabitant. In 2019 (the latest available data), Poland had the lowest number of practising doctors per 10,000 inhabitants at just 24 in the EU, vs. 39 EU average, and one of the lowest number of nurses at 51 per 10,000 inhabitants, vs. 84 EU average. In addition, many doctors and nurses in Poland are approaching retirement age, which deepens concerns about the future supply (OECD, 2021). However, there is no rigid relationship between the number of medical staff and health indicators, because health depends mainly on factors other than medical ones. Therefore, it is a symptom of a deeper systemic problem rather than the cause.

Is low health literacy responsible? Health literacy, as an important public health task, should be seen in the context of social responsibility and solidarity. However, increasing its level is needed both for people seeking information and health services, as well as for institutions, bodies, and people that ensure the availability of services for the entire society, as we found out during the pandemic. The health literacy process should be developed in the family, in kindergarten and at school (not only during PE lessons), and later improved during studies (in all fields) and in the workplace (regardless of its nature). However, for health information to be accepted with confidence by people, it must be understandable, transparent, consistent, free from hyperoptimism, free from stigmatisation of particular groups, and consistent with the principles of health pedagogy (Szymborski, 2012; Szymborski, 2023).

Is prevention better than cure? This obvious truth is used by the neoliberal establishment to shift full responsibility for the dysfunctions of the health system onto the shoulders of citizens. It leads, among others, to wrongly interpreting the so-called Lalonda fields with spreading the claim that lifestyle is 50–60% responsible for health, *ergo*—citizens themselves. The influence of socio-ecological, legal (Gostin et al., 2019), and commercial factors, which are beyond the individual's control, are ignored (Lancet, 2023). At a theoretical level, the logic of economic neoliberalism in health prioritises prevention over cure because improved lifestyles lead to a reduction in excessive demand for health care. However, in Poland prevention accounted for only 2% of total spending on health in 2019 (OECD, 2021) and the health system is thus overwhelmed by restorative medicine—prevention and long-term care are seen of less value for money and remain underfunded.

Instead, we argue that the imposition of neoliberal mechanisms in the health system leads to a vicious cycle: low investment in public health (esp. prevention) causes an increase in morbidity and mortality from effectively preventable diseases, which generates an increase in demand for treatment and rehabilitation, health inequalities growing, treatment costs increase, staff workload increase, and all this entails the need to increase expenditure on medical care, also at the expense of modest funds allocated to prevention (Szymborski, 2023). The example of alcohol-related diseases is a dramatic confirmation of the validity of our considerations (See Zatoński et al., 2023 for a case study of tobacco). The deregulation of legislation surrounding alcohol since the early 2000s permitted a return of beer advertising to television in 2001, reduced the excise tax on vodka by 30% in 2002, and led to increased marketing and availability of small bottles of flavoured vodka since 2010 (on average 3 million units sold daily, including about 600,000 from 6:00 am to noon). Evidence shows that this has caused an increase in alcohol consumption from 6.5 litres per person per year in 2002 to almost 11 litres in 2019 (Zatoński et al., 2022). It is obvious that individual citizens cannot be held responsible for the weakening of anti-alcohol policy.

Instead, we argue that the responsibility lies with the neoliberal turn in the health system after 2002, based on supposedly "no alternative" market mechanisms, with low effectiveness, focused not on the quality but on the number of services, characterised by a lack of coordination between primary health care units, outpatient specialist care, and hospitals (Szymborska, 2023). This has been accompanied by a structural weakness of activities in the field of health promotion, health education, and disease prevention, as well as the low position of health in public policies, problems in the coordination of inter-sectoral activities (especially with the education and social welfare sectors) and in strategic thinking, understanding health expenditure as an investment in the future. The previously announced assurances about increased competitiveness, the right to choose, reduced inefficiency, and increased innovation turned out to be, in fact, marketing slogans, artificially incorporated into a field whose focus is not material profit but the well-being and health of an individual patient and the entire society. In a health system, reformed on the basis of neoliberal ideology, there was no room for maintaining the links between health and social care, which was treated as unnecessary ballast and removed from the structure and name of the ministry. The dysfunctionality of the health system was confirmed in the following years by the Supreme Audit Office in over 70 audit reports (NIK, 2019; Szymborski, 2021).

The introduction of market mechanisms led to the liquidation of the "Korczak's" system of paediatric care developed over many years, referring to the native traditions of social paediatrics, recognised in Europe as exemplary (Szymborski, 2020). Because the Ministry of Health withdrew from creating health policy in mother and childcare and the lack of decision-making centres in the voivodeship, organisational chaos was created, deepened by the process of transformation in the functioning and financing of health care facilities. The deterioration of health care for mothers and children was manifested in many regions of the country by a reduction in the provision of preventive services, especially vaccinations, the abandonment of newborn care visits, screening tests and health assessments, and the deterioration of care for pregnant women. The availability of services in both specialist and primary care has decreased (Szymborski, 2006). A particularly drastic decline occurred in the health care for students in schools, where dentists were withdrawn, school nurses and hygienists were dismissed, and over 300 school medicine clinics were closed. The corrective actions undertaken by the Minister of Health, F. Cegielska, were discontinued at the end of 2001 (Szymborski et al., 2002; Szymborski, 2009). The negative effects of dysfunctional child and youth care systems have been described in numerous scientific studies and control reports (Szymborski, 2012).

The dysfunctions of the neoliberal health system became particularly acute during the COVID-19 pandemic, as shown by the Supreme Audit Office's reports (NIK, 2023). It cannot be excluded that ignoring epidemic threats contributed to this. The recommendations of the Government's Population Council on this matter were secret in 2016 for political reasons (Szymborski, 2023). In the beginning there was chaos, reflecting a lack of adequate national public health leadership. Temporary hospitals in Poland were built in Poland after October 2020 on a scale unseen in Europe, without any plan or reliable analysis of the epidemiological situation or availability of medical staff, and without any cost calculation—as established by NIK. Some assets of the COVID-19 Prevention Fund will have to be considered as a loss. The "financial tool" created by the Minister of Health to support the medical staff taking care of COVID-19 patients was distorted and became a mechanism for transferring "extra benefits" for the hospital personnel who were often not eligible to receive them. These are just some of the numerous irregularities detected by the Supreme Audit Office.

Numerous public opinion surveys conducted by CBOS usually reveal strongly negative assessments of the functioning of the public health system after the pandemic, which can be understood as a consequence of the years of neglect described in this chapter. In a nationwide Ipsos poll from April 2023, 81% respondents assessed that the public health care system functions poorly because it is characterised by low availability of health services, poor organisation of work of public health care entities and too few medical staff. In effect, more than half (56%) of respondents express a lack of trust in the public health care system, and two-thirds (66%) of respondents declare that this system does not provide a sense of security (Makowski, 2024).

The Polish health system is susceptible to corruption threats due to both systemic and cultural sources of corruption. Makowski (2024) reports that public health care system remains, after government policy and administration, the third area of public life most exposed to corruption (32% of responses). Respondents primarily point to the systemic basis of corruption threats: politicisation (46%), poor management of health care entities (43%), lobbying by suppliers of medicines, services, products and medical equipment (42), and underfinancing of the public health care system (40%). Nearly half (46%) of Poles know someone who has ever been forced to give a financial benefit to a medical staff member in exchange for access to health services, and almost one-third (31%) of respondents admitted that in order to gain access to health services, benefited from connections. Bribes are most often paid to attending physicians (69% of responses), department heads (27% of responses), and nurses (27% of responses). Usually for more reliable care (50% of responses), shortening the queue for services (41% of responses) and carrying out a complicated operation or procedure (35% of responses). At the same time, the system does not encourage responding to cases of corruption in public health care. Interviews with representatives of the medical profession and officials of the Ministry of Health and the National Health Fund revealed that in these environments there is a misunderstanding of whistleblowers and their role in counteracting corruption and abuses in the public health care system. Meanwhile, Poland is obliged to implement Directive 2019/1937 of the European Parliament and of the European Council of 23 October 2019 on the protection of persons reporting violations of European Union law. The directive, which places particular emphasis on the protection of whistleblowers in the health care sector, has not yet been implemented. In addition to bribery, there are practices in the public health care system that Makowski (2024) calls legal or quasi-legal corruption. Respondents point out that hospital foundations often facilitate access to health services in public health care entities in exchange for donations, and that there are unclear connections between the work of medical staff in the private and public sectors, as a result of which patients, by paying for services in the private practices, can facilitate access to services within the public system. Non-transparent and corrupt practices are also highlighted in public procurement organised by public hospitals and other health care entities, in a broader context of non-transparent political decisions regarding the shape of the list of reimbursed drugs, as well as conflicts of interest in relations between doctors and pharmaceutical companies and manufacturers of medical equipment and accessories. Makowski's research is of particular relevance to understanding the systemic crisis of the health system in Poland by showing that that the source of most corruption threats with pathological competition for resources and access to medical services is the disorganisation of the entire health system.

Summary

In this article, we presented evidence on the unfavourable development of the health of Polish society since 2002, manifested first by a slowdown in life expectancy increases, then by the pre-pandemic health recession and finally by the pandemic health crisis. We have shown that at the same time, neoliberal market mechanisms were being developed and consolidated in the health system. We also questioned the logic of economic neoliberalism, that public health recession can be resolved by policies that correct market failures and reduce excess demand. It is a kind of circular reasoning: address market dysfunctions by introducing more market mechanisms. There is little truth in the neoliberal discourse that the dysfunctions of the health system are solely responsible for the ageing process of the population, low expenditure on health, the shortage of medical staff and society itself. Social, environmental, legal, and commercial factors are key determinants of public health that are largely ignored by market approaches.

The analysis argues that there is a connection between the dysfunction of the health system and the health deficiencies of the society with the "toxic mixture," served by the neoliberal ideology for two decades. This has been realised through:

(1) marginalisation of socio-environmental, legal, and commercial determinants of health and paying lip service to health promotion, health education, and disease prevention;
(2) overestimation of the importance of remedial medicine while consistently depreciating the role of public health;
(3) misleading interpretation of the Lalonda fields with the creation of a cult of individual responsibility;
(4) a public narrative, entrenched in the laws passed since 2002, promoting the neoliberal health system as an expression of the policy of realism, economic necessity, and the lack of alternatives;
(5) separation of the health system from social policy and the education sector;
(6) withdrawal of social medicine (e.g. medical practices from schools) to reduce costs;
(7) susceptibility to corruption and emergence of conflicts of interest between the profit motive and the duty of care;
(8) disconnection from native traditions of public health and philosophy of medicine, with a lack of reflection on the ontological status of the patient in the health system.

In the spirit of Tadeusz Kowalik's work with Kalecki on the crucial reform of capitalism to achieve a better society, in our view, a "crucial reform" for the health sector should include: Firstly, expanding the debate on public health in Poland, utilising both the international experience and native traditions of public health and social economy and rethinking the role of the state to implement a multifaceted, multi-sectoral reform aimed at a shift away from a profit-driven market-oriented health system towards serving the common good. And, secondly, expanding the ontological understanding of the health system based on four equal pillars of health promotion and health education, disease prevention, restorative medicine and social welfare. This requires structural changes in how public health and social good are valued. The need to analysis and discuss the negative consequences for the health of society of market solutions in the health system in their neoliberal version results from the moral obligation towards the victims of the pre-pandemic health recession and towards people who died during the pandemic from causes that could have been prevented.

References

Boni, M. (Ed.). (2009). *Polska 2030. Wyzwania rozwojowe*. Kancelaria Prezesa Rady Ministrów.

Bourdieu, P., & Wacquant, L. (2001). New Liberal Speak Notes on the new planetary vulgate. *Radical Philosophy, 105*, 2–6.

Browne, J., Cryer, D. R., & Stevens, W. (2021). Is the QALY fit for purpose? *The American Journal of Accountable Care, 9*(2), 8–13.

Commissioner for Human Rights. (2009). Raport z korespondencji i kontaktów z organizacjami pozarządowymi. In *Biuletyn Rzecznika Praw Obywatelskich – Źródła*.

Ćwiąkała-Małys, A., & Łagowski, P. (2013). Ewolucyjny obraz przekształceń systemu ochrony zdrowia w Polsce. *Acta Universitatis Wratislaviensis 3515 Przegląd Prawa i Administracji, XCIII*, 89–101.

European Commission. (2021). *State of health in the EU: Poland. Country Health Profile 2021*. Publications Office of the European Union.

European Commission. (2023). *State of health in the EU: Synthesis Report 2023*. Publications Office of the European Union.

Eurostat. (n.d.) Excess mortality by month demo_mexrt. Retrieved June 5, 2024, from https://ec.europa.eu/eurostat/databrowser/explore/all/all_themes

Frączkiewicz-Wronka, A. (2001). *Reforma systemu opieki zdrowotnej w perspektywie integracji z Unią Europejską: wybrane aspekty zachodzących zmian*. University of Economics.

Golinowska, S. (2000). *Polityka społeczna: koncepcje – instytucje – koszty*. Poltext.

Golinowska, S., Czepulis-Rutkowska, Z., Sitek, M., Sowa, A., & Włodarczyk, C. (2002). *Opieka zdrowotna w Polsce po reformie*. Centrum Analiz Społeczno-Ekonomicznych.

Gostin, L. O., Monahan, J. T., Kaldor, J., DeBartolo, M., Friedman, E. A., Gottschalk, K., Alwan, A., Binagwaho, A., Burci, G. L., Cabal, L., Gostin, K. G., Hossain, S., Koh, H., Ooms, G., Uprimny, R., & Yamin, A. E. (2019). The legal determinants of health: Harnessing the power of law for global health and sustainable development. *The Lancet, 393*, 1857–1910.

Government Population Council. (2016). Prevention and combating infectious diseases in Poland. In *Założenia polityki ludnościowej w Polsce* (pp. 176–185). Warszawa.

Horton, R. (2018). Defending the left hand of the state. *The Lancet, 391*, 2484.

Islam, N., Shkolnikov, V. M., Acosta, R. J., Klimkin, I., Kawachi, I., Irizarry, R. A., Buajitti, E., Kawachi, I., McKee, M., & Stuckler, D. (2021). Excess deaths associated with covid-19 pandemic in 2020: Age and sex disaggregated time series analysis in 29 high income countries. *British Medical Journal, 375*, e066768.

Korzeniewska-Koseła, M. (Ed.). (2020). *Gruźlica i choroby układu oddechowego w Polsce w 2019 r.* Instytut Gruźlicy i Chorób Płuc.

Karwowski, E (2019) Towards (de-)financialisation: the role of the state, Cambridge Journal of Economics,*Cambridge Political Economy Society, vol. 43*(4), pages 1001 1027.

Kowalik, T. (2012). *From Solidarity to Sell Out: The Restoration of Capitalism in Poland.* Monthly Review Press.

Makowski G (2024) Korupcja w polskim systemie ochrony zdrowia. [Corruption in the Polish healthcare system].*Fundacja Akademia Antykorupcyjna*, Warsaw

Marsh, H. (2023, July 4). The NHS at 75—unhappy birthday? *The Lancet.*

Moses, H., III, Matheson, D. H., Dorsey, E. R., George, B. P., Sadoff, D., & Yoshimura, S. (2013). The Anatomy of Health Care in the United States. *Journal of the American Medical Association, 310*(18), 1947–1964.

National Institute of Public Health – National Research Institute. (2022). *Health status of Polish population and its determinants 2022* (B. Wojtyniak & P. Goryński, Eds.) (pp. 16–17).

NIK. (2019). Information on audit results Report: Health care system in Poland – current state and desired directions of changes, Registration No. 8/2019/megainfo/KZD. https://www.nik.gov.pl/plik/id,20223,vp,22913.pdf

NIK. (2023). Przygotowanie i działanie odpowiedzialnych organów państwa, instytucji i służb w sytuacji zagrożenia i wystąpienia chorób szczególnie niebezpiecznych i wysoce zakaźnych, LKA.430.007.2022. 72/2023/P/20/062/LKA. https://www.nik.gov.pl/kontrole/P/20/062/

Norton, A. (2013, November 12). Soaring prices, not demand, behind massive hike in U.S. Health Spending. *HealthDay News.*

OECD. (2021). *Health at a glance: OECD indicators.* OECD Publishing.

OECD. (2023). *Health at a glance 2023: OECD indicators.* OECD Publishing.

Parildar, U., Perera, R., & Oke, J. (2021). *Excess mortality across countries in 2020.* Centre for Evidence-Based Medicine.

Płonka-Syroka, B. (2022). 75 lat polskiej medycyny i farmacji we Wrocławiu. Wybrane elementy historii wrocławskich wyższych uczelni. *Medycyna Nowożytna, 28*(2), 119–146.

Sawhney, T. G., et al. (2023). QALYs: The math doesn't work. *Journal of Health Economics and Outcomes Research, 10*(2), 10–13.

Sejm, R. P. (1991). Act on health care facilities. *Journal of Laws* No. 91, item 408.

Sejm, R. P. (1997). Act on universal health insurance. *Journal of Laws* No. 28, item 153.

Sejm, R. P. (1998). Amendment to Act on general health insurance. *Journal of Laws* No. 117, item 756.

Sejm, R. P. (2004). Act on health care services financed from public funds. *Journal of Laws* No. 210, item 2135.

Szczeklik, A. (2003). *Catharsis: On the art of medicine.* University of Chicago Press.

Szymborska, H. (2021). Polityka gospodarcza a COVID-19. In P. Wielgosz (Ed.), *Ekonomie przyszłości* (pp. 77–96). Biennale Warszawa.
Szymborska, H. (2023). Perspektywy agnostycznego podejścia do wzrostu w Polsce. In M. Sutowski (Ed.), *Obwarzanek po polsku* (pp. 55–76). Krytyka Polityczna.
Szymborska, H. (2024). Fiscal Policy after the COVID-19 Pandemic: Step Change or Status Quo? *International Journal of Political Economy, 53*(3), 272–284. https://doi.org/10.1080/08911916.2024.2391237
Szymborski, J. (2006). Stan zdrowia dzieci i młodzieży. In *Sytuacja demograficzna Polski* (pp. 252–271). Warszawa.
Szymborski, J. (2009). Zdrowie dzieci – zapomniany priorytet. *Polityka Społeczna, 426*(9), 46–51.
Szymborski, J. (Ed.). (2012). *Zdrowie publiczne i polityka ludnościowa*. Government Demographic Council.
Szymborski, J. (2020). Janusz Korczak i aktualność jego filozoficzno-prawnego dzieła okresu Polski Niepodległej. In K. Karaskiewicz (Ed.), *Dokonania kulturowe w Polsce Niepodległej* (pp. 159–166). Kresowa Agencja Wydawnicza.
Szymborski, J. (2021). Poland's population policy during the COVID-19 pandemic. *Journal of Health Inequalities, 7*(1), 18–25.
Szymborski, J. (2023). Kryzys zdrowotny w Polsce w okresie pandemii – wnioski. *Kontrola Państwowa, 1*.
Szymborski, J., & Marciniak, G. (2015). Zdrowotne następstwa przemian demograficznych w Polsce – przyczyna czy usprawiedliwienie problemów w ochronie zdrowia? *Studia Ekonomiczne. Zeszyty Naukowe Uniwersytetu Ekonomicznego w Katowicach, 223*, 11–20.
Szymborski, J., Radiukiewicz, S., & Iwanicka, E. (Eds.). (2002). *Aktualna sytuacja w opiece zdrowotnej nad matką i dzieckiem w Polsce*. Instytut Matki i Dziecka.
Szymborski, J., & Szymborska, H. K. (2025). Public health outcomes and the neoliberal health system in Poland. *Review of Evolutionary Political Economy, 6*, 405.
Szymborski, J., & Zatoński, W. (2017). The activities of the Government Population Council aimed at limiting health care inequalities. *Journal of Health Inequalities, 3*(1), 30–40.
The Lancet. (2018). Editorial Health systems for prosperity and solidarity. *The Lancet, 391*, 2475.
The Lancet. (2023). Editorial Unravelling the commercial determinants of health. *The Lancet, 401*, 1131.
Tymowska, K. (1999). *Sektor prywatny w systemie opieki zdrowotnej*. Instytut Spraw Publicznych.

Włodarczyk, C. W., & Koprowska, I. (2000). Wykorzystanie programu Policy Maker w polityce zdrowotnej. Niektóre aspekty wdrażania reformy opieki zdrowotnej w Polsce. *Problemy Polityki Społecznej, 2*, 63–87.

Woźniak, Z. (2009). Pokłosie Okrągłego Stołu. Przeszłość dla przyszłości. *Ruch Prawniczy Ekonomiczny i Socjologiczny, 71*(2), 349–373.

Zatoński, W. A. (2004). *Demokracja jest zdrowsza*. Centrum Onkologii–Instytut.

Zatoński, W. A., Janik-Koncewicz, K., Neneman, J., & Gruszczyński, Ł. (2023). Tobacco control collapse in Poland after 2015. Alarming increase in cigarette consumption. *Journal of Health Inequalities, 9*(2), 109–114.

Zatoński, W. A., Janik-Koncewicz, K., & Zatoński, M. (2021). Health decline in Poland after 2002: Response to a recent analysis of the changes in disease burden in Poland. *Journal of Health Inequalities, 7*(1), 2–6.

Zatoński, W. A., Janik-Koncewicz, K., & Zatoński, M. (2022). Life expectancy and alcohol use health burden in Poland after 2002. *Journal of Health Inequalities, 8*(1), 4–16.

CHAPTER 8

From Reform to Reality: The Polish Pension System and Socio-economic Justice

Janina Petelczyc

Introduction

Since 1989, Poland has undergone numerous political and economic reforms. Most of these reforms, resulting from the so-called shock therapy (Poznański, 1993; Sachs, 1994; Marangos, 2002), have been characterised by some scholars as neoliberal (Slay, 1993; Shields, 2008; Anioł, 2015). This dramatic shift, implemented through measures like the Balcerowicz Plan, aimed to transition the country from a centrally planned economy to a market-oriented one. The introduction of these rapid changes was marked by significant challenges, including hyperinflation and substantial public debt resulting in severe austerity measures and structural adjustments that fundamentally altered the Polish economy. Analysing these transformations, prof. Tadeusz Kowalik, in his works collected in the book *From Solidarity to Sellout: The Restoration of Capitalism in Poland* (2012), argued that the transformation in Poland resulted in one of the most unjust socio-economic systems in Europe. Kowalik's critique focuses on the social costs of these neoliberal policies, highlighting

J. Petelczyc (✉)
SGH Warsaw School of Economics, Warsaw, Poland
e-mail: jpetel@sgh.waw.pl

G. Konat, G. Rae (eds.), *Exploring the Ideas of Tadeusz Kowalik*,
https://doi.org/10.1007/978-3-032-09283-0_8

the increase in economic inequality and the erosion of social safety nets. This perspective is supported by other scholars who have noted that the rapid privatisation and liberalisation policies led to significant social instability and hardship for large parts of the population (Blazyca & Rapacki, 1991; Koening, 2012; Ghodsee & Orenstein, 2021).

The main pension system reforms occurred relatively late, a decade after the systemic changes. Enacted by laws from 1997 and 1998,[1] they came into effect as part of the so-called four reforms of Jerzy Buzek on 1 January 1999.[2] The main objectives of these reforms were to reduce the costs associated with the demographic aging of society by diversifying the sources of financing for future benefits and shifting part of the responsibility for individual welfare onto the citizens (Góra & Rutkowski, 2000). These reforms, imposed by the rhetoric of the World Bank, did not differ from those in the Central and Eastern European region (Holzmann, 2002). The principles shifted from social solidarity towards a greater dependence of benefits on the individual situation and partial privatisation of the system. This shift reflected broader trends, which prioritised market mechanisms and individual responsibility over solidaristic values of the system.

However, in the following years, there was a partial departure from this model, within the limits possible under the constraints of path dependency. The rollback of some reforms highlighted the difficulties and limitations in the context of pension systems, which inherently require long-term stability and predictability. The partial reintroduction of state involvement indicated a recognition of the need to balance market efficiency with social equity.

The aim of this chapter is to describe this process in Poland, highlighting the extent of these reforms and their subsequent rollback. The hypothesis is that Poland implemented reforms that moved away from the values of social solidarity in the pension system but partially reversed them in subsequent years. To test this hypothesis, I will conduct an analysis of historical documents regarding the reforms and data on changing social and financial indicators. Given that pension systems inherently require long term, many effects of these reforms become apparent only after a significant period. As a result, understanding the full impact necessitates examining long-term trends and outcomes that may not be immediately visible. Furthermore, some aspects of the reforms were partially reversed even before they fully took effect, complicating the assessment of their true impact. Through this analysis, I will demonstrate that the system became unjust but is slowly being corrected.

I will address the following research questions: Which groups were affected the most by the reform? Did the reforms introduce greater inequalities in the pension system? What mechanisms were introduced to mitigate these effects? By examining these aspects, we can gain a comprehensive understanding of the impact of neoliberal policies on Poland's pension system and the measures taken to address the resulting inequalities.

This chapter aims to contribute to the ongoing discourse on the balance between economic liberalisation and social justice.

Theory and Methods

In this chapter, the theoretical approach will centre on institutionalism and path dependency. Historical institutionalism is a framework that analyses how institutions evolve over time and how historical contexts and decisions shape their development and constrain future policy choices. This approach emphasises the importance of established structures, norms, and practices in influencing institutional behaviour and policy outcomes (Steinmo et al., 1992; Steinmo, 1993; Streeck & Thelen, 2005). Political events occur within a historical context, directly influencing the decisions and outcomes (Koelble, 1995). This implies the concept of path dependency, which suggests that once a particular path is taken, it becomes increasingly difficult to diverge from it due to self-reinforcing mechanisms. Initial policy choices create a trajectory that future developments tend to follow, often making substantial shifts challenging and favouring incremental changes instead (Pierson, 2000; Howlett, 2009). This concept is particularly relevant for understanding the evolution of pension systems, where foundational decisions have long-term impacts. Path shifting is possible when a significant external circumstance, a "window of opportunity," or "critical junctures" such as an economic crisis arise (Mahoney, 2000; Pierson, 2000; Djelic & Quack, 2007; Thelen, 2004). This change does not have to be radical; some studies indicate that it is more often a gradual yet transformative process (Campbell & Pederson, 1996; Garud & Karnøe, 2001; Streeck & Thelen, 2005). Applying this theoretical framework to the context of Poland's pension reforms, we can better understand why certain reforms were introduced in the late 1990s, why some of them persisted, and why some were partially withdrawn. While some modifications were implemented, gradually altering the system, the initial choices made during the early transition period established a path that influenced subsequent policy developments. The main principles, though somewhat moderated, remained intact. Thus, referring to Professor Kowalik's work on the general neoliberal shift in Poland (Kowalik, 2012), the Polish pension system was also reformed in this spirit of privatisation, individualisation, and partial departure from the principles of social solidarity. However, changes related to the growing deficit resulting from the privatisation of the system, and later the global economic crisis, served as critical junctures, leading to a partial rollback of these reforms.

The methodology for this study involves analysing legal documents and relevant data from the Social Insurance Institution (ZUS). This approach allows for a comprehensive examination of the effects of the pension reforms on various social and financial indicators over time. Reviewing historical documents and legislative texts provides a clearer understanding of the specific changes introduced by the pension reforms. Additionally, research includes a quantitative analysis of data from ZUS, focusing on pension distributions, demographic shifts, and the financial performance of pension funds. This methodological approach enables to uncover patterns and trends that illustrate the long-term impact of the reforms. Moreover, the analysis considers the broader social implications of the reforms by examining indicators such as income inequality, gender disparities, and age-related differences in pension benefits. Analysing these indicators highlights the differential effects of the reforms on various segments of the population. By evaluating these sources, the study aims to provide a detailed understanding of how the pension reforms in Poland have affected different segments of the population and the overall sustainability of the pension system.

Therefore, analysis shows how the reforms have influenced income inequality among different socio-economic groups. It also examines gender disparities in pension benefits, considering factors such as labour market participation and wage gaps. Furthermore, the study explores age-related differences in pension adequacy and retirement security by comparing the benefits and conditions of pensions granted under the old system versus those under the reformed system. Additionally, the analysis assesses how labour market dynamics, including segmentation and job stability, have influenced pension outcomes for different groups. By examining these indicators, the study provided insights into the long-term effects of Poland's pension reforms and the extent to which they have addressed or exacerbated social inequalities.

Overall, this comprehensive analysis aims to contribute to the understanding of the impact of neoliberal policies on Poland's pension system and the measures taken to address the resulting inequalities.

The Main Principles and Reasons of Pension Reform in 1999

(a) Reasons of Change

Poland is one of the first countries in Central and Eastern Europe to implement such significant pension reforms. Economic and political transformation served as a specific starting point, allowing for path shifting. In the 1990s, Poland faced numerous economic challenges, including hyperinflation, unemployment, and rising public debt. One of the solutions to labour market problems was to encourage early retirement (Cichon et al., 1997). The increase in the number of retirees was accompanied by relatively high benefits. Generous pension benefits in an aging society were associated with an increase in social contribution rates, which reached 45% of the gross wage in 1998. Expenditures on benefits accounted for approximately 15% of GDP, and it was estimated that without reforms, these expenditures would rise to 22% of GDP by 2035 (Rodzinka et al., 2007). Even before the implementation of the major reform in 1999, several parametric changes were introduced. These included extending the reference period for calculating benefit amounts from 1 year to 10 years, reducing the accrual rates for benefit calculations, and phasing out certain sector-specific privileges (Polakowski & Hagemejer, 2018).

The main debate regarding pension system reforms took place between 1996 and 1998. A significant reference point was the three-pillar pension model proposed by the World Bank in 1994 (World Bank, 1994). Although at the beginning some left-wing parties and trade unions opposed the proposed pension reforms, including the partial privatisation of the system, the discourse was predominantly shaped by right-wing and neoliberal ideologies that supported market-based solutions (Williamson & Williams, 2005). Mitchell Orenstein emphasises the significant role played by international organisations, such as the World Bank and International Monetary Fund, and domestic political actors in shaping these reforms. The World Bank de facto financed the pension reform agency in Poland, which was headed by a World Bank official on temporary leave (Müller, 1999;

Orenstein, 2000). As a result, even post-communist, centre-left parties and labour unions supported partial privatisation. The leaders of *Solidarność* trade union believed that the reforms would bring benefits, and some unions even entered joint ventures with financial institutions. For example, *Solidarność* established its own pension fund in collaboration with a Swiss insurance institution (Polakowski & Hagemejer, 2018).

Moreover, there has been frequent emphasis on the economic development potential inherent in the reform, and the possibilities of utilising savings to stimulate economic growth. Such specific terms appeared in the report called "Security Through Diversity" (Biuro Pełnomocnika, 1997), which detailed the concept of changes. The reform was described as "an action to improve Poland's long-term economic growth prospects". Professor Tadeusz Szumlicz (2015), in criticising this approach, pointed out that the new reform, by introducing the principle of full insurance equivalence (defined contribution method, described below) and partially privatising the system, led to a reduction in the amount of benefits and the elimination of the redistributive role of the system.

(b) **Partial Pension System Privatisation**

As mentioned earlier, one of the most important assumptions of the 1999 reform was the transformation of the pension system into a three-pillar model and partial privatisation. This model did not perfectly align with the assumptions of the World Bank's, 1994 proposal (which included group, occupational pension schemes as the second pillar, whereas in Poland, these were individual insurance schemes). The system, introduced under the slogan "security through diversity," aimed to diversify the sources of future pension funding, addressing demographic needs and ensuring financial stability and promoting private savings (Góra, 1999).

The division of contributions and the establishment of the three-pillar pension system in Poland were regulated by the *Act on the Social Insurance of 13 October 1998*. This act, along with the *Act on the Organisation and Operation of Pension Funds of 28 August 1997*, laid the foundation for the pension reform. According to the reform's principles, the first pillar was replaced by two components. A portion of the existing contribution to the Social Insurance Fund (managed by the public Social Insurance Institution, ZUS), amounting to 12.22%, continued to flow into the public first pillar. Meanwhile, 7.3% was allocated to privately managed pension funds, known as Open Pension Funds (OFE). Establishment and operation of the OFEs, including the management and fee structures, were regulated by the *Act on the Organisation and Operation of Pension Funds (1997)*. Its articles 136 and 136 regulated maximum initial (initially set at 7% of the contribution amount) and maximum management fee (set at 0.6% of the net assets per year). The management fees charged by Open Pension Funds (OFE) in Poland have been a significant point of criticism since the inception of the pension reform in 1999. These fees were seen as disproportionately high, reducing the net returns for contributors and diminishing the overall effectiveness of the pension system (Chybalski, 2009; Polakowski & Hagemejer, 2018).

The division of contributions between ZUS and OFE, representing the first and second pillars, signified a partial privatisation of the pension system. This reform linked the amount of future benefits to the performance of investments in the capital market. The investment principles for OFE were also established by the *Act on the Organisation and Operation of Pension Funds*. The regulations required OFEs to diversify their investment portfolios to mitigate risks, mandating investments across different asset classes, sectors, and geographic regions (Art. 139). Initially, up to 40% of the fund's assets could be invested in equities, while foreign investments were capped at 5% to manage currency and international market risks. A significant portion of the funds had to be invested in Polish government bonds and other low-risk securities to ensure stability and liquidity.

The 1999 pension reform in Poland also introduced Occupational Pension Programs (PPE) as part of the third pillar of the new pension system. These programs were designed to provide additional, voluntary retirement savings options through employee-sponsored plans. The establishment and operation of PPEs were regulated by the *Act on the Organisation and Operation of Pension Funds of 28 August 1997*.

The structure of the new pension system introduced in 1999 is illustrated in the following Table 8.1:

A critical challenge of this reform was the partial privatisation of the pension system, which involved transferring one-third of the contribution amount to private financial institutions for investment in the capital market. This created a dual challenge: Firstly, the future pension amount became dependent on the financial results achieved in the capital market, which could lead to significant losses during economic crises (Oręziak, 2014). Secondly, a very serious problem was the reduction of contributions paid to the Social Insurance Fund (managed by the ZUS) by

Table 8.1 Polish pension system in 1999

Polish pension system in 1999		
Mandatory		*Voluntary*
I pillar ZUS	II pillar OFE	III pillar PPE
Public	Public contributions managed by private financial institutions	Private
Contribution 19.52% divided between ZUS (12.22%) and OFE (7.3%)		Declared and paid by employees
Accounts indexed, benefits	Return rates from investments	Return rates from investments
Indexed lifetime annuities	Lifetime annuity bought by members in pension insurance company	Lump-sum payment or a predetermined number of instalments.

Source: Own elaboration based on *Act on the Social Insurance System of 13 October 1998*, *Act on Organisation and Operation of Pension Funds of 28 August 1997*, and *Act on Employee Pension Programs of 22 August 1997*

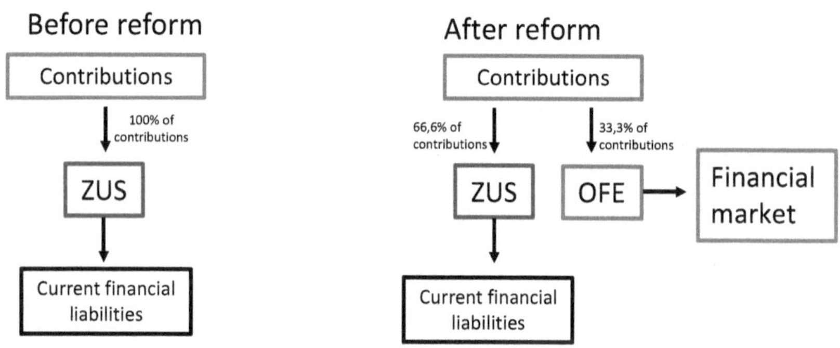

Fig. 8.1 Financial flows from contributions before and after the 1999 pension reform. (Source: Own elaboration)

one-third, while maintaining the same level of existing obligations towards individuals of retirement age at the time of the reform's implementation. This gap was intended to be filled by privatising State Treasury assets, but this solution was far from ideal.

The reform thus constituted a partial privatisation of the system, simultaneously reducing public funds allocated for fulfilling the state's obligation to provide citizens with retirement benefits (Fig. 8.1).

In turn, the introduction of Occupational Pension Programs (PPE) as an additional system resulted in very low participation levels. One of the reasons was that the contributions were initially borne by employees (and not employers), which was later changed. Currently, the basic contribution is on the employer's side (up to 7%), and the employee can pay an additional contribution. In 2004, additional Individual Retirement Accounts (IKE) with tax exemption at the time of payout were introduced, and since 2012, Individual Retirement Security Accounts (IKZE) with tax exemption at the contribution payment stage. In 2019, Employee Capital Plans (PPK) were introduced, with mandatory contributions from both the employer and the employee, along with an auto-enrolment system.[3] However, these additional systems are not the subject of this chapter, and interested parties are referred to the relevant legislation.[4]

(c) From Defined Benefit to Defined Contribution

While the partial privatisation of the pension system had significant implications in the macroeconomic context (increasing system burdens with significantly reduced revenues) and exposed ordinary insured citizens to investment risks, it appears that the most critical and profound change for individual citizens was the transition from a defined benefit (DB) system to a notional defined contribution (NDC) system.

Before 1999 the pension security system in Poland was based on the pay-as-you-go defined benefit (DB) method, where current benefits were funded by the contributions of working-age individuals. The benefit calculation formula consisted of two parts: the social component and the service component. The social component was a fixed part of the pension, constituting 24% of "base amount," which is the average salary in the economy in the previous calendar year (minus insurance contributions). It was an amount effective from 1 March of each year and the same for all insured individuals. The service component was calculated based on the length of service, with 1.3% for each contributory year and 0.7% for each non-contributory year (such as periods of study, sick leave, etc.), multiplied by the pension base, which is the ratio of the beneficiary's wages to the average wages from the period used to determine the base (but not higher than 250% of average earnings). The pension formula was thus presented as follows:

$$P = 24\%BA + (1.3\%CY * P_b) + (0.7\%NCY * P_b)$$

where:

P – amount of pension benefit
BA – base amount (average salary in previous year)
CY – number of contributory years
NCY – number of non-contributory years
P_b – pension base

The existence of the pension base cap at 250% contributed to the flattening of pension amounts. Individuals with incomes exceeding 250% of the average earnings in a given year did not receive a proportional increase in their pensions. In contrast, the presence of a fixed base amount provided a higher level of pension security for individuals with lower incomes.

This benefit calculation formula was quite favourable for the general workforce, guaranteeing an average replacement rate of around 70%. However, it is evident that individuals with the lowest incomes received higher replacement rates compared to those with the highest incomes. For example, after 30 years of service, individuals earning half of the average wage in economy received a replacement rate of 84%. In contrast, those earning an average of 250% of the average wage saw their replacement rate drop to 40% for the same service period. For individuals earning four times the average wage in economy, the replacement rate decreased to only 30% (Czepulis-Rutkowska., 1999). Thus, it can be said that a form of redistribution from wealthier to poorer individuals was inherent in the system. In DB systems, employees' future pensions were calculated based on their contributions during their working life, either over their final years or their chosen highest-earning years. Thus, the final pensions were not directly proportional to the total contributions made by the employees. Therefore, DB systems, including the Polish system before 1999, contain a redistributive element, transferring resources from wealthier to less wealthy employees (Williamson & Williams, 2005).

The new NDC formula significantly more closely ties the amount of the pension benefit to the career trajectory (Cichon, 1999). Each person paying contributions has their own individual account where these contributions are accumulated and indexed. The amount of future pensions is entirely linked to the accumulated capital in the account, as represented by the following equation:

$$P = \frac{\Sigma(Iic + Iis)}{L_{ex}}$$

where:

P – amount of pension benefit
Iic – indexed capital in the individual account
Iis – indexed capital in the sub-account
L_{ex} – life expectancy in months at the time of retirement according to the life expectancy tables for women and men from the Central Statistical Office (GUS)

It is very important to note that for individuals who worked before 1999, the indexed so-called initial capital, calculated using the social part coefficient, is additionally added to this equation:

$$P_{ebr} = \frac{\Sigma(Iic + Iis + Ici)}{L_{ex}}$$

where:

P_{ebr} – amount of pension benefit of a person that worked before 1999
Ici – indexed initial capital

As can be seen, according to the assumptions of the NC model, there is no redistributive element. Instead, the pension is entirely dependent on the individual's situation in the labour market. To protect the most vulnerable participants in the labour market, there is however a minimum pension. Any woman who has worked for 20 contributory years, and any man for 25 contributory years (this difference arises from the unequal retirement ages of women and men, which are 60 and 65 years, respectively), is entitled to a state subsidy if their accumulated capital does not allow for a pension benefit at least equal to the minimum amount.

The introduction of the NDC system was a response to the fiscal and demographic challenges associated with the pension system. Expenditures on the pension system will not increase from 2028 onwards. This solution has reduced system costs, but at the expense of the workers. It is worth noting that the dramatic aging of the population is negatively correlated with the projected increase in pension expenditures. This is because the amount of pensions paid will decrease. The only visible increase will be in costs related to the payment of minimum pensions (Table 8.2).

The problem, however, lies in the fact that the responsibility for social security in old age has largely been shifted onto the shoulders of the individual citizen. As noted by Williamson and Williams (2005), the schemes align with the neoliberal ethos of individualising costs and minimising the redistribution of resources.

The introduction of the notional defined contribution system has led to significant pension inequalities. These arise from two factors. First, the reform divided the insured into two groups: those who worked before 1999 (who receive their pensions entirely within the old system or with very favourably calculated initial capital[5]) and those who entered the labour market after 1999, who operate entirely within the new system without of almost any social element. Projections show that for the generation entering the labour market after 1999, the average replacement rate will be 24% (OECD, 2023). The only component of the system that may prove supportive and maintain some element of redistribution could be the minimum pension, guaranteed to all who demonstrate sufficient work experience (Chłoń-Domińczak & Strzelecki, 2010; Owczarek & Więckowska, 2011).

As shown in the chart below, pensions granted to individuals according to the new rules are significantly more likely to be low. The social element

Table 8.2 Projections of demographics, pension expenditures, and replacement rates for Poland 2022–2070

	2022	*2030*	*2040*	*2050*	*2060*	*2070*
Old-age dependency ratio (65+ / 20–64)	31.9	37.6	42.3	55.4	66	63.7
% GDP spending on pension system	10.2	11.3	10.6	10.7	10.6	10.1
% GDP spend only on minimum pensions	0.1	0.1	0.4	1	1.6	2
% Replacement rate at retirement	58	47	32	27	27	27

Source: Own elaboration, based on Strzelecki and Stachura (2023)

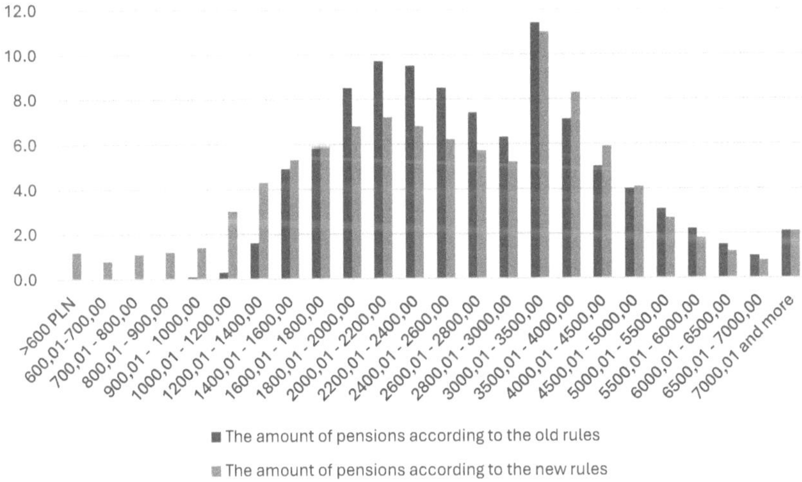

Fig. 8.2 Percentage of individuals receiving pensions of a specified amount from the new and old systems in December 2022. (Source: Own elaboration based on psz.zus.pl)

ensures that there are virtually no pensions lower than 1000 PLN (Fig. 8.2).

Secondly, the system has become, in effect, a reflection of the inequalities presented in the labour market. Thus, individuals with relatively high incomes, without interruptions in employment (e.g., due to unemployment or caregiving for children, the elderly, or disabled persons) and employed under formal contracts, will have relatively high pensions. In contrast, individuals who, for various reasons, were able to save less in their individual ZUS accounts, due to lower salaries, employment gaps, or working under non-contributory contracts, will not accumulate sufficient capital and will only receive minimum pensions based on their length of service.

An example of how the NC system affects pension amounts and reflects the labour market situation is the disparity between the accumulated capital of women and men. There are numerous factors that make women more vulnerable in a defined contribution pension system. Firstly, they simply earn less. Research on income inequality in Poland shows that from 2000 to 2018, women earned on average one-third less than men, and there are especially few women in the highest income group (Bukowski et al., 2023). Lower incomes translate to lower pension contributions. Women are also less likely to hold managerial positions and are more often inactive in the labour market due to caregiving responsibilities, not only for children but also for the elderly (Petelczyc & Roicka, 2015). Even paying contributions for periods of maternity leave does not fully compensate for the so-called child penalty. This is a measure of the impact of parenthood on parents' income and employment (Kleven et al., 2019). In Poland, among parents of children born between 2005 and 2012, women's incomes drop by nearly 20% in the year of the birth of their first child and by over 35% in the year following the birth. Afterwards, incomes stabilise at a lower level. Importantly, men did not experience significant effects of parenthood (Pałka, 2024). We cannot directly compare the pensions themselves due to the fact that the retirement age for women is five years lower, which significantly increases the denominator in the pension calculation equation. For this reason, we compare the accumulated capital (Fig. 8.3).

As mentioned, women in Poland have a retirement age that is five years lower than that of men (60/65), which significantly impacts the reduction of their pensions. Even childless women who earn as much as men and have no career breaks work five years less, meaning their initial capital, reduced by this period, is divided by an additional 60 months. Data shows that the pension gap between women and men currently stands at 35% (it was 25% under the old system). About 8% of female pensioners receive

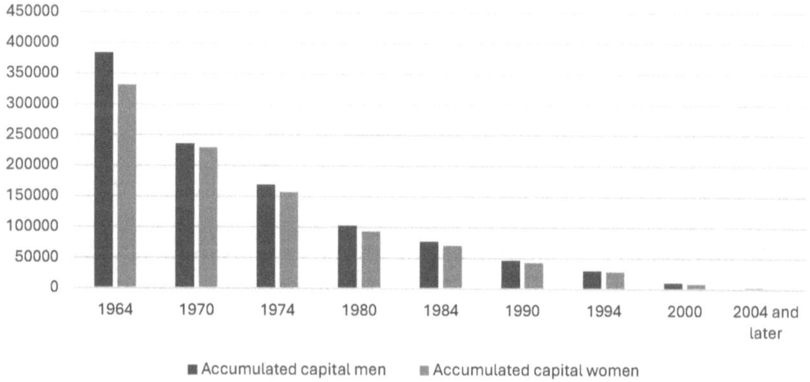

Fig. 8.3 Average accumulated capital (in PLN) by year of birth and gender in the first quarter of 2024. (Source: Own elaboration based on psz.zus.pl)

only the minimum pension because they have not accumulated enough capital for higher benefits (in comparison, this is only 0.3% for men). The problem of an insufficient number of contribution periods is further highlighted by the fact that a growing percentage of all female pensioners receive benefits lower than the minimum, which means they have not accumulated even 20 years of service. For men, this percentage is 3.7% (Ratajczak-Leszczyńska, 2024).

Labour market segmentation, alongside income and gender inequalities, is also influenced by the type of employment contracts prevalent in Poland. Some contracts, such as the "*umowa o dzieło*" (contract for a specific task), are not subject to social security contributions at all, while others, like "*umowa zlecenia*" (contract of mandate), have only recently started to be partially included, and not for all employees. Additionally, self-employed persons face exceptionally low contribution bases. This situation often leads to many people either choosing or being forced to establish their own businesses, even when performing tasks that should be under standard employment contracts. Although this phenomenon is challenging to quantify precisely, estimates from the European Working Conditions Survey suggest that this form of employment constitutes up to 31% of all self-employed individuals in the EU, with Poland being a notable "leader" in this category (Williams & Horodonic, 2018; Nikulin, 2020). Research indicates that self-employed individuals in Poland contribute, on average, from a base that is only 48% of the assessment base for those in regular employment. This discrepancy arises because these contributions are based on flat rates rather than income-related amounts. Consequently, relatively affluent business owners pay the minimum contributions and later receive supplementary payments to reach the minimum pension level due to their insufficient accumulated capital (Bukowski et al., 2023; Petelczyc & Lasocki, 2024). Another issue related to evasion of contributions, which results in lower benefits in the defined contribution (NDC) system, is the presence of so-called contribution convergence ("*zbiegi*"). Briefly, if an individual works under multiple contracts, they only pay contributions on one, typically at the minimum wage level (Iwanowski et al., 2020). Therefore, a significant number of individuals in Poland contribute less than they should, either because they are compelled by the labour market or choose to do so themselves. As a result, they fail to accumulate sufficient capital for higher pensions, leading the state to subsidise their minimum pensions. In the defined contribution system, with the current retirement age, the number of people receiving only the

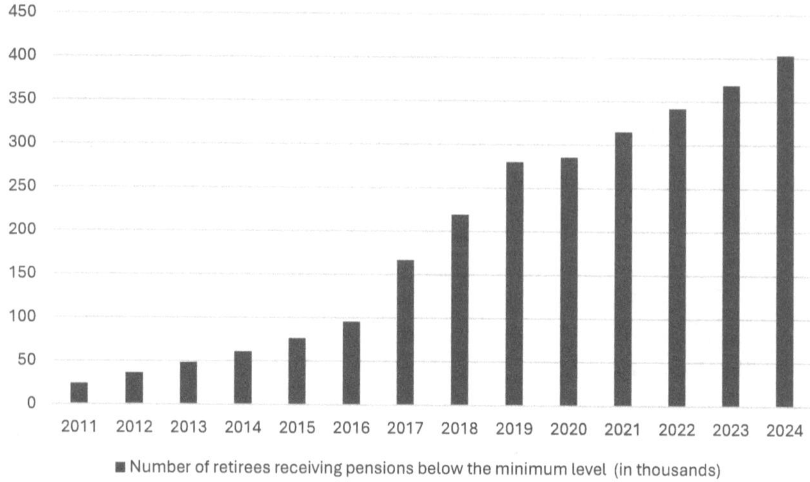

Fig. 8.4 Number of retirees receiving pensions below the minimum level (in thousands). (Source: Own elaboration based on psz.zus.pl)

minimum pension is expected to increase drastically in the coming years, as their capital will not suffice for higher benefits. It is estimated that this will affect approximately 70% of individuals born in the 1970s and 1980s (Bielecki et al., 2017). The escalating costs associated with this challenge are detailed in Table 8.2. Recent years have also seen a dramatic increase in the number of individuals receiving less minimum pension, mostly from the "new" system (Fig. 8.4).

The consequences of the implemented reforms proved to be unfavourable for the state budget and led to a decline in social security standards in Poland. Thus, they were part of reforms leading to one of the most unjust systems (Kowalik, 2012). As Prof. Szumlicz states: *"it can be assumed that the creators of the system and the parliamentarians, enchanted by the expected and desirable capital change, forgot about the existing social functions of the pay-as-you-go solution"* (Szumlicz, 2015).

Partial Retreat from the Reform

According to institutional theories, it is difficult to implement radical reforms due to path dependency, which posits that historical decisions and processes (e.g., the pension reform in Poland in 1999) strongly influence the current and future directions of policies and institutions. Once a particular path is established, switching to a new trajectory requires significant effort and resources. However, sometimes a critical juncture arises, and such a moment in Poland's history after 1989 was the economic crisis post-2007. The burden of this crisis, though not visible in GDP, was borne by the citizens (Theiss et al., 2017). In this sub-section, I show that the growing deficit and the financial crisis contributed to a partial retreat from the privatisation of the pension system in Poland. However, no reforms were undertaken to move away from the defined contribution system, which has the greatest impact on the shape of future benefits. It seems, though, that the ongoing changes make it increasingly difficult to call this model entirely NDC.

(a) **Reasons of Re-reforms**

As previously mentioned, the 1999 reform caused many fiscal and social issues. The most debated issue was the costs associated with the transformation from a public system to a partially private one (see Fig. 8.1). It is estimated that these costs amounted to as much as 16% of GDP between 1999 and 2010, and, without any changes, were projected to reach 79% of GDP by 2060 (Bielecki, 2011). Subsequent governments were primarily focused on financing the transition costs associated with the 1999 reform. These costs were significantly higher than anticipated, and the revenues from privatisation, which were supposed to cover these costs, turned out to be insufficient. Consequently, the reform was financed through public debt, which further burdened the state budget. It should be noted that when Poland joined the EU, the European Commission pressured the country to meet the Maastricht criteria and subjected it to the excessive deficit procedure. This was the main reason for the decision to reduce the size of the privately managed pillar in 2011, followed by the nationalisation of part of its assets (those held in government bonds) and making it voluntary (Polakowski & Hagemejer, 2018). Therefore, it is recognised that the increase in the public deficit and the fiscal costs associated with the transformation resulting from the 1999 reform were the main reasons for the withdrawal from the reform in Poland and other countries in the region (Bielawska et al., 2015).

Another reason for the reforms was the fact that during the financial crisis, the short-term performance of pension funds was unsatisfactory when the Warsaw Stock Exchange was affected by an outflow of investors.

They performed significantly worse compared to the indexation of contributions in ZUS accounts. The global economic crisis of 2008–2009 thus raised concerns about the financial performance of the second pillar, investment risk, and the dependence of future benefits on the financial market situation (Polakowski & Hagemejer, 2018; Oręziak, 2014).

(b) **Re-reforms**

After the economic crisis, several significant changes occurred in the pension system in Poland. The most important years in this regard are 2011–2013. First, the reform introduced by the *Act of 25 March 2011, on amending certain acts related to the functioning of the social insurance system*, significantly reduced the contribution flowing to OFE from 7.3% to 2.3% of wages. This meant that the remaining part of the contribution flowed into the ZUS account, effectively increasing the portion of contributions managed publicly. Finally, this law introduced the voluntary nature of OFE. People who previously had to be in OFE (all born after 1969 who worked and contributed) could now decide whether they wanted to continue in OFE or direct all contributions to ZUS. At the same time, methods of behavioural economics (Thaler & Sunstein, 2008) were applied: If someone wanted to remain in OFE, they had to fill out an appropriate form. If no action was taken, it was automatically assumed that the person wanted to transfer entirely to ZUS. According to data from ZUS, 2,564,072 people submitted declarations, meaning that after the reform, one in six eligible individuals remained in OFE after the first wave of reform in 2014. Finally, this reform also introduced sub-accounts in ZUS. This means that the contribution that previously was supposed to go to OFE (all or part of it, depending on the choice made) was credited to the person's sub-account in ZUS. This part includes elements not found in traditional social security systems, such as the possibility (under certain conditions) of inheriting these funds.

Another reform, introduced by the *Act of 6 December 2013, on amending certain acts in connection with the determination of the rules for paying pensions from funds accumulated in open pension funds*, led to the transfer of part of the government bonds from OFE to ZUS (so-called nationalisation of bonds). It was 51.5% of the assets held by OFE. This amounted to around 153 billion PLN. The transferred bonds were then cancelled to reduce public debt. Following the transfer, OFE were no longer allowed to invest in government securities. This was intended to diversify the investment portfolios of the pension funds and reduce the dependency on government debt. Under these changes, the so-called safety slider was also introduced—a gradual transfer of funds from OFE to ZUS 10 years before reaching retirement age. It aimed to protect the value of pension savings as individuals approached retirement, reducing exposure to market volatility.

Conclusion: Is the System More Just?

I began this chapter with a quote from Professor Kowalik, who claimed that Poland's economic transformation after 1989 led to one of the most unjust systems. There are several arguments to support this view, especially in the context of the 1999 pension reforms (introducing a three-pillar system and NDC). Additionally (which I did not cover in this article due to the breadth of the topic), the post-1989 period saw numerous changes regarding special entitlements for many professional groups, including the withdrawal and reintroduction of early retirement options, the introduction of so called "bridging pensions" (*emerytury pomostowe*) for individuals performing work in special conditions or of a special nature (which, as of 2023, are no longer phasing out as previously), and reforms in the retirement age, which was first raised (albeit over a very long time frame) and then lowered again.

In this chapter, I demonstrated that the 1999 pension reforms were part of the broader reform trend of that era: neoliberal assumptions, shifting responsibility to individuals, partial system privatisation, and reforms dictated by international institutions. This led to a declining replacement rate, increasing pension inequalities, and the elimination of the redistributive element in the Polish pension system. The partial rollback of these reforms was primarily driven by fiscal reasons (rising debt and deficit) due to transformation costs and asset devaluation caused by the financial crisis, rather than social reasons.

However, it is worth noting that despite maintaining the Notional Defined Contribution system within the first pillar, certain measures protect future retirees from poverty. The most important of these is the so-called minimum pension, granted to anyone who demonstrates sufficiently long work experience. It can be said that this tool today and in the future will play a key role in redistribution.

In summary, the system, while still reflecting many of the neoliberal policies implemented during the 1999 reforms, includes mechanisms to address some of the social injustices that have emerged. The minimum pension serves as a critical component in maintaining some level of social equity and redistribution within the pension system, mitigating the full impact of reforms that shifted significant responsibility onto individuals. Additionally, the move away from the partial privatisation of the system reduces the dependence of future benefits on the performance of financial markets. The evolving nature of these reforms indicates an ongoing struggle to balance fiscal responsibility with social justice in Poland's pension system.

Notes

1. Act of 28 August 1997 on the Organization and Operation of Pension Funds. Act of 13 October 1998 on the Social Insurance System. Act of 17 December 1998 on the Social Insurance Fund Pensions.
2. The Buzek reforms, initiated by Prime Minister Jerzy Buzek in Poland in 1999, encompassed four major areas: pensions, healthcare, education, and local government administration.
3. Autoenrolment in Employee Capital Plans (PPK) is a system where employees are automatically enrolled in the PPK scheme by their employers. Exiting the system requires additional effort (submitting a declaration). Autoenrolment is designed to increase participation in retirement savings plans, ensuring that more employees have adequate savings for their retirement.
4. Act of 20 April 2004 on Individual Retirement Accounts (IKE). Act of 20 April 2004 on Individual Retirement Security Accounts (IKZE). Act of 4 October 2018 on Employee Capital Plans (PPK).
5. The significant impact of initial capital on increasing pension benefits was demonstrated by Tomasz Lasocki and me in the report "Dobrowolne ubóstwo - o konsekwencjach dobrowolnego oskładkowania samozatrudnionych" ("Voluntary poverty - on the consequences of voluntary contributions for the self-employed") for ZUS, where we modeled the pension benefits of an individual with the same contributions but paid before or after 1999 (Petelczyc & Lasocki, 2024).

References

Anioł, W. (2015). On three modernization narratives in Poland after 1989. *International Journal of Social Economics, 42*(9), 777–790.

Bielawska, K., Chłoń-Domińczak, A., & Stańko, D. (2015). *Retreat from mandatory pension funds in countries of the Eastern and Central Europe in result of financial and fiscal crisis: Causes and effects*. Warsaw School of Economics.

Bielecki, J. K. (2011). *Pension system reforms in CEE – Example of Poland*. Office of the Economic Council to the Prime Minister of Poland.

Bielecki, M., Makarski, K., & Tyrowicz, J. B. (2017). Obniżanie wieku emerytalnego Jakie będą jego skutki? GRAPE Group of Research in Applied Economics.

Biuro Pełnomocnika Rządu ds. Reformy Zabezpieczenia Społecznego. (1997). *Bezpieczeństwo dzięki różnorodności. Reforma systemu emerytalno-rentowego w Polsce (wersja druga poprawiona)*. Warszawa, Luty.

Blazyca, G., & Rapacki, R. (1991). *Poland into the 1990, Economy and society transition*. Pinter Publishers.

Bukowski, P., Chrostek, P., Novokmet, F., & Skawiński, M. (2023). Income inequality in 21st century. *MF Working Paper Series* 40-2023.

Campbell, J. L., & Pederson, O. K. (Eds.). (1996). *Legacies of change. Transformation of postcommunist European economies*. Aldine de Gruyter.

Chłoń-Domińczak, A., & Strzelecki, P. (2010). The minimum pension as an instrument of poverty protection in the defined contribution pension system – an example of Poland. *MPRA Paper* 25262.

Chybalski, F. (2009). Barriers to increased effectiveness of investment by pension funds in Poland. *The Pensions Institute, Cass Business School, City University*, Discussion Paper PI-0910.

Cichon, M. (1999). Notional defined-contribution schemes: Old wine in new bottles? *International Social Security Review, 52*(4), 87–102.

Cichon, M., Hagemejer, K., & Ruck, M. (1997). Social Protection and pension systems in Central and Eastern Europe. *ILO-CEET Report* 21.

Czepulis-Rutkowska. (1999). The Polish pension system and its problems. In K. Müller, A. Ryll, & H.-J. Wagner (Eds.), *Transformation of social security: Pensions in central-eastern Europe*. Springer-Verlag.

Djelic, M. L., & Quack, S. (2007). Overcoming path dependency: Path generation in open systems. *Theory and Society, 36*.

Garud, R., & Karnøe, P. (Eds.). (2001). *Path dependence and creation*. Lawrence Erlbaum.

Ghodsee, K., & Orenstein, M. (2021). *Taking stock of shock: Social consequences of the 1989 Revolutions*. Oxford Academic.

Góra, M. (1999). Ekonomiczne podstawy funkcjonowania nowego systemu emerytalnego w Polsce. *Gospodarka Narodowa, 3*(150), 9–24.

Góra, M., & Rutkowski, M. (2000). The quest for pension reform: Poland's security though diversity. *William Davidson Institute - Working Papers*.

Holzmann, R. (2002). The world bank approach to pension reform. *International Social Security Review, 53*(1), 11–34.

Howlett, M. (2009). Process sequencing policy dynamics: Beyond homeostasis and path dependency. *Journal of Public Policy, 29*(3), 241–262.

Iwanowski, D., Hetmański, M., Skowron, B., & Wroński, M. (2020). Pełne dochody – niepełne składki. Zbieg tytułów do ubezpieczeń społecznych i konsekwencje dla systemu ubezpieczeń społecznych. *Instrat Policy Paper* 07/2020.

Kleven, H., Landais, C., & Søgaard, J. (2019). Children and gender inequality: Evidence from Denmark. *American Economic Journal: Applied Economics, 11*(4), 181–209.
Koelble, T. A. (1995). The new institutionalism in political science and sociology. *Comparative Politics, 27*(2), 221–244.
Koening, M. (2012). *The failure of neoliberal transition policies in eastern Europe Post-1989.* E-International Relations.
Kowalik, T. (2012). *From solidarity to sellout: The restoration of capitalism in Poland.* Monthly Review Press.
Mahoney, J. (2000). Path dependence in historical sociology. *Theory and Society, 29*(4), 507–548.
Marangos, J. (2002). The political economy of shock therapy. *Journal of Economic Surveys, 16*(1), 41–76.
Müller, K. (1999). *The political economy of pension reform in central-eastern Europe.* Edward Elgar.
Nikulin, D. (2020). *The determinants of false self-employment: A survey of Polish enterprises.* Eastern European Economics.
OECD. (2023). *Pensions at a glance 2023: OECD and G20 indicators.* OECD Publishing.
Orenstein, M. (2000). How politics and institutions affect pension reform in three postcommunist countries. *Policy Research Working Paper.* World Bank.
Oręziak, L. (2014). *OFE – katastrofa prywatyzacji emerytur w Polsce.* Instytut Wydawniczy Książka i Prasa.
Owczarek, J., & Więckowska, B. (2011). Ryzyko dopłaty do emerytury minimalnej w nowym systemie emerytalnym w Polsce. *Zeszyty Naukowe, Uniwersytet Ekonomiczny w Poznaniu, 181*, 331–340.
Pałka, M. (2024). Rodzicielstwo i rynek pracy: child penalty w Polsce. *MF Working Paper Series* 9-2024.
Petelczyc, J., & Lasocki, T. (2024). *Dobrowolne ubóstwo - o konsekwencji dobrowolnego oskładkowania samozatrudnionych.* ZUS.
Petelczyc, J., & Roicka, P. (2015). *Sytuacja kobiet w systemie emerytalnym.* Instytut Spraw Publicznych.
Pierson, P. (2000). Increasing returns, path dependence, and the study of politics. *American Political Science Review, 94*(2), 251–267.
Polakowski, M., & Hagemejer, K. (2018). Reversing pension privatization: The case of Polish pension reform and re-reforms. *ESS – Working Paper* 68. ILO.
Poznański, K. Z. (1993). *Stabilization and privatization in Poland, An economic evaluation of the Shock Therapy Program.* Springer.
Ratajczak-Leszczyńska, J. (2024). Wyzwania w kontekście zabezpieczenia emerytalnego kobiet w Polsce. Conference paper at: *Zabezpieczenie społeczne w Polsce – wczoraj, dziś i jutro. Wyzwania i szanse na przyszłość.* ZUS.

Rodzinka, J., Hady, J., & Hospod, J. (2007). Przyczyny wprowadzenia reformy systemu emerytalnego w Polsce. *e-Finanse* 3.

Sachs, J. (1994). *Shock therapy in Poland: Perspectives of five years*. The Tanner Lectures on Human Values.

Shields, S. (2008). How the east was won: Transnational social forces and the neoliberalization of Poland's post-communist transition. *Global Society, 22*(4), 445–468.

Slay, B. (1993). The Dilemmas of economic liberalism in Poland. *Europe-Asia Studies, 45*(2), 237–257.

Steinmo, S. (1993). *Taxation and democracy: Swedish, British and American approaches to financing the modern state*. Yale University Press.

Steinmo, S., Thelen, K., & Longstreth, F. (Eds.). (1992). *Structuring politics: Historical institutionalism in comparative analysis*. Cambridge University Press.

Streeck, W., & Thelen, K. (2005). Introduction: Institutional change in advanced political economies. In W. Streeck & K. Thelen (Eds.), *Beyond continuity*. Oxford University Press.

Strzelecki, P., & Stachura, J. (2023). *2024 ageing report Poland—Country Fiche*. Directorate-General for Economic and Financial Affairs.

Szumlicz, T. (2015). Reformowanie system zabezpieczenia społecznego. In T. Szumlicz (Ed.), *Ubezpieczenie w polityce społecznej, teksty i komentarze*. Fundacja Instytut Zarządzania Ryzykiem Społecznym.

Thaler, R. H., & Sunstein, C. R. (2008). *Nudge: Improving decisions about health, wealth and happiness*. Yale University Press.

Theiss, M., Kurowska, A., Petelczyc, J., & Lewenstein, B. (2017). *Obywatel na zielonej wyspie, polityka społeczna i obywatelstwo społeczne w Polsce w dobie europejskiego kryzysu ekonomicznego*. IFiS PAN.

Thelen, K. (2004). *How institutions evolve. The Political Economy of Skills in Germany, Britain, the United States, and Japan*. Cambridge University Press.

Williams, C. C., & Horodonic, A. (2018). Evaluating the prevalence and distribution of dependent self-employment: Some lessons from the European Working Conditions Survey. *Industrial Relations Journal, 49*(2), 109–127.

Williamson, J. B., & Williams, M. (2005). National defined contribution accounts, neoliberal ideology and the political economy of pension reform. *The American Journal of Economics and Sociology, 64*(2), 485–506.

World Bank. (1994). *Averting the old age crisis*. Oxford University Press.

CHAPTER 9

The Welfare State and the New World Order

Janusz J. Tomidajewicz

Introduction

One of the most important topics that has preoccupied economists and social thinkers for more than two hundred years has been the consideration of what shape of social order will best realise the expectations and needs of societies. After the emergence of capitalism, its analysis by classical political economists seemed to indicate that it would realise the dream of creating the best social order. Quickly, however, its inadequacies and the resulting negative social consequences led to the emergence of ideas pointing to the need for it to be reformed and improved or even replaced by another better socio-economic system. Throughout the nineteenth century, this strand of thinking about society was developed by various trends in socialist thought. These ranged from the concepts and projects of the Utopian socialists, through the Marxian analysis of capitalism and the vision of a communist society, to the reformist social democratic current on the one hand and the concepts of revolutionary socialism on the other. The development of socialist concepts, competitive with liberal capitalism, was also reflected in the activities of socialist social movements

J. J. Tomidajewicz (✉)
Poznań University of Economics and Business (Emeritus), Poznań, Poland

University of Zielona Góra (Emeritus), Zielona Góra, Poland

G. Konat, G. Rae (eds.), *Exploring the Ideas of Tadeusz Kowalik*,
https://doi.org/10.1007/978-3-032-09283-0_9

and their influence on the transformation of the social order. In the twentieth century, this led, on the one hand, to the emergence, development and finally collapse of the totalitarian system of state socialism[1] and, on the other hand, to transformations within liberal capitalism leading to the formation of a system described as the welfare state, perhaps most fully realised within the Nordic model of the social democratic welfare state.

With the collapse of the 'world socialist system'[2] and the collapse of the USSR, it might have seemed that the dispute over the shape of the future social order was concluded by the victory of neoliberal capitalism and liberal parliamentary democracy. The best-known expression of such a view was the work of F. Fukuyama diagnosing the 'end of history' (Fukuyama, 1992) and the thesis spreading in political and scientific discourse: TINA (*There Is No Alternative*).[3]

In Poland, which embarked on the path of transformation to a market economy in 1989, other roads of transformation, than the neoliberal one, were presented in the public sphere. Such alternative concepts to neoliberalism for the transformation of the Polish economy included:

- Postulating various forms of state interventionism, a programme to pull the country out of its short-term collapse and develop a strategic vision of development, proposed in Drogi wyjścia (1991)
- The programme for the transition to a market economy developed by R. Krawczyk, taking into account the need to use employee ownership (Krawczyk, 1990)
- The visionary concept of building a cessationist system (cessationism), presented by M. Guzek (1991)

However, in view of the worldwide trend towards the dominance of neoliberal concepts in economics and the political and economic pressure from international capital acting through the governments of highly developed countries and international organisations such as the IMF and WTO, basically without any broader ideological and political discussion, the neoliberal model of the market economy, synthetically presented by the so-called Balcerowicz Plan, was chosen.

In Poland, the most active critics of this neoliberal concept of carrying out transformation and the associated target vision of the future socio-economic order included G. Kołodko (cf. Kołodko (1999)) and T. Kowalik, who referred to the Scandinavian social democratic order as the main alternative (cf. Kowalik, 2009, p. 200).

Parallel to the discussions and political problems of choosing an economic model taking place in Poland and other post-socialist countries, in highly developed capitalist countries and in many developing countries, the neoliberal concept of systemic order, due to its negative social consequences, soon began to be contested by international, left-wing social movements and organisations.[4] On the conceptual and theoretical side, on the other hand, the non-alternative vision of a global, neoliberal social order has been subjected to criticism both by some leading economists coming from the mainstream[5] and, above all, by circles of economists associated with leftist and heterodox thinking.[6]

Parallel theoretical and socio-political discussions on an alternative socio-economic order to neoliberalism intensified, especially in the wake of the 2008 global financial and economic crisis. The crisis also gave an additional impetus to the economic policy of developed countries to look for non-liberal tools to combat it. Although within the European Union, the austerity policy pushed by the ECB and the so-called Troika became the dominant response to the crisis, many countries (in particular the USA) also applied quantitative easing policies and eased the conditions for recovery from the debt crisis.

Tadeusz Kowalik was an active participant in these discussions, both on the Polish and European levels (cf. Kowalik, 2009, pp. 68–88), and expressed his opinion both on the issue of what the desired future shape of the socio-economic order should be, as well as on the conditions and methods leading to its establishment. On the first issue, Kowalik strongly advocated the choice of such a model of a market (capitalist?) economy, which would fit into the broadly understood notion of a welfare state, considering the so-called Scandinavian model as a particularly attractive example.[7] On the other hand, referring to the conditions and methods of achieving the desired model of market economy, Kowalik pointed in particular to two factors: the international situation largely expressed in the existence and strength of international systemic competition[8] and the strength and mobilisation of internal and international movements of protest in defence of labour and civil rights. From the latter point of view, he pointed to the appeals of well-known intellectuals and social activists such as G. Soros and J. Sachs, but stressed that 'Of course, there are many similar appeals to reason by the US authorities. But what matters is strength. ... In contrast, the "argument of force" can only be demonstrated by mass movements and organisations. That is why it is worth following the anti-globalisation movements', and pointed out: 'Leftist intellectuals thus have a natural role to perform: to expose myths, to defend workers' rights to self-organisation, to social entitlements, and so on. It is valuable to consider possible systemic changes in the distant future. These changes, however, will depend on the balance of social forces, elements of which can already be discerned today' (Kowalik, 2004, pp. 76–77).

During the last ten years, both of these aspects, important for the direction of systemic transformations and the shaping of the future political order, have undergone significant changes, prompting consideration of their consequences for the shaping of the future political order in Poland and within the European Union. Thus, the following parts of this article will consider:

- Contemporary competing models of economic and social governance
- The emergence of a new, multipolar world order and the resulting conditions of intersystem competition and threats to the maintenance of world peace
- The chances of creating a democratic welfare state in Poland and the EU

Competing Models of Economic and Social Governance

At least from the end of the Second World War, until the collapse of the USSR, there seemed to be only two main socio-economic systems competing on a global scale: capitalism and socialism.[9] In individual countries and regions, within each of these systems there were several specific economic and social models differing, on the one hand, in the manner and mechanisms of political power exercised in them and, on the other, in the role and tools of state influence on economic processes. For the formation of the world order, however, the competition between these two fundamental systems was of crucial importance, leading to the formation of a bipolar balance of power on a global scale. As already mentioned, the collapse of the USSR and the so-called socialist camp seemed to lead to the transformation of the world order into a unipolar system, with the dominant role of the USA and the developed market economy countries imposing a victorious and universal systemic model on the whole world based on the democratic political system and the neoliberal economic model shaped in them.

However, the course of political and economic processes that we have observed in the more than 30 years since the collapse of the 'socialist system',[10] contrary to initial expectations, has now led to the formation of a multipolar political and social system in which there are many, in some sense competing, systems of socio-economic order. These systems can be characterised and distinguished by their location on two relatively independent systemic axes, defining the political system on the one hand and the economic order on the other. It will be assumed here that the actual political system can be shaped on either of the intermediate states between the extremes of dictatorial authoritarianism versus parliamentary democracy. On the other (socio-economic) axis, the system may evolve from extreme neoliberalism (or even libertarianism) to a social democratic welfare state.

Of course, the economic and social systems that actually exist are almost never in a pure form, but a mixture of the four characteristics indicated here: economic liberalism, pro-social interventionism, liberal democracy and authoritarianism (dictatorship). Based on these assumptions, however, it can be taken that the most typical (in a sense, pure) political models are:

- *Neoliberal democracy*. This is a system combining a democratic political system with the functioning of an economy based on the neoliberal doctrine of a minimal state and domination of the market. This system was most successful from the 1980s to the first decade of the twenty-first century and was mainly implemented in the Anglo-Saxon states and imposed on developing countries and transforming post-socialist countries through international economic institutions (IMF, World Bank or WTO and the so-called Washington Consensus, which they have been pushing). At present, neoliberalism is being weakened in many countries through the introduction of pro-social (including pro-environmental) restrictions on economic freedom on the one hand and through the weakening of parliamentary democracy and the progressive oligarchisation and subordination of political power to the strongest interest groups on the other. However, the systems in the USA, Ireland and such Anglo-Saxon countries as the UK, New Zealand and Australia are probably still closest to this model.
- *The democratic welfare state of a managed market economy*. It is an economic and social system mainly shaped in European countries

during the so-called glorious 30 years. On the political side, it is characterised by a relatively well-functioning and generally socially acceptable system of liberal parliamentary democracy. On the economic and social side, it is characterised by significant state interventionism aimed at stimulating development processes on the one hand and ensuring the welfare of the widest possible social strata on the other. At its peak, this system existed in several fundamental varieties, such as the Scandinavian social democratic welfare state, the German ordoliberal welfare state or the republican welfare state in France. In the 1980s and 1990s, this system somewhat eroded under the dominance of the neoliberal approach. However, it still retains its distinctiveness and relative attractiveness in the European countries mentioned above, and is to a large extent a fundamental reference point for the shaping of the socio-economic order of the European Union.

- *Nationalist-neoliberal authoritarianism.* This system developed mainly in countries with no political tradition of parliamentary democracy. There, political power was either established through a coup d'état or even on the basis of a formal electoral process. However, it was then exercised in a more or less authoritarian manner by circles linked to national and/or foreign capital on the one hand and using national and religious ideas to consolidate society on the other. From the economic and social side, in this system the state limited its social and welfare activity, while from the economic side, it tried to pursue mainly the interests of the capital groups linked to it and left far-reaching freedom of action to market mechanisms. The neoliberal economy of Chile under A. Pinochet can be considered the most drastic example of such a system. With a greater or lesser intensity of authoritarian and neoliberal tendencies, this system was also present in some other Latin American countries (e.g. Brazil under the military dictatorship of 1964–1985 and under J. Bolsonaro, or Argentina under the military dictatorship of 1976–1983), as well as in some European and Asian countries (Spain under F. Franco, or the Philippines under the dictatorship of F. Marcos).
- *Populist-welfare authoritarianism.* However, in social systems implementing the assumptions of economic neoliberalism, both in politically authoritarian and democratically governed countries, problems may arise in maintaining even passive social acceptance for them. These occur when economic neoliberalism leads to an excessive

> build-up of phenomena such as growing poverty and social exclusion, unacceptable income and social disparities and a lack of avenues and mechanisms for individual social and economic advancement. This threatens the existing social order with the emergence of protests and rebellion movements against the system. In dictatorial systems, the response to this can be an increase in political terror, but this rarely proves effective in the long run. What often proves more effective is the introduction of solutions that take into account the state's need for welfare and social mechanisms to mitigate the negative effects of economic neoliberalism. Neoliberal democratic systems can also evolve in a similar way. The introduction of selected pro-social institutional and systemic solutions is achieved there, however, not through the seizure of power by political forces advocating the model of a democratic welfare state, but through the acquisition of authoritarian political power by populist national-religious circles, which aim to eliminate the sources of possible social resistance by consolidating societies around specifically understood national and/or religious and sometimes quasi-religious values. A characteristic feature of the social solutions introduced then is their selectivity (targeting specific social groups) and the subjectivity and voluntarism in their allocation. This results in the fact that, although they alleviate the most acute social tensions, they do not allow for their systemic solution.

The systems of some European countries (such as Hungary and Poland during the PiS government) are evolving in this direction. Also, some other post-communist states in which authoritarian rule by the former party and/or post-communist oligarchy has been preserved are converging towards this model. In these systems, specifically understood national ideas of opposing the domination of foreign (imperialist) economic and cultural concepts are used as a tool to consolidate society around authoritarian power. Sometimes a traditional religious or quasi-religious component is used to consolidate society (when the cult of the ruling dictator takes on the character of a specific religion). This phenomenon can most clearly be seen in Putin's Russia or North Korea. To a certain extent, such tendencies also appear in countries such as China and Cuba, but with less of a religious component and more of a nationalist one.

As a nationalist alternative to neoliberal democracy, this model also shows a certain electoral attractiveness in European countries with a

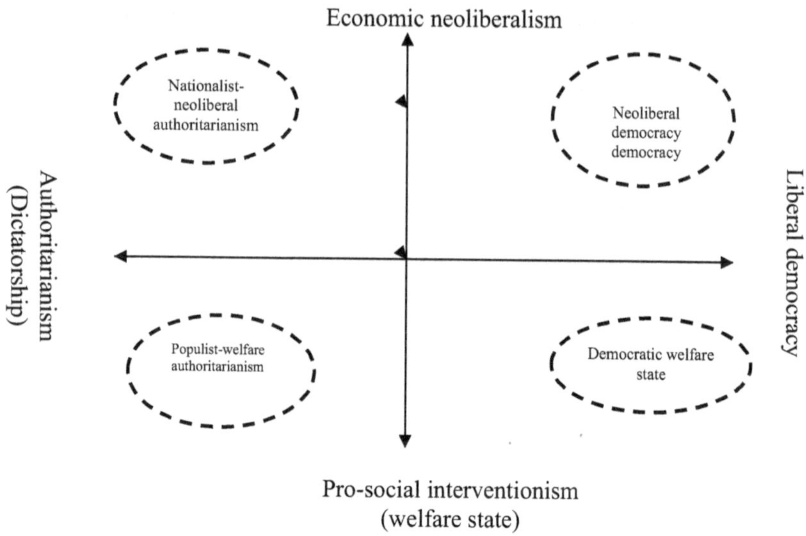

Fig. 9.1 Types of socio-economic governance. (Source: Own elaboration)

seemingly well-established democratic tradition, such as Italy, France or Germany, and even the USA, where it is supported by social movements such as the Brothers of Italy, National Rally, AfD or 'Trumpism'. In all these countries, the specific political and economic solutions can differ quite significantly in both the degree of authoritarianism of the political power and the level of 'welfare' in the social system.

The location of the systemic models thus characterised in the area delimited by the political and economic variables can be depicted as in Fig. 9.1.

The Emergence of a New, Multipolar, World Order and the Conditions for Maintaining World Peace

At the beginning of the twenty-first century, it might have seemed that the only alternative to the victorious neoliberalism was that offered by left-wing protest movements such as the anti- and alter-globalists, ATTAC, Occupy Wall Street or the Spanish indignados movement. However, it quickly became apparent that they all had too little influence to bring about a real (and not just ideological) counterweight to neoliberalism.

Their impact on the socio-economic reality has, however, led to some softening of neoliberal concepts and the introduction (particularly in the EU) of partially pro-social solutions.[11] In contrast, significant changes in the conditions for the formation of the global socio-economic order have occurred as a result of the emergence of new economic and social centres of gravity with the character of global and/or regional powers. The BRICS group of countries and some smaller regional powers, such as Turkey and Iran, have begun to claim this role in recent years. On the one hand, this has resulted in a weakening of the neoliberal dictates of the developed countries (which can be seen as a positive development). However, on the other hand, it has become a source of intensified inter-system competition, sometimes leading to international armed conflicts. The most acute expression of this has been the outbreak of the war over Ukraine and the threats to world peace growing elsewhere in the globe as well. As such potential or already existing sites of conflict, one can point to China's aspiration to annex Taiwan or attempts by terrorist organisations such as Al Qaeda or ISIS to 'export' the principles of Muslim fundamentalism. I have written more extensively about these developments and their consequences (Tomidajewicz, 2024b).

Undoubtedly, the changes in the global balance of power that we are currently witnessing are becoming a threat not only to the dominance of the neoliberal economic and social order, but also to the possibility of reforming it towards a model of a democratic welfare state and towards the creation of a sustainable economy of moderation.[12] We will omit here the details of the rather geopolitical reflections on the possibility of the emergence of such a new world order, in which competition between the systems does not lead to a threat to world peace or even to the outbreak of a world war that would have tragic consequences for humanity.[13] It is worth noting, however, that a necessary condition for the emergence of such a peaceful order is the recognition by all competing powers that the new world order has been formed as a multipolar and multisystem arrangement and that none of the powers claiming to lead can impose their own solutions on the others. From this point of view, the greatest threat to a peaceful world order is, on the one hand, the persistence in the USA and certain European circles of the conviction of absolute superiority and the right to impose a liberal-democratic political order. On the other hand, such a threat is posed by the attempts of powers with authoritarian systems to stop the liberal-democratic transition by force. The most drastic example of this is Russia's aggression against Ukraine.

In view of the changes in the global balance of power and the conditions for the choice of political order in individual countries, which have only been sketched here in general terms, the possibilities and directions of shaping the future socio-economic system in Poland and the EU are also changing. In particular, two questions keep appearing and with increasing intensity:

1. Under these new conditions, is it possible for a country like Poland to independently shape a national socio-economic order with the character of a social democratic welfare state?
2. With the deepening of integration within the EU, are such transformations of the European social order possible, which will lead to the principles of the democratic welfare state being recognised as a characteristic norm for the entire Union? And for individual countries (including Poland), will they become a source of transformation of their national socio-economic models in this direction?

Depending on how these questions are answered, it will also be possible to formulate recommendations and demands regarding our participation in European integration. These problems, under slightly different geopolitical conditions, were addressed by Tadeusz Kowalik in an article published in 2012 (Kowalik, 2012b), which is a polemic with my piece (Tomidajewicz, 2012).[14]

Is There a Chance for a Democratic Welfare State in Poland and the EU?

Today, I agree with most of the theses once presented by Kowalik (2012). On one—but very fundamental—point, however, I have differed with him. For Kowalik wrote: 'Counting on European social guarantees would in practice mean condemning oneself to extreme impossibilism'. On the other hand, I (especially in the current multipolar world) maintain the thesis that the Left should opt for deeper European integration, realising that in the face of the rising tide of nationalism and the power of international capital, it is increasingly difficult, if not impossible, to fulfil its social demands within the framework of individual nation states.

Kowalik, on the other hand, wrote: 'While agreeing that measures are needed to give the current version of capitalism—especially in Poland, but also in Europe—a human face, more friendly to the poorer part of society, we differ on whether this should be sought rather by reforming the social order in individual countries or by striving to give a more pro-social shape to the entire European Union'. At the same time, I think we were both quite pessimistic on this issue. For I thought that the chances of softening the wolfish face of capitalism in individual countries were very limited, while Kowalik did not believe that such an operation could be successfully carried out on an EU-wide scale.

Of course, there are countries in Europe, indicated by Kowalik, which are already an example that a pro-social model of economy can be both highly effective and capable of competing on a global scale. However, in Poland, with the weakness of the politically organised left and the escape of the majority of society from politics into the sphere of individually solving their problems (as it is popularly said, 'everyone is getting by as best they can'), the chances of changing the economic and social model 'chosen' as a result of decisions made (or perhaps imposed on us) in 1989 seem to be at least as small as counting on European social guarantees. Also, the 8-year 'episode' of the PiS governments has shown that in Poland the political power of the left, advocating the model of a democratic welfare state, is too small to significantly influence the systemic character of the Polish socio-economic system 'from within'.

In addition, important factors hindering the internal reform of the social system in Poland are the country's level of development and economic position in the world. In today's globalised environment, whether we want it or not, we must ensure that the economy is highly competitive internationally. The Scandinavian countries mentioned by Kowalik achieve it thanks to their high level of knowledge and social capital, which ultimately translates into very high labour productivity. Poland, however, for the time being, does not possess these qualities and, to a large extent, is condemned to competing through social and tax dumping. This gives additional arguments to those who do not want to allow pro-social reforms of the country's system.

In the face of ever-intensifying international competition on a global scale, I fear that defending (let alone building) capitalism with a human face in a country with a relatively low level of development and a small economy is doomed to failure. In the face of increasing globalisation processes, an attempt to shape a more people-friendly face of capitalism within the European economy as a whole may have a much better chance. In spite of the internal differences rightly mentioned by Kowalik, it is already possible to juxtapose the European social order as a whole, with its still significant share of pro-social institutions and solutions, with the American system or the completely 'uncivilised' systems of many Asian or Latin American countries. In this situation, the shaping of a people-friendly European social order is becoming a component of the struggle for Europe's place in the world as well as for the shape of future socio-economic changes on a global scale.

Therefore, the attempt to influence a revision of the neoliberal paradigm that has dominated the European Union so far is at least as worthy of effort as the action to reform the social systems of individual countries. Even more, for the European Left today, it is an obligation to make such an attempt.

Indeed, the socio-economic and political processes that have taken place in Poland and Europe since my 2012 polemic with Tadeusz Kowalik have led to several contradictory trends in the EU.

On the one hand, resulting from the dominance of neoliberal approaches and austerity policies, the inability of the European Union to solve the social problems caused by the 2008 crisis has led to a tendency to seek solutions at the national level. However, this was done through the introduction of national populist-welfare models rather than through a deepening of the democratic welfare state model. V. Orban's Hungary and PiS's Poland became classic examples of such an evolution. Orban's Hungary and Poland's PiS party, and more recently Italy under the Brothers of Italy and G. Meloni seem to be moving in this direction. Seemingly and in the short term, this allows the social situation of the most needy to improve, but it does not create the conditions for a lasting and systemic solution to the growing social problems.

On the other hand, social pressure expressed in the rise of the 'indignados movement' and such radical and left-wing parties and social movements as Podemos, Syriza or France Insoumise, despite not being allowed to participate directly in power, has nevertheless forced, in some democratic European countries, a certain reduction in the dominance of the neoliberal approach to economic policy. This has been expressed in the suspension, for the duration of the fight against the Covid-19 pandemic, of a restrictive approach to public spending (including that aimed at protecting the material situation of the economically most vulnerable groups of the population) and in a more flexible approach to monetary and budgetary policies.

Thirdly, as a result of these social pressures, initiatives and changes limiting the hitherto neoliberal integration paradigm emerged also at the level of the EU's institutions. In the social sphere, these include, above all, the adoption of the European Pillar of Social Rights and, in the economic sphere, the relaxation of the EU's debt and deficit control rules and excessive deficit procedure, as well as the introduction of a joint EU debt mechanism for the implementation of the European Recovery Plan.

Finally, Russia's aggression against Ukraine and the consequent policy of economic sanctions has placed a question mark over the possibility of the further development of unlimited international exchange between competing (and sometimes hostile) blocs. This has led to a shift away from the neoliberal paradigm of removing barriers to international exchange as far as possible and towards the need for states and economic groupings to have autonomy in order to maintain their economic and political security. Within the European Union, this has been reflected in efforts to diversify the sources of energy resources and in the development of its own potential based on renewable energy sources, as well as in efforts to develop its own arms industry.

As a result, the European Union today faces a choice:

Should we try to continue with the current neoliberal paradigm of European integration? According to the scenario once outlined by Kowalik, and as a result of the growing importance of authoritarian and populist tendencies, this will probably lead to the disintegration of the EU or at least to the halting of further integration and its retreat to the level of a loose association of independent states retaining full sovereignty. Unfortunately, neither from the point of view of the interests of the EU as a whole, nor of the individual states that make it up, is this a particularly favourable scenario. None of the EU states (and Poland, as a medium-sized European country, in particular) has a chance in the emerging multipolar world order to play the role of one of the significant global powers. This is also not a favourable scenario from the point of view of the realisation of social development goals in the EU countries, as the pressure of global competition between the superpowers and the growing importance of supranational capital centres will force restrictions on the pursuit of national welfare programmes and/or the maintenance of democratic welfare states as islands isolated from their surroundings.

Unfortunately, the current balance of social forces in the EU countries seems to indicate that this scenario is highly likely. It is supported, on the one hand, by the power of pressure from international financial circles and, on the other, by the relative weakness of the EU's pro-social agenda and the declining importance of the European left and the orientation of social protest movements towards populist-nationalist solutions.

Should we try to deepen integration, taking much greater account than before of the principles of solidarity and the need for active social policies at a European level? Such a scenario seems much more desirable both for Europe's position in a multipolar world order and for the possibility of solving the social problems that beset us. Only by deepening economic and social integration and broadening it with political and military dimensions can Europe become a significant geopolitical centre in the emerging multipolar world, and the pro-social character of European democracy makes it an attractive development model in the global inter-system competition. Unfortunately, two opposing social forces stand in the way of such a transformation of the European Union.

The first is the international capital centres, which have enormous economic power and do not hesitate to use it to exert formal and informal pressure on the governments of individual countries and the European Union as a whole. The aim and direction of this pressure is to maintain the neoliberal nature of European integration and to halt or minimise the pro-social solutions it introduces, as well as those that aim to strengthen the role of the state in steering the economy. A more or less conscious ally of these tendencies are also those circles of intellectuals and professional economists for whom economic theory has stopped at the neoliberal paradigms of free market, freedom of economic activity and minimising the role of the state in the economy.[15]

The second of the social forces standing in the way of the pro-social transformations of European integration are the national-populist movements and parties, which are gaining increasing popular support. Opposing the deepening of European integration, these movements promise to solve social problems at the national level (mainly by limiting migration and launching internal transfers to selected social groups). Unfortunately, such a policy direction puts the countries pursuing it in a weak position vis-à-vis international capital and does not provide the basis for a sustainable and systemic solution to social problems.

Unfortunately, the strength and capacity of the tendencies opposing the deepening of the EU's pro-social transformation is considerable, and those advocating the building of a democratic welfare state in Europe are as yet poorly organised and do not have sufficient popular support to impose the necessary transformation in the EU.

Translated from Polish by Grzegorz Konat and Gavin Rae

Notes

1. The system that arose and developed in the USSR after the October Revolution and was later extended to the entire so-called socialist camp is also referred to as real socialism. However, T. Kowalik believed it should be referred to as the communist system. He wrote: 'I count myself among those who deny "real socialism" a socialist character, even if it were to be socialism with distortions or degenerations. That is why the term "communism" or "communist system" suits me better than the compromise "real socialism"' (Kowalik, 2004, pp. 69–77).
2. I use this term here realising that it was coined as a propaganda term and that it has largely served to falsify reality. Nevertheless, leaving aside its ideological message, it can be used as a shorthand expression of the real division of the actual socio-economic systems found in the world in the second half of the twentieth century.
3. For the concept of TINA and an overview of the arguments against its adoption, see Żakowski (2005).
4. Such as anti- and alter-globalists, ATTAC (*Association pour la Taxation des Transactions pour l' Aide aux Citoyens*), OWS (*Occupy Wall Street*) and national leftist or populist parties and movements such as Syriza, Podemos, LFI (*La France Insoumise*) and NUPES (*Nouvelle Union Populaire Ecologique et Sociale*).
5. These include J. Stiglitz (2002), P. Krugman (2009) or J. Sachs (2005) and even the declared conservative R. Kagan (2009).
6. In Europe, examples include: The Lisbon Group (Lisbon Group, 1996), the political movement 'Utopia', (Manifeste Europeen, 2008), the association 'Les Economistes attérrés' (Manifeste, 2010), DiEM25 (*A* Manifesto, 2022) and the EuroMemo Group, with which Kowalik was associated.
7. Speaking on the various forms of market economy, he pointed out that: '… by writing a text about the systemic diversity of contemporary capitalism and the possibilities of choosing one of its varieties, we make it easier to understand possible future choices by reducing the welfare state … to an invention of capitalism' (Kowalik, 2004, p. 72). On the other hand, from the Polish point of view, referring to K. Aigenger and M. Landesman, he pointed out that 'In terms of economic dynamism, they divided the EU countries into two groups. One included large countries: Germany, France, and Italy, which have a low economic growth rate. The other included the smaller Northern European countries, which are doing quite well and are even in the foreground in the most modern sectors' (Kowalik, 2012, pp. 271–272).

8. On this subject he wrote: 'And without taking into account the role of the socialist movement and the (largely falsified) economic and wartime success of the USSR, is it possible to understand the astonishing fact that after the Second World War two social systems so different from the American one arose in Germany and in Japan under the tutelage of the occupying powers (in Germany – mainly American)? Also the "Scandinavian model", from the beginning described as a third way, arose not without connection to the international situation' (Kowalik, 2004, p. 73).
9. These terms are a far-reaching simplification and often mischaracterise the essence of both systems. Against the systems shaped in the former USSR and in other countries of the so-called people's democracies, although they were inspired by socialist concepts, accusations were levelled with regard to both the mechanisms of exercising political power and its representation of social interest versus the interest of the party-bureaucratic ruling class, as well as the degree of implementating the postulate of socialising the management of the means of production, constitutive for socialism. As a result, these systems, as opposed to 'theoretical' socialism, were often referred to as 'real socialism', while Kowalik advocated their designation as communist. On the other hand, with regard to capitalism, particularly in the period of transition, a term was sought to avoid the negative connotations associated with the word, and to describe it as a liberal or market economy system. Consequently, to characterise the competition between the two systems, pairs of terms such as: real socialist (communist) versus liberal system or centrally controlled versus market economy system were also often proposed.
10. These phenomena and processes include, on the political side, the failure of Western attempts to impose a liberal-democratic social order in countries such as Iraq and Afghanistan and the emergence of new economic and political powers such as China and, to a certain extent, India and Brazil and, above all, Russia's triggering of the war over Ukraine. On the economic and social side, on the other hand, it was the occurrence of such negative consequences of the functioning of the neoliberal economy as: growing social inequalities and related social protest movements, the economic consequences of the financial and economic crisis in 2008 resulting to a large extent from the functioning of the neoliberal economy as so-called casino capitalism (Kowalik, 2009) and threats to the ecological balance—the threat of climate catastrophe.
11. This has been particularly evident in the EU's socio-economic policies with regard to climate policy (Energy Roadmap, 2011) and in the assumptions of the European Pillar of Social Rights (2021).

12. The concept of the economy of moderation is formulated among others by G. Kołodko (cf. Pach et al., 2016) and it is also discussed in (Gorynia & Śliwińska, 2024).
13. I wrote about this in Tomidajewicz (2024a).
14. The main subject of our polemic was the question: Should (as I argued in my article) the pursuit of a pro-social political order in Europe be based on reforming the EU towards its further integration and giving it the character of a democratic welfare state? Or should (as Kowalik argued), in view of the dominance of neoliberal tendencies in the EU, pro-social social and economic reforms be introduced primarily at the level of individual nation states, which would retain considerable autonomy in this regard.
15. In Poland, L. Balcerowicz, among economists, and R. Petru, among politicians, can be considered the flagship representatives of these circles.

References

Drogi wyjścia z polskiego kryzysu gospodarczego. (1991). Polskie Towarzystwo Ekonomiczne—Zarząd Główny.

Energy Roadmap. (2011, December 15). *Plan działania w zakresie energii do roku 2050.* Komisja Europejska.

European Commission. (2021). *European pillar of social rights booklet.* European Commission.

Fukuyama, F. (1992). *The End of history and the last man.* Free Press.

Gorynia, M., & Śliwińska, M. (2024). Economics of moderation as a foundation of sustainable development. In M. Baudry, S. I. Bukowski, & M. B. Lament (Eds.), *Financial stability, economic growth and sustainable development* (pp. 13–29). Routledge.

Grupa Lizbońska. (1996). *Granice konkurencji.* Poltext.

Guzek, M. (1991). *Ekonomia przejścia. Od kolektywizmu do systemu przyszłości.* Instytut Koniunktur i Cen Handlu Zagranicznego.

Kagan, R. (2009). *The return of history and the end of dreams.* Vintage.

Kołodko, G. (1999). *Od szoku do terapii: ekonomia i polityka transformacji.* Poltext.

Kowalik, T. (2004). Państwo dobrobytu – druga fala? *Problemy Polityki Społecznej, 6*, 69–77.

Kowalik, T. (2009). Kapitalizm kasyna. In *Kryzys. Przewodnik Krytyki Politycznej.* Wydawnictwo Krytyki Politycznej.

Kowalik, T. (2012a). *From solidarity to sellout: The restoration of capitalism in Poland.* Monthly Review Press.

Kowalik, T. (2012b, March 11). Niechlubne rekordy Polski na tle Unii. *Przegląd*, 10.

Krawczyk, R. (1990). *Wielka przemiana. Upadek i odrodzenie polskiej gospodarki.* Oficyna Wydawnicza.

Krugman, P. R. (2009). *The conscience of a liberal.* W.W. Norton & Co.
Manifest Utopia. (2008). *Manifeste Utopia.* Parangon.
Manifeste. (2010). *Manifeste d'économistes atterrés.* https://www.atterres.org/manifeste-deconomistes-atterres/.
Manifesto. (2022). *A manifesto for democratising Europe.* https://diem25.org/wp-content/uploads/2023/05/DiEM25-Manifesto-2022_pages.pdf.
Pach, J., Kowalska, K., & Szyja, P. (2016). *Ekonomia umiaru – realna perspektywa?* Wydawnictwo Naukowe PWN.
Sachs, J. (2005). *The end of poverty: Economic possibilities for our time.* Penguin Books.
Stiglitz, J. E. (2002). *Globalization and its discontents.* W. W. Norton & Company.
Tomidajewicz, J. J. (2012, February 5). Fałszywe recepty na kryzys. *Przegląd* 5(631).
Tomidajewicz, J. J. (2024a, March). *Społeczno-gospodarcza polityka UE wobec wyzwań walki o nowy podział świata. Biuletyn PTE* 1(104).
Tomidajewicz, J. J. (2024b, May 3). W przedwojennych czasach—nowe pokojowe współistnienie. *Studio Opinii.* https://studioopinii.pl/archiwa/242105.
Żakowski, J. (2005). *Anty-TINA: rozmowy o lepszym świecie, myśleniu i życiu.* Wydawnictwo Sic!.

PART III

Kowalik on Kowalik

CHAPTER 10

Three Against One. Mustard Before Dinner

Tadeusz Kowalik, Edward Chudziński, Filip Ratkowski, and Paweł Kozłowski

Edward Chudziński *I read in one of your biographical notes that you were attracted to the hat-making profession in your early youth. How did this come about?*

Tadeusz Kowalik Yes, I'm an apprentice hat-maker and an apprentice leather-maker. The first profession was a means to get out of the countryside, out of rural

The interview, conducted by Edward Chudziński, Filip Ratkowski and Paweł Kozłowski, took place on 14 May 2004, in Cracow. It was published in 2004, in *Zdanie* (no. 3/4, pp. 3–19), and then republished in 2013 in: T. Kowalik, *O lepszy ład społeczno-ekonomiczny* [For a Better Socio-economic Order], Warsaw: Polskie Towarzystwo Ekonomiczne & Instytut Nauk Ekonomicznych PAN, pp. 618–652. This translation is based on the latter version.

T. Kowalik (Deceased)
Warsaw, Poland

E. Chudziński • F. Ratkowski
"Zdanie", Kraków, Poland

P. Kozłowski (✉)
Centre for Europe, University of Warsaw, Warsaw, Poland
e-mail: p.kozlowski@uw.edu.pl

G. Konat, G. Rae (eds.), *Exploring the Ideas of Tadeusz Kowalik*,
https://doi.org/10.1007/978-3-032-09283-0_10

poverty. And as for the leather-making, I had learnt it for the needs of my work cooperative, and I never worked in that profession, because at the end of the war our cooperative fell apart.

I was born into a peasant family and in such a godforsaken village near Lublin where there was no post office, church, school or shop. I had to go to three schools to finish a full primary school. A four-year school was nearby, then a six-year school, and a seven-year school was even further away. It wasn't until the early 1950s that my parents moved to work at an aircraft factory in Świdnik near Lublin. And that's when my social background changed. My mother was a factory cleaner, my father a warehouseman, and later he even became the manager of a warehouse, so I already had a peasant-worker-intellectual background! Both my professions [hatter and leather maker] are connected with the war and the extermination of the Jews. In 1942, it suddenly turned out that the region had been completely emptied of craftsmen, because the Jews had been deported to the Lublin ghetto.... It was a horrible sight, by the way—a procession of Jews, old people, children on foot, rushed through our village by "navy-blue" police and German gendarmes. I had this image before my eyes for a long time.

Soon afterwards, announcements were made about various apprenticeship courses, so I signed up for a hat-making course, which protected me from being sent to forced labour in the Reich. I treated it as a temporary profession, so I chose an easy one (not tailoring, for example). And to my surprise, this choice was met with my father's fierce opposition. I remembered his words for a long time: "Suit yourself, but we won't help you". Although I am convinced that there was no anti-Semitism in this, both my parents were very tolerant, open-minded (I heard from them many times that all people are equal), I am also convinced that the reason was an ingrained dislike of these professions, intended rather for the Jewish poor, or perhaps non-Jewish poor, not for those who were to achieve [social] advancement.

Filip Ratkowski *So where did you get the inclination to skip over this, shall we say, stage of contentment with every day?*

Kowalik Here I must make a longer digression about my father, because I have often wondered what he could have been if he had had the chance to learn. My mother remained "illiterate", while my self-taught father owed his first social skills to the peasant movement (he belonged to the "[PSL] Wyzwolenie" party). But what a self-taught man he was! Not only did he write applications and official letters for the whole village with some knowledge of the law, but he created a kind of mini-literacy centre. On winter evenings, we read books aloud. He must have had some knowledge of literature, because he borrowed books by [Stefan] Żeromski, [Bolesław] Prus and [Władysław] Reymont from school, rather than books by, for example, [Maria] Rodziewiczówna, [Wacław] Berent or the then-fashionable [Tadeusz] Dołęga-Mostowicz. We were the first family in the village to have a headphone radio ("a crystal set"), which the neighbours were also allowed to use in the evenings. It was a nuisance because we lived in a one-room house (its other half was a cowshed). On many Sundays, we would cut the peasants' hair (free of charge, of course, and only until the "high mass", i.e. the 12.00 mass, although the church was far away). My father was also very open to various craft activities. It was thanks to him, his self-taught skills, that I too knew how to make flick-knives, skates (both things from old sickles and scythes), lighters (from rifle thimbles), skis. Quite a few of the neighbours used milk jugs (made from old buckets) that I had made. But I was supposed to be a teacher, a clerk. Not a priest, because my father was anticlerical. It was progress, because my grandmother used to say to me: "you study and study, but you could already be an organist" [*łucys się i łucys, musi jus mug byś być łorganistom*].

Precisely for such a social advancement, so that his children could "further their education" (both my sisters are university graduates, one a lecturer in econometrics at the University in Lublin), my father drove or walked (over 20 km) to Lublin for many years to check if there was an opportunity to buy a caretaker's flat with a job for our two hectares of land. But no one wanted to buy the land, nor was it possible to find a vacant caretaker's flat.

Ratkowski *Buying back the caretaker's flat along with the caretaker's post? Like buying an office under Louis XIV in France.*

Kowalik It was different, because there you had bought among your own, and for us, the city, the "town dwellers" [*mieszckie ludzie*], was a completely different entity, closed to us, a dream world! Let me tell you about my first encounter with city food. Shortly before the war, some daredevil opened a shop in a small rented room, which a couple of us boys helped to finish off (we carried boards, rammed sand for the cement floor). Incidentally, the shop did not last because the village then returned to a natural economy. He gave us a choice as payment: sugar cubes or mustard. I, for one, chose mustard because I was educated: I knew that it was not eaten after dinner ("mustard after dinner")[1], so I decided to try the delicacy before dinner, which I did in the field, probably so as not to share it with anyone. I didn't use the delicacy for a long time afterwards.

Sad to say, it was only the war and the new regime that opened up avenues of promotion, yet no one from my village but me and my sisters graduated from university until the 1960s.

Chudziński *So your "class background", the term that is so unfashionable today, strongly influenced your opportunities and ideological choices?*

Kowalik Of course, with class-based resentments and even class-based dreams. Our village was adjacent to a large landed estate of a Count's family. My father had vehemently supported land reform, so in accordance with his beliefs didn't go there to earn money, but my mother did. She went for what are known as quarters [*ćwiercie*]. Her work mainly consisted of picking and carrying in quarter-quart (25 kg) baskets of beets and potatoes. That's how she knew that after the wheat was harvested and raked, there were short ears left that were not picked up by the rake. We would go at dawn "for the ears", from which you could make white bread that "smelled like the city" (we ourselves only grew rye, cabbage and potatoes on the poor land). Mother was a deeply religious person, but at the same time she had a cult of bread, of grain, so that nothing would go to waste. So she didn't think she was committing a sin. I didn't confess to that either, although of stealing one sugar beet (a delicacy roasted on the fire) I did. But the governor (that's someone between the landlord and the carver) didn't like it. He had a habit of going round the estate in the morning in a two-horse carriage, and when he saw us, he would drive swiftly straight at us. This very dream haunted me for years: horses rushing at me, and it was a matter of jumping off not too early because he could still turn on us and not too late. My mother did not curse, but spoke with a sense of wrongness: "He won't take it himself and he won't give it to us" [*Taki to sum nie weźnie i num nie do.*] (her language only improved considerably thanks to radio and then television).

Paweł Kozłowski *One of those choices you made was to go to the school for training scientific personnel at the KC [the Central Committee of the Communist Party]?*

Ratkowski *This school was also a response to the dramatic situation of Poland, which had lost three-quarters of its intelligentsia during the war.*

Kowalik That was the motive of the managers, of those in power. In my case, it was an ideological choice. I believed in socialism at the time. I had evidence of this [that socialism works]: the parcelling out of the estates of a rather parasitic social stratum, which its most enlightened representatives admitted. This is what Paweł Czartoryski—with whom I worked for a long time at the Institute of the History of Science of the Polish Academy of Sciences—called it in a conversation with me. And above all, universities [were] open to the poor and [there were] jobs for everyone, [just like] health care, holidays, sanatoriums. In 1948, I myself travelled around villages and small towns in the Podkarpacie region, and sought out talented poor young people [*Janków Muzykantów*] for preparatory courses at universities [*Kursy Przygotowawcze na Wyższe Uczelnie*]. I travelled as an activist of the Cracow AZWM "Życie" [Akademicki Związek Walki Młodych "Życie", Academic Association of Young Fighters "Life"].

But I still want to mention my cooperative adventure, because it influenced my choices. I think it was at the end of 1942 or the beginning of 1943 that I started to work in a labour cooperative already established in Bychawa, hidden from the Germans under a private company. Partly because of the building we were housed in, and partly because of our views, way of life, way of remuneration; we were called the "Judenrat", which was the equivalent of the pre-war Judeo-Communism [*Żydokomuna*]. For indeed we were an ideological community believing in Edward Abramowski's

"Cooperative Republic". We also benefited from some correspondence courses combined with ideological pamphlets. It was in this milieu that I received a booklet by Ludwik Krzywicki, which made a great impression on me. Its original title was: "Sic itur ad virtutem", better than the later Polish one ("Such shall be your ways" [*Takiemi będą drogi wasze*]), while it should have been: "Behold the path to virtue (but probably also valour)". Have ambition. Be proud. Have a name. In deeds strike steel. A debtor are you. Because of its Young Poland-esque, almost Nietzschean language, it is difficult to digest when reading it today. But during the occupation—as it was written during Russian captivity for the frustrated youth after the fall of the 1905 revolution—it spoke to me better than a catechism. As a matter of fact, these were my commandments. Especially as my last actual confession in Lublin next to the smoking Majdanek [concentration camp] became an outburst of rebellion against a God who allows such things.

Kozłowski *What memories have you retained from the Institute of Social Sciences at the Central Committee of the Communist Party* [Instytut Nauk Społecznych przy KC PZPR, INS]?

Kowalik As good as it gets. First of all, for me, it was a liberation from a job for which I was absolutely unsuited. I studied law. First, I did a three-year programme at the Teodor Duracz Law School in two years. Then I went on to a fourth (master's) year at the University of Warsaw. But I got an assignment to work at the court after [only] two years. Two months of apprenticeship and an appointment as an assessor with the right to try cases (mainly so-called squabbles, of course, but also on the basis of the draconian Socialist Labour Discipline Act). After six months, I ended up in the Ministry of Justice, developing scripts.

However, all the time I wanted to move away from law, to become an economist. I was also already an assistant at Duracz School. The post-graduate studies [*aspirantura*] at the Institute were liberating. And the environment turned out to be exceptionally interesting: Bronisław Baczko, Leszek Kołakowski, Tadeusz Kroński, Helena Eilstein, Włodzimierz Brus, Kazimierz Łaski, Stanisław Kuziński. Adam Schaff deserves credit for creating conditions conducive to relatively free intellectual development. He shielded us when we were attacked by the party hardliners [*beton*]. We had greater access to literature, time to study, and a lot of free discussion, though, of course, this took place within a certain framework which was broken at the beginning of 1956 by Khrushchev's famous speech on Stalin's crimes. It turned out that the Institute was a breeding ground for revisionism.

I was also fortunate in that, due to the subject of my thesis—I wanted to write about Ludwik Krzywicki as an economist—Oskar Lange became my supervisor. He was a fully assimilated Pole/European with German roots, a polyhistor like my hero [i.e. Krzywicki]. Lange was a bad [public] speaker, but in an intimate setting an extremely interesting interlocutor. I went to see him at the end of 1951 with an arrogant attitude. For, in accordance with the general belief in party circles, I had been warned that I was going to a bourgeois economist. It was believed that, although a socialist, he was not only a great expert in neoclassical economics but also its committed practitioner, that is a bourgeois economist.

I always feel ashamed when I think back to my first conversations, when I arrogantly opposed him with "true" Marxism or socialism. And he, with Olympian calmness, usually began his long monologue: "Perhaaaps [*Być moooże*] you are right ...

[*macie rację*]" (he always used this formal form of "you", by the way, also with his friends from the 1930s), and the argument would follow in such a conciliatory tone that sometimes only after I left did I realise that I had been wrong.

Studying Krzywicki facilitated my entry into the unknown world of non-communist socialism, mainly into the milieu of the pre-war Institute of Social Economy [*Instytut Gospodarstwa Społecznego*, IGS], which he headed. Initially, it was Lange who opened the door to this community for me, followed by Tadeusz Szturm de Sztrem. The latter was the actual organiser of the Institute, its scientific secretary, editor of most publications, and its soul. He was a legendary man and Piłsudski's aide-de-camp in the Legions (a.k.a. "Little"). He was a socialist of the early Christian type, known as a "little Christ" [*Chrystusik*] due to his attitude and anchoritic lifestyle. I came to Szturm de Sztrem shortly after his release from prison (convicted in a brass trial together with Kazimierz Pużak). Through him I met Edward Strzelecki, Jan Topiński, Stanisław Szwalbe, Wincenty Jastrzębski (one of the heads of the IGS, formerly a participant in the Russian Revolution, whom I persuaded to write his memoirs), general Adam Uziembło, economic historian Natalia Gąsiorowska, statistician Edward Grabowski. Also socialists from outside the "licensed" Polish Socialist Party [*Polska Partia Socjalistyczna*, PPS]: [Józef] Grzecznarowski, [Antoni] Pajdak. They all sharply opposed socialism to communism.

In 1956 or 1957, as soon as the political atmosphere improved, we made an attempt to recreate the IGS, but we ended up creating a unit with that name at the Main School of Planning and Statistics [*Szkoła Główna Planowania i Statystyki*, SGPiS]. We also attempted, mainly with the aforementioned Uziembło, to recreate the Free University of Poland [*Wolna Wszechnica Polska*], where I was to take up the Chair of Economics.

So when I left the INS in 1956 (already as an employee), not only had the communist environment of the INS changed significantly under the influence of events, but I also had many acquaintances and friends who were non-communist socialists.

Kozłowski *And who taught you economics?*

Kowalik Lange taught me less about economics, he talked more about people in economics, about the centres where he studied, about different approaches. And above all, about politicians and socialists, socialist thinkers. I had come across economics earlier, for the first time in Lębork-Wejherowo, in 1947. And in what capacity! I worked in Lębork in the political department of the district office, but as a censorship officer. What I didn't tell you before was that I had already worked as an accountant in this institution for six months in Lublin, and I left for the Western Territories[2] offended that they didn't want to give me a political job. And I wanted to "serve the revolution", not the party. A vacancy in neighbouring Wejherowo meant that [I finally took up the position of censor and] I received the manuscript of *Introduction to Economics* [*Wstęp do ekonomiki*] by the Poznań [neoclassical] scholar Edward Taylor. I gave my consent to print it without realising that I was exceeding my authority. Books and newspapers were reserved for provincial offices.

The next step was Kraków, where I completed my first year at the High School of Social Sciences [*Wyższa Szkoła Nauk Społecznych*], founded by the Workers' University Association [*Towarzystwo Uniwersytetów Robotniczych*] (mainly by the Białas brothers). It was taught by interesting people: Stefan and Konstanty Grzybowski. The latter, who was rather conservative, gave interesting lectures on socialist theories, and Zygmunt Gross was supposed to teach "exercises in the theory and practice of socialism", but left or fled abroad. Bolesław Drobner taught rhetorics. Economics was taught by Adam Krzyżanowski's not-very-intellectually-sophisticated [*średniego lotu*] brother, Witold. Jan Czarkowski taught economic policy.

In the Duracz school, I passed economics under Professor Jan Zygmunt Wyrozembski. And at the University, Edward Lipiński was still teaching (in 1951). He no longer taught economics at this time, even though he later became dean of the economics faculty. He had been "relegated" to history [of economic ideas]. At that time, he dealt with the history of Polish economic thought after Copernicus. He wrote a book on the latter's economic views. But he also dealt with little-known figures. That is why it was later joked that he not only wrote the history of Polish thought but created it.

The first encounter was funny. I went to him with a very good grade in my index to ask for my credit. He gave me a "3" [the lowest passing grade]. When I pointed out to him that he had made a mistake, he said: With me, you can only get a "3".

Chudziński *It started not very encouragingly …*

Kowalik I came into closer contact with him when Lipiński was already dean of the Faculty of Economics at the University of Warsaw [Uniwersytet Warszawski, UW]. From my conversations with Lange about Keynes and Kalecki, I understood that everything had to be done to get the English economist's major work—*The General Theory…*—published quickly. The long-overdue Polish translation was the property of the Polish Economic Society, which Lipiński had presided over for several decades. From him I received the typescript of the translation made by Michał Kalecki and Stanisław Rączkowski. Jan Drewnowski edited the text. It was also to him that I owed my first personal contact with Kalecki. During our initial meetings, I realised that Kalecki resented the fact that few people knew about his precedence [over Keynes], and especially that those in Keynes's circle who knew about it from Kalecki had not told him.

Chudzinski *When was this book published in Polish?*

Kowalik As early as 1956, published by PWN [publishing house], of course, with an "appropriate" [*ekwilibrystyczna*] preface setting Keynes against Marxism. This was the beginning of my twelve-year collaboration with PWN, mainly in the publication of the *Library of the Works in Economics* [*Biblioteka Dzieł Ekonomii*] (Adam Smith, David Ricardo, John S. Mill and others) and the *Works* [*Dzieła*] of Ludwik Krzywicki (where we managed to employ Tadeusz Szturm de Sztrem).

In order to not return to publishing matters, I will mention that from Lange I derived a kind of mission to assimilate the thinkers of the past into Polish literature. I also collaborated with Książka i Wiedza [publishing house, KiW]. I was one of the initiators and editors of the *Library of Socialist Thought* [*Biblioteka Myśli Socjalistycznej*], and I initiated the publication of the *Library of Studies on Marxism* [*Biblioteka Studiów and Marksizmem*] (the only country in the "camp" where studies ON Marxism were possible). This came to an end in 1968, when Adam Bromberg of PWN [Polish Scientific Publishers] and Mieczysław Orlański of KiW ["Książka i Wiedza" publishing house], who was the main inspiration of the two Libraries mentioned above, were expelled from Poland.

This was also the time of my, quite peculiar, farewell to PWN. In 1967, a textbook on the *History of World Economic Thought 1870-1950* [*Historia powszechnej myśli ekonomicznej 1870-1950*] by three authors, including me, was published. After the March "anti-revisionist/anti-Zionist" campaign of 1968, a new edition appeared without my name, and with the assurance that it was the first textbook of its kind in socialist countries ....

The aforementioned experiences and relationships determined that I was entrusted to lead the team preparing the critical edition of the *Works* [*Dzieła*] of Oskar Lange (eight hefty volumes) and of Michał Kalecki (six volumes in Polish edited mainly by Jerzy Osiatyński, and in English—exclusively by him).

Kozłowski *Lange, Brus, Lipiński. You had the good fortune to move in a circle of exceptional people.*

Kowalik Well, "A debtor you are ...". Of the "locals" I should also add Czesław Bobrowski and Michał Kalecki. I think I owed my close contacts [with them], which turned into friendships of varying closeness, to two circumstances. I was always interested in the biographies, the becoming of intellectuals, scholars, and economists. This gave me a title to a certain impertinence. Biographical questions have something of a confessional quality about them. The questioner becomes a confidant, which is generally hugely conducive to rapprochement.

Sometimes such questions had an unexpected effect. It was Lange who drew my attention to how Rosa Luxemburg's work and theory are, in a sense, a precursor to Keynesian theory. He told me that Rosa Luxemburg's theory of markets (about which I wrote my habilitation thesis), and in relation to Congress Poland, the theory of "organic incorporation", had been taught to him by his not-very-literate [*mało piśmienny*] father, who was a textile factory owner. His factory produced for eastern markets. He believed that without access to the Russian market, his factory could not exist. And indeed, after the 1905 revolution, when there was a downturn, and at the beginning of the interwar period, a lot of factories were set on fire in order to at least receive insurance compensation. This was the result of cutting off the Polish lands from the Russian market.

Ratkowski *A similar situation arose after the 1863 uprising, when a customs border between Privislinskiy kray*[3] *and the empire was erected as repression. Then part of the textile industry from Łódź moved to Białystok.*

Kowalik The second circumstance conducive to rapprochement is my tendency to "argue and persist". To argue with the great ones as well. With all of those mentioned above, it ended well. But not, for example, with Julian Hochfeld, although I tried. He never treated me other than as one of the seminar participants. I myself also gave up after the first meeting on recording Władysław Bieńkowski's memoirs, because I got the impression that he was playing with me, manipulating me. I recorded more than 20 tapes with Czesław Bobrowski, from which he later made a book (*Memories from the Century* [*Wspomnienia ze stulecia*]). But I couldn't say that this paved the way for our friendship to develop. On the contrary, I felt that I shouldn't have asked some questions. Let me tell you about one, which has a more general value. At the end of our conversations, I asked how he, a social liberal, explained his collaboration with the communists. He replied that he had to think about the answer. He began the next meeting, to my great surprise, by reading out his *credo* from a sheet of paper. There was something about this gesture that precluded conversation. Almost like a statement. But at the end, he added: "Sir, the pre-war governments were also abhorrent, and yet I cooperated with them".

Chudziński *And then, wherever you took your studies, you became a lecturer immediately after graduating ....*

Kowalik Times were such that this occurred even before I graduated. During my final year of law studies at the UW, I taught economics at the "Duracz

School". Also, after finishing my studies at the INS, I taught economics.

Kozlowski *In those dangerous times, did these giants of our economy say anything that would have been frowned upon at the time?*

Kowalik Before 1956, it was difficult to have frank conversations. Here I would contrast Lange with Lipiński. Lange was always cautious in his judgements; he did not lie, but he kept quiet about many things. In fact, it was in Lange's very nature to avoid harsh judgements, as he was an incredibly kind-hearted man. There was once a nasty article by [Wacław] Zbyszewski about Lange in "Kultura" in Paris, with a passus stating that "like every cripple, Lange hated normal people" [*"jak każdy kaleka Lange nienawidził normalnych ludzi"*]. Well, indeed, an idea not of this earth! Henryk Dunajewski's reaction best captures the essence of Lange's benevolence: he recalled that in our circle we used to repeat: "How lucky it is that Lange is not a woman, because he would have been pregnant every nine months".

Lipiński was different. He always said what he thought, ranted at the bureaucrats, used strong words, including on the phone, and also towards himself. In a file entitled "The Polish Ball" [*"Bal Polski"*], he collected various errors, paradoxes ridiculing the system. Once, out of ignorance, I said something stupid about Katyń[4], for which he reprimanded me, but it was in such a tone that it was not taken too painfully. He was a member of the PZPR for a long time, but his whole behaviour contradicted party discipline, hierarchy. When he signed the famous Letter 34 in the early 1960s and then revoked it at the behest of the party, he was ashamed, saying, for example: "I behaved like the rag that lies there".

Kozłowski *And Kalecki?*

Kowalik Yet another personality. Kalecki returned to the country for the first time in 1946, and many things troubled him. Not only the reaction to the Kielce pogrom, anti-Semitism, but he was also concerned about the immaturity of the ruling cadre. He saw himself as an advisor to the most important people in the state, but found it difficult to talk sensibly with them. He repeated to me, for example, a conversation he had with Eugeniusz Szyr, who outlined before him huge plans for industrialisation. To Kalecki's reaction that there would be a shortage of food, that this would cause inflation, Szyr said: "Then we will take the peasants' grain by force". Kalecki replied: "If you take it one year, the next year you won't have anything left to take". Discouraged, he left and did not return until 1955. In the USA, in turn, he took a hard look at MacCarthyism and the infiltration of the UN by US secret services. At the time, he worked at the UN, led by Dag Hammarskjöld as secretary, and considered him a poor economist. Anyway, he resigned after some conflict around communist China, which he wanted to include in reports.

Kozłowski *And here in Poland, the thaw was beginning …*

Kowalik At the end of 1955, it was even more than a thaw, especially in the literary circles, because there was a considerable mental ferment. Kalecki's first speeches were a revelation to us. That precision of language, an impressive knowledge of facts subjected to leftist analysis, especially of the American economy. He won the hearts and minds of almost everyone, and while Lange did not actually have a school, because he was too universal, with views that were not very profiled, the "Kalecki school", known for its sharply defined views, was quickly established. Two teams worked under his leadership: one on capitalist economics and the other on socialist economics.

Kozłowski *What was Kalecki like in private?*

Kowalik

[He was characterised by] Absolute integrity and modesty, but modesty about things other than scientific theory. He believed that what he propounded was simply the truth. He was angry with Lange, who, after presenting Kalecki's business cycle theory, wrote more or less as follows: Many such models can be made, which depends on the assumptions made. Kalecki, on the other hand, believed that he had not presented a model, but a theory, implicitly the only theory that was true. He hardly consulted literature. He had a few economics books in his library, but they were read from cover to cover .... It was as if he was taking the book apart. I once saw at his place, I think, a book by Sen, later a Nobel laureate, heavily crossed, with numerous remarks. Kalecki lectured only himself, his own views, hence his great reticence to accept lecture assignments, because he could not lecture much if he only preached his own views. His lecture at the SGPiS usually lasted half an hour, and he wanted to fill the rest of the time with questions and answers. But—as Kazimierz Łaski, perhaps his most faithful and eminent pupil, once said—he "explained" with the same words, only louder.

He once stated that when it comes to investment decisions, there are at least three theories. At this I whispered to a colleague that we had an extraordinary event: Kalecki was starting to become a historian of economic thought. But after a moment, he added: "I created them all myself". And here he lectures on these three theories.

In general, Kalecki was incredibly critical of capitalism. He believed that there was a strong tendency for capitalism to stagnate. One cannot therefore take the development, the dynamism of capitalism, for granted. It was in this connection that he used to say: "I go further than Marx" (because Marx assumed that the rush to accumulation was unstoppable until it collapsed). He had a particular aversion to American capitalism, mainly because of its imperial tendencies. The peak of his dislike was triggered by the US intervention in Vietnam. I have met no one else who took that war more emotionally than Kalecki. It was as if this war was going on right next door, across our border. He spoke repeatedly of the killing of innocent Vietnamese peasants, of settlements destroyed by napalm. And then there was the shameful March '68 [events in Poland], which Kalecki called the "Reichstag for the poor". The more strongly he committed himself to socialism, the deeper his disillusionment became. He asked: Can "they" withdraw my books from libraries? Or: "The only optimistic thing is that I am already 70 years old". And indeed he died before reaching the age of 71.

Returning to capitalism, perhaps the most enduring element of his aversion to this system was the issue of unemployment, brought up from the Great Depression of the 1930s. It was actually the obsession of his life.

Ratkowski *How right!*

Kowalik Well, yes, but he also saw that danger in socialism, which for us "Young Turks" was pure abstraction. In 1956, I was editor-in-chief of *Życie Gospodarcze* [Economic Life], and we fought for workers' self-government, although he opposed this for going too far. For us, the Yugoslav model was the pinnacle of dreams at the time, and he [would say]: Self-government breeds unemployment, because the workforce is not interested in sharing the wealth earned with the growing number of workers.

Kozłowski *But after all, he wrote the text …*

Kowalik Yes, he wrote an excellent article on the balance between self-government and planning, but that was the result of long discussions, mainly with

Brus, who was perhaps the only one in our environment who influenced him. In defending the compromise between planning and local government decentralisation, Kalecki was, of course, more right than we were.

Kalecki was a difficult debater, incredibly distrustful of acknowledged truths. A certain Yugoslavian reflected his character well. When he came from him to Lipiński, he said of Kalecki: "What a strange man, as soon as you start agreeing with him, he no longer agrees". Anyway, there were many anecdotes about this.

As a person, he was exemplary in his personal interactions, modes and honest. After giving his lecture, when he drove from SGPiS to the Planning Commission in his work car, he would give us a lift, but only to Hoża Street, and not two hundred metres further, to the Palace of Culture and Science, where our offices were located, apologising that he did not want to abuse the company car.

Kozłowski *Almost at the same time as Kalecki, Bobrowski returned to the country.*

Kowalik Czesław Bobrowski is the most colourful character I have ever known. Brilliant intelligence, golden-tongued and, in addition, a beautiful man. After he was removed from the presidency of the Central Planning Office, he first "ambassadored" in Stockholm, then settled in Paris. In 1956, he began to be encouraged from many quarters to return. I myself wrote to him on behalf of the renewed *Życie Gospodarcze* team with the rather obsequious: "Your place in the country".

Bobrowski enjoyed great authority as the creator of the successful three-year plan[5] and the associated myth of the émigré exile, a dismissed activist after the ideological vendetta known as the "Central Planning Office Discussion" [*Dyskusja CUP-owska*]. I was all the more surprised when he finally arrived in the country in September or

October 1956. During a prolonged conversation in the editorial office [of *Życie Gospodarcze*], he suddenly said that we had to finish now because he had an appointment with Hilary Minc. I experienced a great lesson in tolerance, in openness. Here was Bobrowski taking almost the first steps towards his (already in the offing) conqueror. From later conversations, I know that he was fascinated by Minc. He saw something of the Polish nobleman or romantic in him. This obsession with heavy industry stemmed from Minc's experience of the 1939 war. He reportedly regretted that in 1939, Polish soldiers had to go to the front without weapons; he even said: barefoot. He said that such a situation must not be allowed to be repeated.

Ratkowski *Was he treating this formulation as a metaphor, or did he really have this view of some fraction of pre-September [1939] reality?*

Kowalik I have no idea, maybe they didn't go to the front barefoot, but that they volunteered for the army barefoot, I believe it (I myself deprived my mother and then my father of shoes when I went to school in winter). At the very least, according to Bobrowski, Minc's obsession with forcible industrialisation stemmed from just that ….

Chudziński *Bobrowski, as I recall, was a supporter of workers' self-government. He promoted the Yugoslav model.*

Kowalik Yes. We read in the editorial office a reproduced Polish translation of his French book [entitled] "Socialist Yugoslavia" ["Socjalistyczna Jugosławia"]. That's also why we wanted to have him in Poland, because it was he who discovered Yugoslavia for us, the model for the "Polish road to socialism". Nevertheless, despite Tito's authoritarianism, this version of the system was much more democratic than the Soviet model.

Chudziński *With these great figures in the background, your scientific path was shaped …*

Kowalik At first, my ambitions were not academic. I think that if conditions had been better, I would have preferred to edit a left-wing monthly or quarterly magazine, possibly with a book and brochure publishing arm. I wanted to be useful mainly on the borderline between science and journalism. At the time, I was not familiar with the message at the end of Keynes' work, that essentially the world is ruled by ideas. Science, if it wants to be useful, has to wade through "directional ideas" [*"idee kierunkowe"*], as Stefan Czarnowski called them. I think I learned this from reading Krzywicki, who for many years played such a role. He did not become a scientist until he was middle aged.

My academic career was pretty standard. First, I was an assistant at the Duracz School, then I did my post-graduate studies at the Higher School of Social Sciences [Wyższa Szkoła Nauk Społecznych, WSNS], while also teaching journalism at the University of Warsaw. Among my students were Hanna Krall and Jerzy Urban. I remember that, probably during the holidays in 1957, the latter went to Egypt and Israel, and published a highly critical confrontation in "Po prostu" [magazine] of what I was teaching him and what he saw there, how the economy functioned there. In spite of his scepticism, he is grateful to me, I think, because then, when he dropped out of university (he was too intelligent to be a student), and when he was forbidden to work, I tried to help him somehow ….

Chudziński *This is after the article about Dr Marcinkowski from Kraków ….*

Ratkowski *It was said of him: "His totality Dr Marcinkowski" ["Jego totalność dr Marcinkowski"][6]. Anyway, the protagonist of this text was a tragic figure.*

Kowalik Yes, that was the point. He [Ubran] wrote for a while a column entitled "Dumping words" [*"Dumping słów"*] in *Życie Gospodarcze*, no longer under my direction, by the way.

Chudziński	*Let us return to your scientific career …*
Kowalik	I obtained my PhD for a book on Ludwik Krzywicki as an economist. I still managed to teach at the party's Institute of Social Sciences for a year or two before it was abolished. Then I taught at the Higher School of Social Sciences at the Central Committee of the Communist Party (until 1959). First studies abroad: I spent most of 1960 in Vienna to study Austro-Marxism. I continued this at the Amsterdam Institute of Social History, which houses a rich archive of Austrian and German social democracy. On my return I was no longer wanted at the party school because of my views. Well, precisely as a result of studying a different Marxism.
Kozłowski	*The fashion for revisionists was over.*
Kowalik	I was publicly attacked together with Juliusz Wacławek from the newspaper "Trybuna Ludu" [People's Tribune] by the secretary of the Central Committee, [Witold] Jarosiński. Somehow, by mutual agreement, I was transferred to the Polish Academy of Sciences. I landed in the Department of Economic Sciences, headed by Bronisław Minc (by the way, [he was a person of] much lower [intellectual] calibre than [his] brother Hilary). He was afraid of my writing, and I happened to be preoccupied with Rosa Luxemburg, her book *Accumulation of Capital*. He wanted me to make a declaration that I was a Marxist. Although in my mind I was one ("a real one!"), I found such a declaration derogatory. In 1963, he dismissed me, even though I had written my habilitation thesis by the deadline he had set for me. After the interventions of Kalecki and Lange, [Stefan] Żółkiewski arranged for me to be transferred to the Department of the History of Science, Education and Technology. Professor Bohdan Suchodolski demanded that I deal with the nineteenth century. And that's when I wrote *The History of Polish*

Economic Thought After 1865 [*Historia polskiej myśli ekonomicznej po 1865 r*]. I finished it in 1973, but at that time, even without being read, it was not included in the [publishing] plan. It was not published until nineteen years later, in 1992. The habilitation thesis was more fortunate: it was published after eight years. It was translated into Italian, then into Spanish.

I consider it fortunate that my book on Lange, which was submitted to the head of department in 1974, was never published. It was rejected by several publishing houses, sometimes without being read. I haven't gotten around to modifying it yet. Actually to re-writing it. A difficult task, because it has to be, at least indirectly, a reckoning with oneself.

The next stage was to work on lectures for the semi-legal "Flying University" ["Uniwersytet Latający"], which I co-organised. Of the three intended, only the first part was published: "Spory o ustrój społeczno-ekonomiczny w Polsce, 1944–1948" [Disputes over the Socio-economic System in Poland, 1944–1948]. It was published illegally by Mirosław Chojecki, who once told me that he had 500 copies stashed away somewhere in his cellar, but cannot remember where. So maybe they will be found one day. The second part has already been written and a third is planned. After martial law and my two-year stay in the United States, I took up comparative economics, which is examined in the book "Współczesne systemy ekonomiczne" [*Contemporary Economic Systems*].

Chudziński *What were the twists and turns of your political affiliations?*

Kowalik For a long time, I didn't want to be in any party. In the beginning, I rather looked up to the peasant parties, because my father was a peasant. And then I liked PPS [*Polska Partia Socjalistyczna*, Polish Socialist Party] better, but it was becoming more and more (due to its social composition) an intellectual-bourgeois party. When I was accepted into the PPR [*Polska Partia Robotnicza*, Polish Workers' Party], I was even asked why I would join them and not the PPS. I think I said something about the embourgeoisement [*zmieszczanienie*] of the latter party. Perhaps there was a peasant anti-intellectual resentment behind it. It was probably no coincidence that at university I was called a "a smallholder shepherd" ["pastuszek małorolny"] .... I think an anecdote about Włodzimierz Reczek—a PPS activist—would be spot on. When a lady asked him about the difference between the PPS and the PPR, he replied: Just look at their faces.

So then I joined the PPR. Then, as a natural progression, I became a member of the PZPR [*Polska Zjednoczona Partia Robotnicza*, Polish United Workers' Party], paradoxically two weeks before the row over Yugoslavia.

In the summer of 1948, another episode occurred that gave me much food for thought. On my way to the unification congress of the youth movement in Wrocław, where ZMP [*Związek Młodzieży Polskiej*, Polish Youth Association] was established, I met Tadeusz Hanuszek in the Planty park in Kraków. He was sitting on a bench, sad and depressed. I asked why, and he replied that he felt as if he was putting his organisation in a coffin. At the unification congress, he presided over the ceremony.

Kozłowski *He was in the Union of Independent Socialist Youth?*

Kowalik No, he was chairman of the AZWM "Życie" [*Akademicki Związek Walki Młodych "Życie"*, Academic Youth Fighting Association "Life"] and a PPR activist. But he reacted badly to the levelling [*glajchszaltyzacja*] of the youth movement. A few days after coming to the Institute of Social Sciences, Seweryn Bialer (he fled to the West in

1955) told me in the corridor about the suicide of Tadeusz Borowski. With the comment or suggestion that it was a political suicide. This made a strong impression on me. I was enthralled with Borowski as a reader and listener when I attended the lively discussions of the young artists and writers club (I think that was its name) in 1948 or 1949. It was he and Stefan Żółkiewski that I remember most from there. The meetings were held in the Jewish theatre, on the site where the "Victoria" hotel now stands. When he spoke, he would spread and fold his arms, as if seizing people and saying: "To the gas Gentlemen, to the gas…". That is how I remember him.

Chudziński *But there are no traces of an ideological crisis in Borowski's work. We talked about this in the 1980s with Andrzej Wasilewski, who considered himself one of his closest colleagues; they worked together on the editorial board of "Nowa Kultura" ["New Culture"]. Wasilewski said that Borowski was going through a serious personal drama. He had fallen in love with some journalist from the "Sztandar Młodych" ["Banner of the Young"] and was, after all, involved with his Maria, whom he immortalised in literature. He dragged her from Sweden, she had just been in hospital, giving birth to a daughter, and he committed suicide exactly one day before he was to pick them both up from hospital …. Wasilewski claimed that Borowski could not cope with this dilemma.*

Kowalik I don't think it is an unfounded rumour. My point is different. Here I came full of faith to the forge of party cadres, and the first thing I found out is that a man of such prominence, for me a paragon of ideology, can commit political suicide. The first strong blemish on my faith.

Kozłowski *And soon afterwards, your fight for reform began.*

Kowalik A very moderate reform. In May 1956, a group of colleagues from the INS, due to my editorial interests, and perhaps a little literary ones, persuaded me to become the editor of a biweekly magazine they had their eye on: "Życie Gospodarcze". With the intention of rejuvenating and radicalising the magazine, we carried out a kind of fusion of our team of young economists with the newspaper's team. Our group marked its arrival with a declaration entitled "Our position" [*"Nasze stanowisko"*]. Years later, one has the urge to summarise it by saying: "I would like to, but I am afraid" [*"I chciał(a)bym i boję się"*]. The direction of the reforms was, however, quite clear: a reduction in the ubiquity of the state, workers' participation, greater autonomy for enterprises.

This began in May 1956, and I was dismissed already in 1957, at the same time as *Po prostu* [weekly] was closed down and 34 other editors-in-chief were "removed" by the Secretariat of the Central Committee. We were exceptionally allowed to choose my successor from among ourselves. We proposed Jan Główczyk from Kraków.

Kozłowski ... *Who then ran the magazine for many years.*

Kowalik He was a great editor. But was he too much of a procrastinator [*kunktatorski*], and opportunistic? It is not for me to judge. He certainly could not have continued my political line, openly fighting for reforms, attacking the conservatives [*konserwa*] longer than until the aforementioned turning of the screws [*przykręcenie śruby*] in 1959. Well, perhaps the example of *Polityka* [weekly] shows that he could have behaved better in March 1968. Especially since even Gomułka (I know this from Bobrowski) thought that an economic magazine should have more freedom in its criticism. That was when I said goodbye to *Życie Gospodarcze* for many years.

The reason for the change was, in my opinion, primarily a conflict with the then deputy prime minister Piotr Jaroszewicz. I remember two significant conversations. Bobrowski repeated his words to me: "If you don't calm them down, I will stifle them". I myself also had the opportunity to hear from Jaroszewicz: "You, with our money, are undermining the party and the government!" ["*Wy, za nasze pieniądze, podgryzacie partię i rząd!*"], and it was the phrase "on our money" that stuck in my memory the most, although the system of settlement was such that it was not clear whether the magazine benefited from subsidies.

In the middle of 1957, I went to Moscow, convinced that the thaw was happening there too. With all my naivety, in their publishing office, of which I was a guest, I gave a lecture on the Polish transition, the June workers' revolt, the Polish October. I heard no questions, apart from perfunctory praise. [Perhaps due to] Coldness or fear. Only a few days later, when Khrushchev got rid of Molotov, Malenkov and others from the party leadership, did tongues wag a little. But, for example, I was simply not believed that in Poland land is privately owned....

Kozłowski *You had contacts with the "Crooked Circle" Club [Klub „Krzywego Koła"]?*

Kowalik: Almost from the beginning, until its dissolution in 1962, I was a member, an active participant, representing rather conciliatory views, initially pro-Gomułka. There I met Aleksander Małachowski, Jan Józef Lipski and many others, but only with Jan Strzelecki did I become friends. It was certainly one of the most interesting circles, although unofficially, it was constantly being said that it was created by people connected with the secret police.

Chudziński *When did the paths of the scientific community in Poland and the authorities of the time finally diverge?*

Kowalik As far as the economy is concerned, it is quite simple. All of Gomułka's reformist achievements were prepared before his return to power. Let me remind you: the drafts of the law on workers' councils, the law on the company fund and the regulation of the Council of Ministers increasing the powers of enterprise directors were prepared in September and October 1956 by Kalecki, Brus and Szymon Jakubowicz, the most active members of the Commission chaired by Jaroszewicz. Gomułka himself was distrustful of workers' self-government and the independence of enterprises, but he could not fail to give these projects a go. He had to give something to society.

But from 1957 onwards, Gomułka began to withdraw decisively from all these reforms. He ignored the Economic Council. Its chairman, Oskar Lange, who in public opinion was regarded as his advisor, told me that the only one-on-one conversation he had with Gomułka took place in a parliamentary corridor. The gist of it boiled down to the sentence [spoken by Gomułka]: "While you were touring Western universities, I was in prison". In 1959 came the decisive turning of the screw. Also on the cultural "front".

Chudziński *But these precautions did not save you from being expelled from the party.*

Kowalik Well, those were very different times. I was suspended in March 1968 and expelled in October. I was thrown out, incidentally, by Zofia Gomułkowa [wife of Władysław Gomułka] herself, who clearly regretted that with such a good background I had wasted away like that. She said half-heartedly something like this: "He had entered a rotten intelligentsia environment" ["*Wszedł w zgniłe środowisko inteligenckie*"]. I defended myself until the last moment, claiming that my place was in the party, because I was the one who represented true socialism. And then Jan Rychlewski, invited on behalf of the POP PZPR PAN [basic party organisation of the Polish United Workers' Party in the Polish Academy of Sciences] to a meeting of the

Provincial Party Control Committee, said to me: "Tadeusz! Brus, [Leszek] Kołakowski, [Bronisław] Baczko, Zakrzewska—all of them are already out of the party. What will you do in the party without your friends?". That was the final argument!

But those were different times, a different party, we were different. I remember the first threat of removal in 1957. When I told Brus about it and he responded: "So what?", I was relieved, because it still seemed to me that it would be tantamount to being "blacklisted" [*"wilczy bilet"*]. This time [in 1968], it had a small practical consequence: I was no longer formally in charge of the workshop for editing the works of Lange and Kalecki, a workshop I have already mentioned. But I remained its actual head. I was also not allowed to complete my research on the state of economics in the world, conducted for UNESCO. Previously, we had extremely interesting discussions on this topic in Paris with eminent scientists from other disciplines. This is how I met [Claude] Lévi-Strauss and [Jean] Piaget, for example. This was research that was initially headed by Lange, with Brus and Ignacy Sachs taking part. And I also had to give up a year's grant from the Ford Foundation [as a result of expulsion from the party].

Anyway, parallel to our presence in the party, we had semi-legal meetings in the 1960s, attended by Brus, Kołakowski, Baczko, Krzysztof Pomian, [Jerzy] Tepicht, Janina Zakrzewska, Flora and Władysław Bieńkowski, Ryszard Herczyński and (I think) Stefan Żółkiewski. These were interesting discussions in private flats. Then we came up with the idea of mystifying the meetings with neutral topics in my workshop dealing formally with the edition of Kalecki's works. Secretary of the Department I [of the Polish Academy of Sciences], Żółkiewski would sign camouflaged, academic-sounding invitations.

Ratkowski *It was not a bloody regime.*

Kowalik It wasn't. I had a lot of freedom to study, the barrier was the issue of publication, also problems with passports, trips abroad, but even that worked. Lange's intervention and, after his death, Lipiński's or Żółkiewski's worked at least half the time. In the 1970s, for example, I travelled several times to Italy for a few days of Marxist studies organised by the well-known socialist Lelio Basso. With limited opportunities to work in the country, I took advantage of scholarship trips. Among other things, this enabled me to spend more than ten years in six different Western countries. In Czechoslovakia, I would probably have been a tram driver, or returned to cap making.

Kozłowski *However, you did not have classes with students?*

Kowalik In a way, fortunately. When Professor [Edmund] Dąbrowski of SGPiS died in 1965[7], I was offered the chair of comparative economics, which was pioneering at the time. Minister [Henryk] Golański signed the appointment after consulting with the Provincial Committee of the party. But when the Vice-Dean, in a conversation with Andrzej Werblan, then head of the Science Department of the Central Committee, said in passing: "Kowalik is taking over the chair after Dąbrowski", Werblan was to respond: "Kowalik to the students? Never!". And the already signed appointment was withdrawn, as it was to turn out, happily for me. For I had somehow managed to hold on at PAN after 1968, and if I had been at the university, especially at SGPiS, I would certainly have lost my job, like many others even less critical [of the regime].

"To the students" I went at the Faculty of Economics, at the University of Warsaw, in the early 1970s. We also camouflaged this. I taught a special course for final-year students, as I had suggested, entitled "Economics and Socialism". But the program listed it as "Economics and Sociology" .... However, I wanted the students to meet outstanding people, so I invited Edward Lipiński to give a lecture. Immediately afterwards, the secret services took action, and I was not offered any lectures for the following year.

Again, I found myself with students, but also with many people of mature age at the "Flying University", which I have already mentioned. This involved a lot of emotions, fear, groups [of hostile people] being sent [against us] and detentions. Fortunately, with me it was done without brutality, rather in the form of asking numerous questions without waiting for an answer. I also invited Lipiński, Bobrowski and a few others. When I was detained in Poznań, a colonel from Warsaw flew in to talk to me. Sometimes there were paradoxical situations. I was not allowed to go to Wrocław, where I was supposed to give a lecture in a [catholic] cathedral about ... Rosa Luxemburg.

Chudziński *How did your milieu relate to Gierek and his ideas in the 1970s?*

Kowalik It's difficult for me to talk about my milieu, because after 1968, it disintegrated. Many friends went abroad. It wasn't just those who were brutally reminded that they were Jewish, and regardless of the degree of assimilation. It is often forgotten that this was an anti-revisionist fuss [*heca*]. For example, Janusz G. Zieliński of the SGPiS, one of the first to openly proclaim liberal views, also left. In 1970, Kalecki died. Brus lasted in the country until 1972, when he left for England in the dramatic circumstances of his son's illness. Bobrowski spent more time abroad (mainly in Algeria) than at home. That left Lipiński, whom I often visited at that time, Helena Hagemejer and Jerzy Osiatyński, still young at the time, who had been expelled from the SGPiS, and with whom I was then collaborating on the edition of the aforementioned two economists.

An unforgettable scene: In April 1968, Brus and I were walking down Nowy Świat Street [in Warsaw]. Brus was tall. And a prominent economist was walking towards us, equally tall and well acquainted with us both. He must have been looking for stars in the sunny sky not to spot us. When we reached the University, we met Klemens Szaniawski; he greeted us with a firm handshake and, silently turning his head quickly, walked away to hide his tears .... (This was, of course, about Brus, who had already been kicked out of the University). You Cracovians can have no idea what that vendetta meant socially. Some of my former colleagues didn't recognise me on the street either.

In 1971, we did a two-volume "Festschrift" (in one copy) for Brus's 50th anniversary. Both among the authors and at the "presentation ceremony" for the jubilarian; of the economists there were probably only Lipiński and Helena Hagemejer. People like Jadwiga and Jan Strzelecki, the Bieńkowskis (old) [Flora and Władysław], Nina and Witold Kula were dominant. In economic circles I was isolated. I tended to hang out with [*obracałem się*] sociologists and historians. A new milieu was slowly emerging, from which grew KOR [*Komitet Obrony Robotników*, Workers' Defence Committee], other seminar or political groups, the Society for Academic Courses [*Towarzystwo Kursów Naukowych*, TKN]. It was only after a few years that the atmosphere warmed up. Probably later in the capital than elsewhere. There was liberalisation without democratisation.

As for Gierek's reforms—an improvement in economic prospects based on credit—they confounded even economists like Stanisław Gomułka. Brus was sceptical because he constantly emphasised political democratisation as a condition for improving efficiency [of the economy]. We could not like the reform involving the creation of WOGs [*Wielkie Organizacje Gospodarcze*, Large Economic Organisations] borrowed from the GDR. After all, it was then that a "Poland of the industries" [*"Polska branżowa"*] was created, and dominated by interest groups.

The only prominent figure who wanted and knew how to play with the authorities was Józef Pajestka. Admittedly with huge compromises, he still defended, shall we say, the reformist-revisionist concept of reform. It was well known that he was in favour of some kind of participatory socialism.

Chudziński *And so we come to the second half of the 1970s, when you get close to KOR and, as a result, become an advisor to the Strike Committee at the Gdańsk Shipyard.*

Kowalik It was more of a closeness to certain people, because KOR was made up of very different individuals. With the main figures, the Commandos [*Komandosi*], cooperation was difficult. They liked to present us with a fait accompli. To manipulate. A well-known historian from the opposition once said to one of them: "It is difficult to work with you, and it is difficult to operate without you" [*"I z wami trudno współpracować i bez was trudno działać"*]. This was perfectly expressed in Andrzej Kijowski's diary. He wrote something like that he felt pressure to go into illegal activity. We also felt something like that. Each of us deluded ourselves that one was doing something useful, something one didn't want to give up. For example, an activist comes to our house, somewhat friendly with us, as she is expecting a call, probably from the Daily Express, to give an interview from our phone. It turns out that she had already arranged for this phone call. It was a form of treating us, shall we say, quite instrumentally. On another occasion, I remember, [Zbigniew] Bujak came to us together with [Helena] Łuczywo with some text to sign. But the text was already sealed; I had no influence on its content. At first I signed, and then I cancelled. For there was something humiliating about it for me. Although I was also afraid for my papers and books, among other things. It was through such carelessness that a search was caused, and so many things (bags) were taken from me that the officers conducting the search had to call for reinforcements.

Kozłowski *But you did, however, cooperate with KOR.*

Kowalik I worked most closely with KOR at the time of its transformation into KSS KOR [*Komitet Samoobrony Społecznej KOR*, KOR Committee for Social Self-Defense]. Kuroń, the writer Anka Kowalska, and I, after a stormy discussion, were obliged to write a new programme declaration. I prepared a draft, which Kuroń rejected outright, because (in the words of Waldemar Kuczyński, with whom I was then close, although now we hold opposing views) "the text smelled of socialism a mile away".

Chudziński *The moment you joined the team of advisors …*

Kowalik The trip to Gdańsk by a group of intellectuals was my idea. Helena Łuczywo, who came from Gdańsk, was terrified by the growing radicalism of the strikers. She said it was boiling there [*tam wrze*] and there could be a massacre. She mentioned something about Andrzej Gwiazda pushing for a confrontation. She said, "Do something or there will be a disaster". She praised my idea of having a couple of "authorities" go there. But my first thought was of real authorities, such as Bieńkowski, [Aleksander] Gieysztor, [Stefan] Kieniewicz, [Witold] Kula and [Tadeusz] Mazowiecki. My proposal was accepted by [Bronisław] Geremek; he was to persuade historians, I was left to convince Mazowiecki and Bieńkowski. However, when I went to Mazowiecki, he changed his mind. He was particularly afraid of the very authoritarian Bieńkowski. He suggested that we, the signatories of the "Letter of 64", should go. I described the twists and turns, the negotiations, my admiration for the workers and their sense of responsibility, as well as moments of terror, in *Przegląd* [weekly]. Perhaps to liven things up, I will repeat the shortest dialogue. When we were going from the shipyard to the Pauline Fathers to sleep at night, we could hear something like a rumbling, probably a freight train, I thought it was tanks. I say to Geremek: "What do you think, fifteen?". Geremek: "Per person?".... And then a great relief, a great compromise, albeit briefly.

Chudziński *We once asked Karol Modzelewski, in a similar conversation, whether the course of events inevitably led to what happened. Was it possible to reverse the tide? I am referring to 1981, martial law and its consequences. Because this is still a matter of dispute ...*

Kowalik I was pessimistic. Both sides in the conflict were incapable of a more lasting compromise. Besides, we acted too early. If only it had happened at least five years later, under Gorbachev. But then both sides were still immature, both mentally and intellectually unprepared. Russia was unwilling, or perhaps unable, to tolerate such an alien body [as Solidarność]. If I had not been so pessimistic, I would not have gone to the United States, where I spent the whole of martial law.

The Russians had some idea of how to solve the problem. I cannot recall, and my notes are lost, whether it was already during martial law or before. Seweryn Bialer, who had a very high standing both in Moscow and in the [US] State Department, and probably not only, once came to see me in Washington with an urgent proposal that the Russians wanted to organise a meeting with the oppositionists on "neutral" ground, that is on US soil.

Kozłowski *This is a fantasy!*

Kowalik Absolutely! I laughed at it, but I believe there was nevertheless an attempt by some faction whose aims were, by the way, completely unclear.

This was somehow connected with the fact that, at the time of my departure for Washington, I was obliged to prepare Wałęsa's visit to the USA. In fact, we interrupted these preparations at the beginning of November, because both [Zbigniew] Brzeziński and [Jan] Nowak-Jeziorański suddenly began to convince me that Wałęsa's arrival could end badly both for him and for Solidarity. That, in the best-case scenario, "that pack of journalists" [*"ta sfora dziennikarska"*] (as Brzeziński put it) would lash out at poor Wałęsa, who would utter silly things that would make his return difficult. Today, by the way, I think that they already knew from [Ryszard] Kukliński about the preparations for martial law.

Kozłowski *When did you come to the conclusion that something like martial law had to happen?*

Kowalik Already on 9 September 1980, in fact just after the signing of the Gdańsk Accords, I returned home devastated. There was a deep conflict between Wałęsa and [Anna] Walentynowicz and both Gwiazdas [Andrzej and Joanna], in which people from KOR were still involved. There was, in fact, an attempt by the Gdańsk radicals to break the August Agreements.

Ratkowski *What did they actually want?*

Kowalik That's a good question—what did they actually want?

Ratkowski *After Mickiewicz: "For the war of nations we beseech Thee Lord" ["O wojnę narodów błagamy Cię Panie"]?*

Kowalik Maybe, but it was an expression of the public mood. The workers had a huge distrust of authority. They feared that it wanted to trick them. And there was incessant worrying news coming from the authorities. We travelled all over the country to put out strikes, and it was getting more and more difficult. As a result, we supported some of them, thinking that in this way we were weakening even more radical sentiments! Newer and newer people were coming into Solidarity who wanted to show off, to disown us, including the KOR people. I was together with people like [Jan] Olszewski, [Wiesław] Chrzanowski, [Jan] Strzelecki, [Władysław] Siła-Nowicki and Kuroń, demanding that the agreements be respected. But confrontational winds prevailed in Solidarity.

Ratkowski *Wasn't there a provocation in this? After all, Solidarity was probably very strongly infiltrated by the [secret] services?*

Kowalik Of course. Even during the negotiations, I had to keep the notes, the proposals, under my feet. I have the soul of a historian, and I wanted to keep them for myself, and they kept vanishing into thin air. That was the first sign that something wrong was happening.

Chudziński *How did you react to the attributes of national mourning displayed by some artistic circles during martial law?*

Kowalik I spent the entire period of martial law abroad, mainly in Washington. I received rather reassuring signals from home. I remember giving a presentation at Columbia University (in New York) in a conciliatory spirit. Among other things, I read out a letter from [Ryszard] Herczyński received immediately after his release from internment, describing the sense of uncertainty felt by the officers. They made it clear that they did not like it either, but they had to follow orders.

Ratkowski *And the internment of Gierek and his comrades was a clear signal that the thing was verging on the grotesque!*

Chudziński *How did you know that—to use Wiesław Górnicki's words—martial law was more like a Boy Scout alert than a bloody Pinochet-style coup d'état?*

Kowalik I received letters, but also first-hand reports from journalists. One of the founders of CNN, and an acquaintance of mine, as sort of friend, travelled from Moscow to Warsaw and was with Lipiński, among others. As he said, they both agreed that it was rather Russia that was under martial law.

Chudziński *And meanwhile, the communist regime is slowly coming to an end. And a new problem emerges: After the June [1989] elections, the Solidarity bloc begins to crack. How did you find your place at that moment, when the paths of various Solidarity people were diverging?*

Kowalik I took the political turn made by Solidarity in the summer of 1989 with the utmost anxiety. It so happened that I was teaching the summer trimester at the New School in New York. I returned at the end of August just in time for a meeting of the OKP [*Obywatelski Klub Parlamentarny*, Civic Parliamentary Club] in the Sejm's Column Hall, where Jeffrey Sachs was presenting his concept of a leap into a market economy for an hour and a half. I was struck by the presence—emphasised by their prominent seating—of the later Republican presidential candidate, Senator Robert Dole, whom I knew as a slayer of the welfare state, and his wife. The total freeing of prices, the immediate internal convertibility of the zloty and the opening up to the world were, according to Sachs, to bring stability after six months and set the country on a path of rapid development. Although no one, apart from Kuroń, supported this idea, no one, including none of the invited economists, took up the polemic. It was as if there had been no earlier Round Table Agreements, which announced the creation of a "new economic order", but with gradualism and the electoral declaration of

Solidarity maintained in that spirit. This was striking to me, because I was convinced of the great popularity in Poland, within the ranks of Solidarity, of the West German model of the "social market economy". I also knew that, earlier that year, a study group of several people had visited Sweden, on behalf of the Economic Consultative Council [*Konsultacyjna Rada Gospodarcza*], to explore the possibility of using the Swedish experience [in Poland]. It was a terrible pity that the Germans were so preoccupied with themselves at the time, and the former invaders, the Swedes, had become so timid.

The abrupt turnaround was made in the summer of 1989, with a great deal of complicity in this by the expanding number of self-appointed American advisers. I know of a case where a graduate student wanted to reach the government through me with his revelatory ideas. Shortly thereafter, the Minister for Privatisation, Waldemar Kuczyński, would boast that in his department, in the corridor, English is heard just as often as Polish. Let us add: with an American accent.

Kozłowski *They were called the "Marriott [Hotel] Brigade".*

Kowalik And they encountered the prevailing atmosphere of bravado bordering on social irresponsibility in power circles. It even shocked a World Bank expert. When he asked a senior official at the Ministry of Finance about predicted unemployment, he was told: We don't know how many there will be, maybe a million, maybe two, maybe three, or maybe none at all. Recounting this, he added in a faltering voice that these people do not know what they are talking about.

In this atmosphere shaped by the ease of political victory (Russian: *szapkami zakidajem*[8]), the fiendish idea of a great leap into the market economy, known as shock therapy, was born. The result was bound to be lamentable, in a laboratory-like confirmation of Karl Popper's view that socio-technical projects of great change bring equally great changes that are unexpected and undesirable. The gap between stated goals and results was several hundred per cent. No communist plan experienced such a gap as the Balcerowicz Plan.

Chudziński *Even the six-year plan?*

Kowalik Even this one. Examples? National income was supposed to fall by 3%; it fell by 11% in the first year and by 8% in the second. Industrial production was predicted to fall by 5%; the result was a 25% drop. There was talk of 400,000 unemployed; it ended up with unemployment of three million; not temporary but permanent. In all these cases, a discrepancy of more than 500%. Inflation was already supposed to be in single digits at the end of this "year zero", and only it became so after nine years!

You asked me how I got into this. It seemed to me that I was doing the right thing. I took part in the discussions. I delivered the memorandum, signed by [Wiktor] Herer, Władysław Sadowski and myself, which could be summed up in the cry: "Not everything at once!", to the reception offices of the prime minister, the minister of finance, the head of the CUP and Geremek as head of the OKP faction in the Sejm. And only the latter, on the steps of a church, during the funeral of a mutual friend, thanked me and even said: "We need to talk about this". The silence was all the more meaningful because all these people were my colleagues or friends. But when you are outside the power structures, you can talk to a brick wall.

Kozłowski *At the time, the prevailing conviction among those in charge of the great change was that a certain critical mass had to be exceeded for a return to real socialism to be impossible.*

Kowalik That is agreed, but success was ultimately determined by the quality of this critical mass. After all, psychologically, real socialism is back. In surveys, the majority of respondents believe that life was better then. And there were other factors besides. Also neophyteism. It turned out, as Karol Modzelewski perfectly showed in his book[9], that the leading intellectuals, who were considered to be representing labour interests, changed their views by 180 degrees. We were in a debt trap, which entitled our creditors to a certain amount of boisterousness, eagerness and ease in imposing certain solutions. Although I believe we had strong bargaining chips and could have used them. But we did not want to. Again, to the surprise of IMF experts accustomed to the fact that negotiations with Third World authorities are very difficult, out of the three options presented by these experts at the time, the Polish government unanimously chose the toughest, most far-reaching one. Even knowledge of the common canons of negotiation failed. The extreme option is usually presented in order to have something to give up during negotiations. In general, there was surprise after surprise. Workers' leader Lech Wałęsa accepted the Balcerowicz Plan before it was finally formulated, and a few years later, when asked whether Mazowiecki or Balcerowicz had provided him with this programme, fundamental after all for the standard of living of millions of people, he carelessly replies: "I don't remember, I think not…". And parliament, I remind you, was a contractual Sejm dominated by the old regime, which passed a package of laws comprising this programme. The only "rational" explanation for all of this was given by the then deputy speaker of the Sejm, Aleksander Małachowski, who stated: "We were like sheep being led to their slaughter…" [*"Byliśmy jak barany prowadzone na śmierć …"*]. However, a group of MPs and senators quickly emerged—the aforementioned Małachowski,

Modzelewski, Bugaj—increasingly openly critical of government policy. Unfortunately, without Kuroń, who declared that he was suspending his leftist views for the period of building the foundations of capitalism. He later admitted in one form or another that this was the greatest mistake he had made in his life!

Chudziński *He also told us this in a similar conversation.*

Kowalik He has repeatedly said that the workers' defeat keeps him awake at night.

Ratkowski *Then there was an explosion of our "bed capitalism" ["kapitalizm łóżkowy"]*[10].

Kowalik Folding beds, [the so-called] jaws [*szczęki*][11], exchange offices, in a word: an Eldorado for the new private sector was one side. The other was the deluge of untariffed, untaxed imports, which destroyed Polish crafts, cooperative and state trade. Together with a few other measures and processes, such as the drastic reduction of monetary savings, the famous "*popiwek*", a draconian tax on wage increases with high "corrective inflation", gave birth to a highly polarised society, a society of primitive capital accumulation. The share of wages in the population's income fell from over 46% to 28% in four years, farmers' incomes fell by a half, and the incomes of the self-employed more than doubled. Thus, this deep recession, often referred to as "transformational", that is considered as a necessary cost of change, was rather a recessionary transformation, that is change through recession as a tool for building a new social structure. This, of course, regardless of whether it corresponded to the original intention of the authorities.

Kozłowski *At that time, the idea took hold that capitalism was simply a good thing, and that the disastrous reality of socialism was equated with communism. So, the further we move towards a free market, the better!*

Kowalik It was also thought that the further we jumped into the free market, the more financial aid we would receive from the West. But after all, we are talking about changing institutions, and therefore the rules of behaviour of people, not changing machines. It also had the fatal effect of destroying the Solidarity trade union, on whose behalf these changes were made. Without taking this fact into account, it is impossible to understand the ongoing degeneration of this social movement.

Ratkowski *And a whole new class emerged. They were no longer the communist-era* badylarze[12] *or craftsmen. These groups in fact also disappeared in the process of change ….*

Kowalik Interestingly, and perhaps uniquely, at least in Central Europe, as many as 40% of new business owners (whose numbers quickly doubled) were people with only a basic education. This explains, among other things, the nineteenth-century labour relations in many small and medium-sized companies.

Kozłowski *Don't you have the impression that some important public debates have not taken place? Around 1990, it was the choice of system and the way out of the previous regime, and now it is the attitude towards Maastricht [Treaty]. Meanwhile, we are discussing the preamble [to the 1997 Constitution] and not talking about what is most important at all.*

Kowalik I totally agree. In 1989, there was no possibility of a serious discussion about the choice of system. At the time, haste prevailed, but that does not explain everything, since it is difficult [to discuss about it] even now, when social criticism is enormous. Only a few per cent of respondents believe that the transition is going in the right direction. As with the Iraq War, the majority of the public is against what is happening. But when it comes to formulating an agenda of what to do, it is extremely difficult to break through with sensible solutions.

The draft European Constitution was a good opportunity to address serious issues. After all, already at the outset (in Article 3), the draft declares a policy of full employment and a social market economy, as in the Polish Constitution. A good opportunity, then, to claim these values. To consider what this would look like. To confront the social order that has emerged in our country. Organised pressure on the authorities, demanding a change in socio-economic policy, is even worse. With the "messengers" [*"przekaziory"*; meaning mass media] in their grip, neoliberals are skilfully using the aversion to the state in general, the necessity—often alleged—of adapting to the rules of the European Union and the bogeyman of the financial crisis, learned from the past, to defend the *status quo* and even further reduce social transfers. The state is being weakened, tacitly assuming that it is still a state with roots in communism.

Ratkowski *But having joined the European Union, we are becoming part of a huge mechanism which, by its very size, already acts as a stabiliser.*

Kowalik A political stabiliser, yes, but an economic one? The main countries of the Union, apart from England, have been semi-stagnating for years. Cyclical fluctuations have resurfaced and deepened. But the bottom line is that the EU is advocating a suicidal, pro-recession macroeconomic policy. Stable prices at all costs, cuts in social spending, this is supposed to be the medicine from the pharmacy in Maastricht. We are currently observing an interesting paradox. If budget deficits had been used early enough to stimulate the economy, we would not now have deficits in many countries forced by a protracted recession. Why did the UK avoid it? Because when the stock market bubble burst overseas, when the recession started there, it was the [Tony] Blair government that increased social spending (on education and on health), so it stimulated domestic demand. Blair is lucky to have such a great finance minister as Gordon Brown.

Chudziński *And we have opened the floodgates wide.*

Kowalik Not only us. Actually, all post-communist European countries, except Slovenia. This is why the effects of the influx of foreign capital are so depressing. According to a study by the Institute for Social Research and Initiatives on the impact of foreign direct investment on economic growth in the eight post-communist countries joining the EU, apart from Hungary, the greater the amount of foreign investment (relative to GDP) the … lower the growth rate. Why? Because privatisation, not new investment, prevailed, and mainly in trade, not manufacturing.

Ireland is often cited as a model for us, but Ireland was fortunate in that it started its acceleration programme before the Maastricht Treaty, and especially the Amsterdam Treaty, came into force. It knew how to use EU funds. It made the leap in development not by applying the EU recommendations but, on the contrary, by an incredibly interventionist policy in its first phase. It promoted foreign capital only in the four most modern sectors, giving indeed great privileges, discounts, tax exemptions, but only to selected, desirable foreign capital.

Kozłowski *From the point of view of economic development, our entry into the EU does not necessarily mean that we will be a less peripheral country, in fact quite the opposite!*

Ratkowski *I do not believe it!*

Kowalik I would also like not to believe it. Joining the EU restricts us from pursuing our own separate economic policy, and here is the big challenge. If the Polish authorities had presented the dramatic situation of Poland to the EU, with its 20% unemployment, and over 40% among young people, then perhaps we would have been allowed, or even helped, to get out of this dramatic situation for a certain strictly defined period of time. And this presupposes far-reaching interventionism. We have strong arguments. But it is necessary to stop proving that Poland is a transformational success story, and instead loyally inform (warn) the EU authorities that Poland, with such high unemployment, especially among young people, could infect the Union with pathologies, crime! We are already good at manufacturing amphetamines, stealing cars. And yet we can move *en masse* to the West not only in search of work. This assumes, of course, also the wisdom and determination of the Polish authorities. Meanwhile, the postulates, even of Grzegorz Kołodko, which I no longer understand at all, go in the opposite direction. We are in a hurry to join Euroland, that is, to abandon our own monetary policy. This is good for stabilised countries with an unemployment rate of a few per cent, but not for us.

Kozłowski *But financial assistance …*

Kowalik This is yet another pro-EU myth: hopes for significant development effects from the inflow of structural funds. Meanwhile, there are already numerous studies showing that the EU's hitherto policy strategy of equalising regions has failed completely. The gap between rich and poor regions has not narrowed. And it used to, before they joined the EU. It has also narrowed under EFTA.

I'm talking about regions, not countries, because the economies of Portugal and Spain have come somewhat close to the level of the EU. But beware: They now have economic growth rates that are lower than before they joined the Union! The statistics here are ruthless! Portugal, Spain and even Greece were catching up with the more developed EU countries faster than they are now. And yet we will receive less funds than those countries did at the beginning.

The danger of further peripheralisation of Poland is real. I have just returned from an international conference in Poznań, where research, with appropriate simulations, was presented by two Frenchmen from the "regulation" school of economics. They argue that regional disparities within the EU are growing. In their opinion, only the most developed countries among the new members, namely the Czech Republic and Hungary, have a chance of catching up in the future.

Chudziński *Does that mean we are doomed to "two speeds"?*

Kowalik Perhaps here it is worth clarifying what we mean by "two speeds". It [the term] arose in connection with the question of the pace of deepening integration. France and Germany want to do it faster. The UK and probably Sweden are resisting it the most. They don't see a purpose when they are doing better economically outside the Euroland than the twelve with the euro. Few hope that the countries now joining are capable of really reducing systemic differences, unless the degree of marketisation, especially of the public service sphere, is taken as a measure of integration.

The second understanding of "two speeds" can be related to the rather drastic division between the large countries of the Union, suffering from semi-stagnation (euro-sclerosis), and a few small countries, such as Denmark, Finland, Sweden, the Netherlands and Ireland, which cannot be accused of this. What is more, Finland, followed by Sweden, ranked first among "knowledge-based" economies. And yet another interpretation of the two speeds is linked to the desire of economically weaker countries to catch up with, or at least close the gap in terms of per capita income, with the leading Western countries, as we have discussed.

Kozłowski *So what system have we chosen?*

Kowalik Nineteenth-century capitalism. Heavily corrupt and clientelistic.

Ratkowski *Have other countries joining the EU chosen a different solution?*

Kowalik The Polish shock therapy syndrome (Kołodko rightly wrote about shock without therapy) was of great importance as a model for other countries. Besides, with the participation of the same experts, so it was also an imposed model. But there is one country in Europe and two in Asia that have chosen a different path and are following it with great success. Slovenia did not go through the transformation shock. Much of the credit for this goes to Jože Mencinger, a former deputy prime minister who is an economist and econometrician by education and profession. A man of character who knew how to leave the government when he disagreed with Sachs' prescription. Mencinger repeatedly described the experience of this small but most developed country among the post-communist countries. If this experience is taken into account, one cannot dismiss China's evolutionary experience by referring to the specific characteristics of a backward, predominantly agricultural country, or Vietnam, which has a similar structure.

Chudziński *What can realistically be done to improve our situation?*

Kowalik Develop large-scale housing construction with significant state involvement. We also have a lot of work to do with road repairs and construction, afforestation, river regulation …

Ratkowski *Sorry, but housing, as the flywheel of the economy, was written into the SLD's [Sojusz Lewicy Demokratycznej; Democratic Left Alliance] programme.*

Kowalik But that's where it ends. For many, it's all about balancing the budget, and I even argue about that with my friends.

Ratkowski *We need to build roads ...*

Kowalik Exactly. Roads, just ordinary roads, are much more important in our country than motorways from many points of view. The repair and construction of ordinary roads is more labour-intensive, more important and helps absorb unemployment. But here everything depends on the state. By demanding this, I am in good company. Joseph Stiglitz, Nobel laureate, former Clinton chief of advisors and vice-president of the World Bank, recently declared that there are two main coordinators of the economy: the market and the state, adding that it was a mistake to treat the latter as something intrinsically inferior. It is the state, central and local government that would have to take it upon itself to co-finance, for example, everything in housing that is underground [*wszystkiego co w mieszkaniówce jest pod ziemią*].

Kozłowski *The top leaders of the SLD and, of course, other parties, when they hear such views, they say: "You want a return of socialism"!*

Chudziński *In our country, it is considered an obsolete road.*

Kowalik Well, the question is whether these two visions—let's call them the Reagan-Thatcher vision with the free market on the one hand and Lepperism[13] on the other—leave room for anything else in Poland? And as for the leaders of the SLD, the desire to buy into the favors of liberal salons, the complexes of former communists still prevail. They naively attempt to show that they are modern.

Chudziński *Many say that we have to go through this purgatory! Aren't you afraid of finding yourself in bad company?*

Kozłowski *Professor Kowalik has always been in "bad company"!*

Kowalik [Andrzej] Lepper's advisor phoned me to ask if I would like to cooperate ... I replied that I was still loyal to the Unia Pracy [UP, Labour Union] party (although I had ceased to be a member).

Chudziński *But you need money for public works too! Where to get it from?*

Kowalik Paweł Kozłowski and I are both "Kaleckians", and we know that investments finance themselves. Only the first start-up money is needed, [then] people produce national income, wages ... The multiplier calculation of these processes improves the situation [even more]. I remember that back in 1991, at a congress on evolutionary economics in Vienna, when mass unemployment was beginning in our country, one of the world's prominent economists even shouted at us Poles (Hausner was present there): "You have steel, you have cement, a huge unused productive apparatus, a surplus of labour. Build housing, roads. What else do you need? Money? But these are technical problems!". And in the Polish parliament around that time, the biggest applause went to MP Jerzy Osiatyński when he said: "We need three things: money, money, money!".

We don't have to succumb to the magic of budget balance at all. For the entire eight years of the Reagan administration, the average (!) budget deficit was just under 5%!

Ratkowski *The Czechs had an 8.4% budget deficit last year. The Hungarians had 5.2, we had 5.7 .... And I haven't heard the Czechs despair.*

Kowalik We should have and can borrow for this purpose, especially with the current low interest rate in the West, and increase the deficit a little. By increasing employment, increasing national income, increasing budget revenues, we can bring about an improvement in public finances. This path is much safer, more sustainable. It is the path that is well known and tried. The Kalecki way, the Keynes way, today used by Alan Greenspan and Gordon Brown.

Kozłowski *If you had to decide, which would you choose? The Scandinavian model? Can we afford the*

Scandinavian model, regardless of the insistent propaganda that it is falling apart or is a thing of the past?

Kowalik Can we afford it? When Sweden started it, it was as poor as Poland at the time, much poorer than today. But I see a lot of good—in some things better than in Sweden—solutions also in Austria, in the German model of social market economy. We could benefit from the experience of all three models. I mean a type of cooperative, participatory and solidarity system.

Kozłowski *So a different way of accumulation, a different way of distribution.*

Kowalik Also another way of using modern information technology. It may as well serve to stupefy, mainly by the financial markets that are destabilising the world. But it can also be used mainly for schools and adult education, hospitals, pulling villages out of isolation, expanding democracy. How symbolic it was that some time ago, the saturation of schools with computers in Sweden was greater than in the home of computers, California. And while we are mentioning the two countries, let us add that if Sweden has less than 3% of children living in poverty and the USA more than 20%, they are two different civilisations. I have observed on the outskirts of Stockholm how Arab, Asian children integrate quickly because they have the opportunity to spend time in reading rooms, predominantly smart game houses, rather than on the street. By contrast, in Washington and Los Angeles, where I spent a total of three years, whites form a completely different, closed community. Only slightly less so for Spanish speakers. So what if a Swede's per capita income is significantly lower than in the USA, when all quality of life indicators are better for Sweden.

Kozłowski *You spent ten years in the West, what main lessons do you draw for Poland?*

Kowalik And this in countries as diverse as Austria, Sweden, England, Canada, Switzerland (at least one academic year in each). Admittedly, only at universities and institutes, but I had the opportunity for good observation. The most important conclusion is: There is no single market economy, no single capitalism. I feel like repeating after Wiesenthal, who said in another context: We live under the terror of general terms. The market, capitalism, the state, globalisation are our prisons of thought. And the world is diverse and continues to diversify. We are not moving towards a single socio-economic system. Even within the European Union, a specialist (Bruno Amable) lists four "types" of capitalism: market, social democratic, continental, Mediterranean. So it is not that joining the EU solves for us the problem of choice, of forming our own institutional and organisational system.

Kozłowski *Well, and there is the problem of Poland after its entry into the European community.*

Kowalik Here the ideas are crazy. Minister Danuta Hübner concluded an agreement with the private Institute for Market Economy Research [*Instytut Badań and Gospodarką Rynkową*] on behalf of the UKIE [*Urząd Komitetu Inegracji Europejskiej*, Office of the Committee for European Integration], that is the "left" government, creating the Polish Lisbon Strategy Forum. The institute has a reputation as an intellectual appendage of Gdańsk's former conservative liberals. The aim of this strange alliance is clear: to join the EU with a mission to further liberalise the economies of the European Union. The head of this appendage, Jan Szomburg, has repeatedly recommended the American model, an idealised version found in textbooks, because in reality it is far from the textbook ideal. The main focus is on limiting social transfers, commercialising public services and making the labour market more flexible.

Chudziński *What you are saying resonates with the arguments of populists who are trying to scare people about the EU.*

Kowalik But also with the voices of a huge number of American, English, Swedish economists. Also with the position of Vaclav Klaus. I am in favour of the Union as a cooperative union of nation states. In economic terms, [it should be] little more than the common market of the USA, Mexico and Canada (NAFTA), but much less than a single, unified socio-economic system. I defend systemic diversity, which I see as a value worth striving for. I appreciate in the long run the cultural and civilisational benefits, but of just such a diverse Union: a union of cooperating nation states. But not a new European superpower. Just think what would have happened if the pre-war League of Nations had led to the creation of a United States of Europe. Would the "Genevocrats" have allowed such epoch-making systemic innovations as the Scandinavian model, the social market economy in Germany, the partnership system in Austria?

Anyway, in this respect, I am optimistic: The world is globalising, (mainly in terms of technology, consumption patterns), but also diversifying. Whether, in systemic terms, the tendency towards convergence is stronger than towards divergence, it is difficult to say at the moment. What is rather certain, however, is that the blinding light of unifying hyperpower is fading, making it easier to see and appreciate diversity.

Ratkowski *But after all, Polish society is moving towards a welfare, social democratic EU, the kind we remember from a few years ago.*

Kowalik Unfortunately, there is (no longer, or still?) such a Union. Jacques Delors failed, and the brief episode of Social Democrat rule in the thirteen countries of the fifteen was not used to return to Delors' concept.

Kozłowski *Could you look at post-1945 Poland as a string of difficult modernisations, including the systemic transformation?*

Kowalik I have spoken and written enough about the current transition. And about the previous one? Up until the 1960s, there was educational progress and a huge civilisational advancement of the countryside. Mainly the countryside, at the expense of the former labour aristocracy. The professionals of the big factories, the railwaymen. This is unquestionable. But the problem is in something else. The party-state bureaucracy created to meet the needs of imposed industrialisation no longer gave way. It was incapable of reforming the system, and it did not allow itself to be reformed either. In fact, this was the greatest cost of that transformation and modernisation. It was not socialism, but a communist substitute for capitalism, whatever it proclaimed about itself.

Ratkowski *Djilas's new class?*

Kowalik Something like that. In Poland, it is called the nomenklatura. The reformers in the party and the government were held hostage by this nomenklatura, which is why they eventually had to resort to democratic opposition.

Chudziński *What part does the Polish left have in all this? What could it have done during the transition period? President [Aleksander] Kwaśniewski claims …*

Kowalik I will surprise you. In June 1990, we found ourselves—Brus, Kwaśniewski, [Wiesława] Ziółkowska and I—at a European Union conference in Brussels on the Polish transformation. The conference was chaired by Jacques Delors. After the speech of the representative of our government, I made a very sharp criticism of the Balcerowicz Plan, and I was supported only by John K. Galbraith. Even my friend Brus said that I underestimated the difficulties. During the break, Aleksander Kwaśniewski (then head of the SdRP [*Socjaldemokracja Rzeczypospolitej Polskiej*, Social Democracy of the Republic of Poland]), with whom I had never spoken before, approached me and started like this: "It may be unpleasant for you—*at the time I had the Gombrowicz-esque mouth [gęba] of a 'Solidarity guy' ['solidaruch'] who should feel badly about compliments from a 'commie'*—but I completely agree with you". I think, by the way, that he must have spoken to Delors in this spirit, because the latter would not have written to the Polish authorities like that just after my speech. And he wrote something like: "The operation may succeed, but the patient will pass away" (this was revealed by "ResPublica"). A few years later, President Kwaśniewski would repeat that Balcerowicz would permanently enter the history books, as ... and so on. He became one of the more fervent proclaimers of "Polish success".

What should the left have been doing? Be left-wing. To speak out like Aleksander Małachowski, Karol Modzelewski, Ryszard Bugaj, a little later (and until entering the Monetary Policy Council) Wiesława Ziółkowska, the pre-government Marek Pol. And act in that spirit.

Chudziński *President Kwasniewski claims that in 1990, the Polish left had no other option but to support the Balcerowicz Plan!*

Kowalik But you probably do not assume that President Kwaśniewski is a leftist. After all, it was the president who rewarded Leszek Balcerowicz with the presidency of the NBP [*Narodowy Bank Polski*, National Bank of Poland] for his aborted programme to dismantle the welfare state (called the Medium-Term Financial Plan). And in an interview, he said that burdening the central bank with the task of maintaining growth, employment is "some kind of absurdity". Although it is not absurd for Alan Greenspan, a rather conservative liberal, and the USA is coming out of this quite well. It was the President who rewarded one of the main authors of the disastrous neoliberal pension reform, Marek Góra, which will put a serious strain on the budget for years to come. And he made one of the most free-market economists, Witold Orłowski, the head of [the group of his] economic advisers. At one conference, he asserted that Poland has (not just in the constitution, but in reality) a social market economy system. He believes that the welfare state should be abandoned, that the scope of the state should be reduced, although there is no evidence that any country on the European continent is doing this effectively. That the question of "tenure" [*etat*]—work, employment, unemployment—is a matter of individual responsibility. That the state has nothing to do with it. If only he had at least preached the views of Western European liberalism…

Kozłowski *So where is the Polish left?*

Kowalik Certainly not in the presidential palace. The left is scattered in small parties and associations. There is no left in the larger parties. Because even the Labour Union has drifted together with the SLD to the political and economic centre. All that can be said of the SDPL [*Socjaldemokracja Polska*, Social Democracy of Poland], if one wants to give it a chance, is that it is as yet undefined. On social and economic issues, the left is most present in schizophrenic populism, in trade unions, in the silent majority. Jacek Kuroń's words remain valid: "The defeat of 'Solidarity' occurred because the state authorities that emerged from it, instead of spearheading a mass movement of reconstruction, acted above society. Above its heads, they pursued a statist-technocratic programme, which pushed the majority into a claimant leftism that became all the more radical the more acutely the costs of the fall of communism were felt." Let us repeat these words [with a rephrased] beginning: "The defeat of 'Solidarity' and the SLD occurred because ...". And whether some more permanent, larger left-wing party will emerge from this populist magma, or whether a group or party will be found to begin with that can manage this vast field, only the future will tell. One thing is certain, at the moment the organised forces of capitalist transformation are repeating the primer of the flaws and mistakes of communist transformation. Both lack internal forces and opportunities for reform, and therein lies the vicious circle that some kind of upheaval might break. Let us hope it is civilised.

Chudziński *Thank you for a long and inspiring conversation on many issues.*

Translated from Polish by Grzegorz Konat and Gavin Rae

Notes

1. This phrase is used metaphorically in Polish to express that an action or decision was taken too late to have the desired effect (this and all subsequent notes are provided by the editors of this volume).
2. The Western Territories refers to the western and northern regions of Poland that were incorporated into the country after World War II, following the decisions of the Potsdam Conference (1945). These lands were previously part of Germany (East Prussia, Pomerania, Silesia and parts of Brandenburg) and were transferred to Polish administration as compensation for the eastern territories lost to the Soviet Union (modern-day western Ukraine, Belarus and Lithuania).
3. Privislinskiy Kray (Russian: Привислинский край, Polish: Kraj Nadwiślański) was the name given to territories of Congress Poland (the Russian-controlled partition of Poland) after its autonomy was abolished by the Russian Empire in the late nineteenth century.
4. The Katyń massacre (1940) was a mass execution of nearly 22,000 Polish military officers, intellectuals, and prisoners of war by the Soviet NKVD (Stalin's secret police) during World War II. The killings took place in the

Katyń Forest and other locations. The USSR initially denied responsibility, blaming Nazi Germany, but admitted guilt in 1990.

5. The Three-Year Plan (*Plan Trzyletni*) was Poland's first post-war economic recovery program, implemented by the communist government under Soviet influence. Its main goals were: rebuilding the economy, nationalising industry and redistributing land from pre-war landowners to peasants.
6. In 1963, Jerzy Urban, later to become a communist-era spokesman and then editor of the satirical magazine *Nie* [*No*], wrote an article about the well-known doctor from Kraków, Włodzimierz Marcinkowski (who was involved in anti-alcohol activities, which he wanted to carry out using radical methods, including organising labour camps for alcoholics and sterilisation), for which, under the instructions of Gomułka, he was fired and not allowed to publish for 3 years.
7. It was actually in 1964.
8. Literally: "we'll throw a lot of hats".
9. Kowalik is most likely referring to the book published in 1993 entitled *Dokąd od komunizmu?* [*Where to from Communism?*], in which Modzelewski attempts to explain the changes taking place in Poland after 1989.
10. "Bed capitalism" refers to the folding beds that were often used to display goods being sold on the streets during the transformation period.
11. "Jaws" was a street stall made of metal sheets, consisting of two parts, the front of which, when unfolded, formed a canopy.
12. "*Badylarze*" (singular: *badylarz*) is a colloquial and somewhat derogatory term in Polish, originally referring to small-scale, unprofessional farmers or gardeners who grow plants (often vegetables) in a makeshift or amateur way. The word comes from "badyle", meaning "stalks" or "weeds".
13. "Lepperism" refers to Andrzej Lepper (1954–2011) a Polish politician, farmer, and leader of Samoobrona RP (Self-Defense of the Republic of Poland), an agrarian party founded in 1992. Known for his anti-establishment rhetoric, Lepper gained support among struggling farmers and workers by protesting against economic liberalisation, EU policies and unemployment.

Index[1]

A
Alienation, 59, 60

B
Barker, C., 68, 76–93, 96, 96–97n1, 99n15
Biographical sketch, 14n1
Bourgeois revolutions, 67–96

C
Capitalism with a human face, 181
Comparative analysis, 68, 88–91, 96
Crucial reform, 40

E
Economic sociology, 58, 60
European social order, 180, 182

H
Health crisis, 122, 127, 140
Health system, 122, 123, 127–141
Humanism, 104

I
Intellectual history, 6

K
Kalecki, M., 19–40, 43–53
Kowalik, T., 1–14, 19–40, 43–53, 67–96, 103–116
Krzywicki, L., 55–58, 61, 62

L
Lange, O., 43–53, 56–62, 64, 64n1, 64n2
Luxemburg, R., 45, 48, 50–52

[1] Note: Page numbers followed by 'n' refer to notes.

G. Konat, G. Rae (eds.), *Exploring the Ideas of Tadeusz Kowalik*,
https://doi.org/10.1007/978-3-032-09283-0

M
Marxist political economy, 52
Mooers, C., 68, 76–93, 96, 96–97n1, 99n15
Multipolar world order, 174, 178–180, 183, 184

N
Neoliberalism, 121–141

P
Pension inequalities, 158, 165
Pension privatisation and rollback, 148, 151, 153, 163
Pension system, 147–166
Personality, 103–116
Personal recollection, 13, 14
Poland's social order, 172, 174, 180
Polish socialism, 55, 59, 61, 62
Political Aspects of Full Employment, 19–40
Post-socialist pension system, 147–149
Private correspondence, 13, 14

S
Social security in Poland, 161, 162
Socio-economic governance, 174–178
Systemic transition, 108, 116

T
Toporowski, J., 19–40

W
Welfare state, 111, 112, 116n3

FSC
www.fsc.org
MIX
Papier | Fördert
gute Waldnutzung
FSC® C083411

Kolibri 360 GmbH
Ferdinand-Jühlke-Straße 7
99095 Erfurt, Deutschland
produktsicherheit@kolibri360.de